# INTERNATIONAL LIBRARY OF
# AFRO-AMERICAN LIFE
# AND HISTORY

# THE AFRO-AMERICAN
# IN
# MUSIC AND ART

Compiled and Edited with an Introduction by
## LINDSAY PATTERSON

THE PUBLISHERS AGENCY, INC.
CORNWELLS HEIGHTS, PENNSYLVANIA
*under the auspices of*
THE ASSOCIATION FOR THE STUDY OF AFRO-AMERICAN LIFE AND HISTORY

*To*

AUNT TOY *and* EMERSON

*for their more than half-century*

*of care and assistance to young artists*

# *Preface*

THE Association for the Study of Afro-American Life and History joins with Pubco Corporation in presenting this new series of volumes which treat in detail the cultural and historical backgrounds of black Americans. This Association, a pioneer in the area of Afro-American History, was founded on September 9, 1915, by Dr. Carter G. Woodson, who remained its director of research and publications until his death in 1950.

In 1916 Dr. Woodson began publishing the quarterly *Journal of Negro History*. In 1926 Negro History Week was launched, and since that time it has been held annually in February, encompassing the birth dates of Abraham Lincoln and Frederick Douglass. The *Negro History Bulletin* was first published in 1937 to serve both schools and families by making available to them little-known facts about black life and history.

During its sixty-one years of existence, the Association for the Study of Afro-American Life and History has supported many publications dealing with the contributions of Afro-Americans to the growth and development of this country. Its activities have contributed to the increasing interest in the dissemination of factual studies which are placing the Afro-American in true perspective in the mainstream of American history.

We gratefully acknowledge the contributions of previous scholars, which have aided us in the preparation of this *International Library of Afro-American Life and History*.

Our grateful acknowledgment is also expressed to Charles W. Lockyer, president of Pubco Corporation, whose challenging approach has made possible this library.

Though each of the volumes in this set can stand as an autonomous unit, and although each author has brought his own interpretation to the area with which he is dealing, together these books form a comprehensive picture of the Afro-American experience in America. The three history volumes give a factual record of a people who were brought from Africa in chains and who today are struggling to cast off the last vestiges of these bonds. The anthologies covering music, art, the theatre and literature provide a detailed account of the black American's contributions to these fields—including those contributions which are largely forgotten today. Achievement in the sports world is covered in another volume. The volume on the Afro-American in medicine is a history of the black American's struggle for equality as a medical practitioner and as a patient. The selected black leaders in the biography book represent the contributions and achievements of many times their number. The documentary history sums up the above-mentioned material in the words of men and women who were themselves a part of black history.

CHARLES H. WESLEY

Washington, D.C.

# *Editor's Note*

I WISH to thank the following people for assistance in compiling this book: Emily Evershed for her superb editing and design; Allan Kullen for his all-around expert services; George Tichenor for his research and other services; Mary Beattie Brady for her generous suggestions and for supplying materials from the Harmon Foundation; members of the Schomburg Collection of the New York Public Library; Margaret Bonds, Elton Fax and Hale Woodruff for their sources and their contributions; Duncan Schiedt, Merton Simpson, Barbara Cooksey, Carroll Greene, Jr., and Ed Carroll; and Dr. Charles Wesley and Patricia Romero for their generosity and help.

LINDSAY PATTERSON

New York City

# Acknowledgments

WE ARE grateful for permission to use the following material in this book.

"The Meaning of Spirituals," from *Deep River: An Interpretation of Negro Spirituals,* by Howard Thurman. Copyright © 1945, by the Eucalyptus Press. Reprinted by permission of the author.

"Of the Sorrow Songs," from *The Souls of Black Folk,* W. E. B. Du Bois. Copyright © 1961, by Fawcett Publications. Reprinted by permission of the author's estate.

"Spirituals and Neo-Spirituals," by Zora Neale Hurston. Copyright 1933, by Zora Neale Hurston. Reprinted by permission of the author's estate.

"The Source," from *Negro Musicians and Their Music,* by Maud Cuney Hare. Copyright © 1936, by the Associated Publishers. Reprinted by permission of the Associated Publishers.

"The Age of Minstrelsy," from *The Negro and His Music,* by Alain Locke. Copyright © 1936, by the Associates in Negro Folk Education. Reprinted by permission of the author's estate.

"Negro Songmakers," from *Black Manhattan,* by James Weldon Johnson. Copyright © 1930, by Alfred A. Knopf. Reprinted by permission of the author's estate.

"Negro Producers of Ragtime," by Sterling A. Brown, from the Myrdal–Carnegie Study, 1940. Copyright 1940, by the Carnegie Foundation. Reprinted by permission of the author.

"The Blues," by E. Simms Campbell, from *Jazzmen,* edited by Frederic Ramsey and Charles Edward Smith. Copyright © 1939, by Harcourt, Brace. Reprinted by permission of the author and Harcourt, Brace.

"Memphis Blues: A Bungled Bargain," from *Father of the Blues,* by W. C. Handy. Copyright © 1941, by the Macmillan Company. Reprinted by permission of the Macmillan Company.

"Rock, Church, Rock!" by Arna Bontemps, from *The Book of Negro Folklore,* edited by Arna Bontemps and Langston Hughes. Copyright © 1958, by Arna Bontemps and Langston Hughes. Reprinted by permission of the author.

"New Orleans Music," by William Russell and Stephen W. Smith, from *Jazzmen,* edited by Frederic Ramsey and Charles Edward Smith. Copyright © 1939, by Harcourt, Brace. Reprinted by permission of the authors and Harcourt, Brace.

"New York Turns On the Heat," by Wilder Hobson, from *Jazzmen,* edited by Frederic Ramsey and Charles Edward Smith. Copyright © 1939, by Harcourt, Brace. Reprinted by permission of the author and Harcourt, Brace.

"Modern Jazz Is a Folk Music That Started with the Blues," by Frank M. Davis, published in *The Worker,* December 25, 1955. Copyright 1955, by Publishers New Press. Reprinted by permission of *The Worker.*

"Rhythm and Blues (Rock and Roll) Makes the Grade," by Ralph J. Gleason, from *Jam Session: An Anthology of Jazz,* edited by Ralph J. Gleason. Copyright © 1958, by G. P. Putnam's Sons. Reprinted by permission of the author.

"Popular Negro Composers," by Jack Yellen. Copyright 1967, by Jack Yellen. Reprinted by permission of the author.

"Bessie Smith," by George Hoefer, from *The Jazz Makers,* edited by Nat Hentoff and Nat

# Table of Contents

# Introduction

IN 1893, a German musicologist, Richard Wallaschek, published a book entitled *Primitive Music,* in which he challenged the authenticity of Afro-Americans as creators of spirituals. The book hit like a bombshell. Factions were drawn. One contingent said that the spirituals were purely African in origin. Another stated that their origins lay in Scottish and English ballads. Still others claimed that the source was French opera in New Orleans. The argument raged for several years but eventually petered out. No conclusions were reached, though each of the sides was confident that its theory was the correct one. Specific influences aside, musicologists today generally agree that the spirituals were born of the Afro-American's sufferings in slavery, and can truly be called America's genuine folk music.

It was not until 1871 that the spirituals were introduced to the general public by the Jubilee Singers of Fisk University. At first their repertoire consisted largely of classical songs; however, the spirituals proved to be the success of their program, and from 1871 to 1875 they toured America and Europe bringing dignity and public acceptance to this music.

Both the spirituals and Negro folk songs have, for almost a century, formed the basis of much of the world's popular music. These songs, together with the later musical trends to which they gave rise, have been America's greatest and most welcome cultural export. Unfortunately, the Afro-American as performer and composer, in the light of the enormity of his gift to the world, has not derived the full benefit from his music. Most appalling of all, there are those who, even today, challenge his right to be called the creator of so much that is irrefutably his. Why? A partial explanation lies in the fact that the Afro-American has not documented his own contributions to most of the musical forms he has spawned. This has resulted in a great deal of distortion historically, some of which has stemmed from persons who have had their own vested interests at heart. It is the intelligentsia who usually provide the most accurate records, but our intelligentsia have concentrated their efforts and energies on the Afro-American in classical music—a form alien to America. It should be noted that no classical composer of color has employed the Afro-American idiom in the way that Bartok made use of Hungarian folk music.

Happily, the black artist has not suffered this scholarly neglect. Through the years there have been such fine critics and writers as James A. Porter, Hale Woodruff, Romare Bearden and Elton Fax, themselves first-rate artists, who have kept the record straight. Nevertheless, the black painter or sculptor's struggle for recognition has not been easy. Fellowships and other aids have been few, but the black artist has managed, in the face of impossible odds, to keep producing. It is gratifying to know that in recent years there has been a definite upsurge of interest in the artist. Galleries owned and operated by Afro-Americans are springing up all over the country. Individuals have taken it upon themselves to act as representatives for groups of artists —to arrange shows and to contact potential buyers. But the final tribute should be paid to the artists themselves, who have persevered despite formidable obstacles, and who, as this volume will attest, came of age a long while ago.

In the interest of broader coverage, and to avoid repetition, it has been found necessary to edit and delete portions of some of the articles which appear in this anthology. Certain movements in music (bebop, for example) have been touched on in passing only, because I failed to uncover any accounts which dealt accurately with the Afro-American's contribution to this music.

Pictorially, this volume should be considered a companion piece to the *Anthology of the Afro-American in the Theatre*. Performers such as Lena Horne and Harry Belafonte, who appear several times in the theatre anthology, are not included in this volume. I have included only a few of the many well-known current popular singers and musicians—partly in the interest of space and partly because the public is familiar with them through newspaper and magazine articles.

LINDSAY PATTERSON

New York City

*Spirituals*

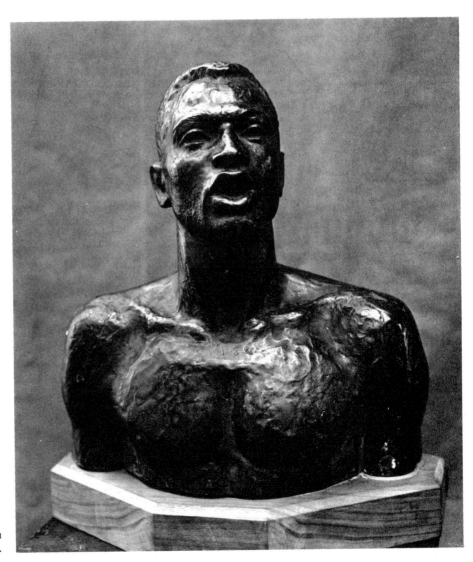

Richmond Barthé. "The Birth
of the Spirituals." Bronze.

Haywood L. Oubre, Jr. "The Prodigal Son." Oil.

# The Meaning of Spirituals

by Howard Thurman

THE ANTE-BELLUM Negro preacher was the greatest single factor in determining the spiritual destiny of the slave community. He it was who gave to the masses of his fellows a point of view which became for them a veritable Door of Hope. His ministry was greatly restricted as to movement, function, and opportunities of leadership, but he himself was blessed with one important insight. He was convinced that every human being was a Child of God. This belief included the slave as well as the master. When he spoke to his group on an occasional Sabbath day, he knew what they had lived through during the weeks; how their total environment had conspired to din into their minds and spirits the corroding notion that, as human beings, they were of no significance. Thus his one message, repeated in many ways over a wide range of variations, was this: "You are created in God's image. You are not slaves; you are not 'niggers'; you are God's children." Many weary, spiritually and physically exhausted slaves found new strength, power and inspiration in the words which fell from this man's lips. He had discovered that which religion insists is the ultimate truth about human life and destiny. It is the supreme validation of the human spirit. He who knows this is able to transcend the vicissitudes of life, however terrifying, and look out upon the world with quiet eyes.

It is out of this sense of being a Child of God that the genius of the religious folk songs is born. There were three major sources from which the raw materials of Negro spirituals were derived: the Old and New Testaments, the world of nature, and the personal experiences of religion which were the common lot of the people, emerging from their inner life. Echoes from each source are present in practically all of the songs. We shall examine all of these somewhat in detail, with reference to the use to which they were put and the end result.

## THE BIBLE—OLD TESTAMENT

The Christian Bible furnished much of the imagery and ideas with which the slave-singers fashioned their melodies. There is great strength in the assurance which may come to a people that they are children of destiny. The Jewish concept of life as stated in their records made a profound impression upon this group of people who themselves were in bondage. God was at work in all history: He manifested Himself in certain specific acts which seemed to be over and above the historic process itself.

The slave caught the significance of this truth at once. He sang:

> When Israel was in Egypt's land,
> Let my people go;
> Oppressed so hard they could not stand,
> Let my people go;

*Refrain*

Go down, Moses, 'way down in Egypt's land;
Tell ole Pharaoh,
Let my people go.

"Thus saith the Lord," bold Moses said,
"Let my People go;
If not I'll smite your first-born dead,
Let my people go.

"No more shall they in bondage toil,
Let my people go;
Let them come out with Egypt's spoil,
Let my people go."

The Lord told Moses what to do,
Let my people go;
To lead the children of Israel thro',
Let my people go.

When they had reached the other shore,
Let my people go;
They sang a song of triumph o'er,
Let my people go.

The experience of Daniel and his miraculous deliverance was also an ever-recurring theme:

My Lord delivered Daniel,
My Lord delivered Daniel,
My Lord delivered Daniel,
Why can't He deliver me?

The experiences of frustration and divine deliverance as set forth in the stories of the Hebrews in bondage, spoke at once to the deep need in the life of the slaves. They were literalists in their interpretations, not only because such was the dominant pattern of the religious thinking of the environment, but also because their needs demanded it. It is a commonplace that what we have need to use in our environment, we seize upon; it is a profound expression of the deep self-regarding impulses at the heart of man's struggle for the perpetuation of his own rights.

Many liberties were taken with the religious ideas. For here we are not dealing with a conceptual approach to religion but an intensely practical one, based upon the tragedy of great need.

Before passing from this aspect of our discussion, it is interesting to point out that the life and the mind were ever on the alert for the dramatic quality in the Bible story. The outstanding significance of the Bible was that it provided inspiration and illumination to the slaves as they sought to thread life's mystery with very few clues. What they had found true in their experience lived for them in the Sacred Book. God was at work in history. One of the oldest songs said:

Who lock, who lock de lion,
Who lock, de lion's jaw?
God, lock, God lock de lion's jaw.

The point is relevant!

God was the deliverer. The conception is that inasmuch as God is no respecter of persons, what He did for one race He would surely do for another. Daring to believe that God cared for them, despite the cruel vicissitudes of life, meant the giving of wings to life that nothing could destroy.

## THE BIBLE—JESUS OF THE GOSPELS

Few of the spirituals have to do with the nativity of Christ. This has given rise to many speculations. James Weldon Johnson was of the opinion that the reason lay in the fact that Christmas Day was a day of special license, having no religious significance to slaves. My own opinion somewhat concurs. It should be added that, in teaching the Bible stories concerning the birth of Jesus, very little appeal was made to the imagination of the slave, because it was not felt wise to teach the significance of this event to the poor and the captive. Even now these implications are not lifted to the fore in much of the contemporary emphasis upon Jesus. It is of first-rate significance to me that Jesus was born of poor parentage; so poor, indeed, was He that His parents could not offer even a lamb for the sacrifice but had to use doves instead. Unlike the Apostle Paul, He was not a Roman citizen. If a Roman soldier kicked Jesus into a Palestinian ditch, He could not appeal to Caesar; it was just another Jew in a ditch. What limitless release would have been available to the slave if the introduction to Jesus had been on the basis of His role as the hope of the disinherited and the captive! In the teaching of the Christian religion to the slave this aspect of the career of Jesus was carefully overlooked.

When I was a boy, it was my responsibility to read the Bible to my grandmother, who had been a slave. She would never permit me to read the letters of Paul except, on occasion, the 13th chapter of First Corinthians. When I was older, this fact interested me profoundly. When at length I asked the reason, she told me that, during the days of slavery, the minister (white) on the plantation was always preaching from the Pauline letters—"Slaves, be obedient to your masters," etc. "I vowed to myself," she said, "that if freedom ever came and I learned to read, I would never read that part of the Bible!"

Nevertheless, there are a few Christmas spirituals that point out the centrality of the significant event that took place in Bethlehem. There is one which connects the birth of Jesus with His coming into the life of the individual—an inner experience of the historical fact:

> When I was a seeker,
> I sought both night and day,
> I asked de Lord to help me,
> And He show'd me de way.
>
> Go tell it on de mountain,
> Over de hills and everywhere,
> Go tell it on de mountain,
> That Jesus Christ is born.

Another of these songs celebrates the star leading to Bethlehem. It is like finding the pearl of great price, or the treasure hidden in the field—for which the finder leaves all else:

> Dere's a star in de east on Christmas morn,
>     Rise up, shepherd, an' foller.
> It'll lead to de place where de Savior's born,
>     Rise up, shepherd, an' foller.
> Leave yo' sheep an' leave yo' lambs,
>     Rise up, shepherd, an' foller,
> Leave yo' ewes an' leave yo' rams,
>     Rise up, shepherd, an' foller.

William H. Johnson. "The Nativity."
Oil. Harmon Foundation.

In many of the songs the majesty of Jesus stands forth in a striking manner. In fact, in most of the songs that treat Jesus as a religious object, He is thought of as King. In these, Jesus and God are apparently synonymous. This may have been a form of compensation, an effort to give to the spirit a sense of worth and validation that transcends the limitations of the environment. For if Jesus, who is Savior, is King, then the humble lot of the worshipper is illumined and lifted. The human spirit makes a dual demand with reference to God—that God be vast, the Lord of Life, Creator, Ruler, King—in a sense, imperial; and that He also be intimate, primary, personal. The contrast is most marked:

> He's the lily of the valley,
>   O my Lord,
> He's the lily of the valley,
>   O my Lord,
> King Jesus in His chariot rides,
>   O my Lord,
> With four white horses side by side,
>   O my Lord!

Or sense the majesty of these lines:

> He's King of Kings, and Lord of Lords,
> Jesus Christ, the first and last,
>   No man works like Him.
> He built a platform in the air,
>   No man works like Him.
> He meets the saints from everywhere,
>   No man works like Him.
> He pitched a tent on Canaan's ground,
>   No man works like Him.
> And broke the Roman Kingdom down,
>   No man works like Him.

In the spirituals, the death of Jesus took on a deep and personal poignancy. It was not merely the death of a man or a God, but there was in it a quality of identification in experience that continued to burn its way deep into the heart of even the most unemotional. The suffering of Jesus on the cross was something more. He suffered, He died, but not alone—they were with Him. They knew what He suffered; it was a cry of the heart that found a response and an echo in their own woes.

The most universally beloved of all the hymns about Jesus is the well known "Were You There When They Crucified My Lord?" Some time ago, when a group of Negroes from the United States visited Mahatma Gandhi, it was the song that he requested them to sing for him. The insight here revealed is profound and touching. At last there is worked out the kind of identification in suffering which makes the cross universal in its deepest meaning. It cuts across differences of religion, race, class and language and dares to affirm that the key to the mystery of the cross is found deep within the heart of the experience itself:

> Were you there when they crucified my Lord?
> Were you there when they crucified my Lord?
> Oh! Sometimes it causes me to tremble, tremble, tremble,
> Were you there when they crucified my Lord?

The inference is that the singer was *there*: "I know what He went through because I have met Him in the high places of pain, and I claim Him as my brother." Here again the approach is not a conceptual one, but rather an experimental grasping of the quality of Jesus' experience, by virtue of the racial frustration of the singers.

## THE WORLD OF NATURE

The world of nature furnished the spirituals with much that was readily transformed into religious truth. The material was used in terms of analogy solely, with no effort to work out any elaborate pattern with regard to the significance of nature and man's relation to it. Most often the characterizations are simple and to the point.

For instance, in the South there is a small worm that crawls along in a most extraordinary manner. He draws his little tail up to his head, making his body into a loop, then holding himself by his tail, he extends his head into the air and forward. He is familiarly known as an "inch worm." His movement is slow, deliberate, formal and extremely dignified. Often with his entire body lifted, he seems uncertain as to the way to go, swinging himself from side to side in the air, until at

William H. Johnson. "The Descent from the Cross." Oil. Harmon Foundation.

last he lets himself straighten out on the ground.

Observing this creature in the early morning on the cotton leaf, the slave felt that here was characterized much of his own life; hence the song:

> Keep a-inchin' along,
> Massa Jesus comin' by an' by,
> Keep a-inchin' along like a po' inch worm,
> Massa Jesus comin' by an' by.

In the spiritual "Deep River," there is a full development of analogies drawn from nature.

## RELIGIOUS EXPERIENCE

The religious experience of the slave was rich and full, because his avenues of emotional expression were definitely limited and circumscribed. His religious aspirations were expressed in many songs delineating varying aspects of his desires. The other-worldly hope looms large, and this, of course, is not strange. The other-worldly hope is always available when groups of people find themselves completely frustrated in the present. When all hope for release in this world seems unrealistic and groundless, the heart turns to a way of escape beyond the present order. The options are very few for those who are thus circumstanced. Their belief in God leads quite definitely to a position which fixes their hope upon deliverance beyond the grave. What a plaintive cry are these words:

> Don't leave me, Lord,
> Don't leave me behin'.

There is desolation, fear, loneliness, but also hope—at once desperate and profound!

Even a casual bit of reflection will reveal just how important it was for the slave to run no risk of missing the joy of the other world. What soul searching must have been present in a song like the one which follows:

> Good Lord, shall I ever be de one
> To get over in de Promise' Lan'?
> God called Adam in de garden,
> 'Twas about de cool of de day,
> Called for old Adam,
> An' he tried to run away.
> The Lord walked in de garden,
> 'Twas about de cool of de day,
> Called for old Adam,
> An' Adam said, "Here I am, Lord."

Religion was a source of consolation that had power to raise endurance to scintillating quality. It supplied a social milieu in which the lyric words were cast. Here we are not dealing with a philosophy of unyielding despair, but a clear sharing by the members of the group of the comfort and strength each found in his religious commitment:

> Let us cheer the weary traveler,
> Cheer the weary traveler
> Along the heavenly way.

Yet there was always present at the same time the element of solitariness, a sense of individual responsibility for life which nothing could offset. The sense of personal spiritual need was deeply voiced in the song:

> 'Tis me, O Lord,
> Standing in the need of prayer.
> It's not my brother but it's me, O Lord,
> Standing in the need of prayer.

For sheer loneliness of heart, felt when, one by one, all social reinforcements in being a member of a religious community have disappeared, and the human spirit is left stranded on the shores of its own spiritual desolation, how true is the sentiment:

> And I couldn't hear nobody pray,
> O, way down yonder by myself,
> Couldn't hear nobody pray.

These songs were rightfully called "sorrow songs." They were born of tears and suffering greater than any formula of expression. And yet the authentic note of triumph in God rings out trumpet-tongued!

> Oh, nobody knows de trouble I've seen;
> Glory Hallelujah.

Freedom from slavery and freedom from life were often synonymous in the thought of those early singers. With actual freedom no closer, and the years slipping away with steady rhythmic beat, death seemed the only hope. Again, God is their answer:

> Children, we shall be free
> When the Lord shall appear.
> Give ease to the sick, give sight to the blind,
> Enable the cripple to walk;
> He'll raise the dead from under the earth,
> And give them permission to talk.

But occasionally a new note is struck—powerful and defiant:

> Oh freedom! Oh freedom!
> Oh freedom over me!
> An' befo' I'd be a slave,
> I'll be buried in my grave,
> An' go home to my Lord an' be free.

"Steal Away to Jesus" belongs in the group of those songs dealing with release. It is release in death. The same is true of "Swing Low, Sweet Chariot."

There is at least one hymn that belongs to that moment of heartfelt realization when it finally dawned upon the slave that he was *free*. Even here, God is given the credit:

> Slav'ry chain done broke at las',
> Goin' to praise God 'til I die.

I shall conclude this discussion with a word about the great hymn "We Are Climbing Jacob's Ladder." There is a great wide stride in this song that catches all the fragmentary aspects of one's yearnings and pours them into one great throbbing channel of triumph. It sums up all the hope for a better day for individuals and groups together. It gathers in its march the entire column of progress and advance, sensing the haunting dream of mankind for something better beyond today, disappearing in the hope of an infinite series of tomorrows. Saint and sinner, Jew and Gentile, Easterner and Westerner, all who love life and seek to understand its mysteries and its possibilities, at long last find their place in its rhythmic ranks:

> We are climbing Jacob's ladder;
> Every roun' goes higher and higher.

—1945

# Of the Sorrow Songs

by W. E. B. Du Bois

THEY THAT walked in darkness sang songs in the olden days—sorrow songs—for they were weary at heart. Ever since I was a child these songs have stirred me strangely. They came out of the South unknown to me, one by one, and yet at once I knew them as of me and of mine. Then, in after years, when I came to Nashville, I saw the great temple builded of these songs towering over the pale city. To me, Jubilee Hall seemed ever made of the songs themselves, and its bricks were red with the blood and dust of toil. Out of them rose for me morning, noon and night, bursts of wonderful melody, full of the voices of my brothers and sisters, full of the voices of the past:

> I walk through the churchyard
>   To lay this body down;
> I know moonrise, I know star-rise;
> I walk in the moonlight, I walk in the starlight;
> I'll lie in the grave and stretch out my arms,
> I'll go to judgment in the evening of the day,
> And my soul and thy soul shall meet that day,
>   When I lay this body down.

Little of beauty has America given the world save the rude grandeur God Himself stamped on her bosom; the human spirit in this New World has expressed itself in vigor and ingenuity rather than in beauty. And so by fateful chance the Negro folk song—the rhythmic cry of the slave—stands today not simply as the sole American music, but as the most beautiful expression of human experience born this side the seas. It has been neglected; it has been, and is, half despised, and above all it has been persistently mistaken and misunderstood; but notwithstanding, it still remains as the singular spiritual heritage of the nation and the greatest gift of the Negro people.

Away back in the Thirties the melody of these slave songs stirred the nation, but the songs were soon half forgotten. Some, like "Near the Lake Where Drooped the Willow," passed into current airs and their source was forgotten; others were caricatured on the minstrel stage, and their memory died away. Then in wartime came the singular Port Royal experiment, after the capture of Hilton Head, and, perhaps for the first time, the North met the Southern slave face to face and heart to heart with no third witness. The Sea Islands of the Carolinas, where they met, were filled with a black folk of primitive type. Their appearance was uncouth, their language funny, but their hearts were human and their singing stirred men with a mighty power. Thomas Wentworth Higginson hastened to tell of these songs, and Miss McKim and others urged upon the world their rare beauty. But the world listened only half credulously until the Fisk Jubilee Singers sang the slave songs so deeply into the world's heart that it can never wholly forget them again.

There was once a blacksmith's son born at Cadiz, New York, who in the changes of time taught school in Ohio and helped defend Cincinnati from Kirby Smith. Then he fought at Chancellorsville and Gettysburg and finally served in the Freedmen's Bureau at Nashville. Here he formed a Sunday-school class of black children in 1866, and sang with them and taught them to sing. And then they taught him to sing, and when once the glory of the jubilee songs passed into the soul of George L. White, he knew his life-work was to let those Negroes sing to the world as they had sung to him. So, in 1871, the pilgrimage of the Fisk Jubilee Singers began. North to Cincinnati they rode—four half-clothed black boys and five girl-women—led by a man with a cause and a purpose. They stopped at Wilberforce, the oldest of Negro schools, where a black bishop blessed them. Then they went, fighting cold and starvation, shut out of hotels and scornfully sneered at, ever northward; and ever the magic of their song kept thrilling hearts, until a burst of applause in the Congregational council at Oberlin revealed them to the world. They came to New York, and Henry Ward Beecher dared to welcome them, even though the metropolitan dailies sneered at his "nigger minstrels." So their songs conquered, till they sang across the land and across the sea, before Queen and Kaiser, in Scotland and Ireland, Holland and Switzerland. Seven years they sang, and brought back $150,000 to found Fisk University.

Since their day they have been imitated— sometimes well, by the singers of Hampton and Atlanta, sometimes ill, by straggling quartets. Caricature has sought again to spoil the quaint beauty of the music, and has filled the air with many debased melodies which vulgar ears scarce know from the real. But the true Negro folk song still lives in the hearts of those who have heard it truly sung, and in the hearts of the Negro people.

What are these songs, and what do they mean? I know little of music and can say nothing in technical phrase, but I know something of men, and knowing them, I know that these songs are the articulate message of the slave to the world. They tell us in these days that life was joyous to the black slave, careless and happy. I can easily believe this of some, of many. But not all the past South, though it rose from the dead, could gainsay the heart-touching witness of these songs. They are the music of an unhappy people, of the children of disappointment; they tell of death and suffering, and unvoiced longing toward a truer world, of misty wanderings and hidden ways.

The songs are indeed the siftings of centuries; the music is far more ancient than the words, and in it we can trace here and there signs of development. My grandfather's grandmother was seized by an evil Dutch trader two centuries ago; and coming to the valleys of the Hudson and Housatonic, black, little and lithe, she shivered and shrank in the harsh north winds, looked longingly at the hills, and often crooned a heathen melody to the child between her knees.

The child sang it to his children, and they to their children's children, and so 200 years it has traveled down to us and we sing it to our children, knowing as little as our fathers what its words may mean, but knowing well the meaning of its music.

This was primitive African music; it may be seen in larger form in the strange chant:

> You may bury me in the East,
> You may bury me in the West,
> But I'll hear the trumpet sound in that morning.

—the voice of exile.

Ten master songs, more or less, one may pluck from this forest of melody—songs of undoubted Negro origin and wide popular currency, and songs characteristic of the slave. One of these I have just mentioned. Another is "Nobody Knows de Trouble I've Seen." When, struck with a sudden poverty, the

Fisk Jubilee Singers

United States refused to fulfill its promises of land to the freedmen, a brigadier general went down to the Sea Islands to carry the news. An old woman on the outskirts of the throng began singing this song; all the mass joined with her, swaying. And the soldier wept.

There are many others of the Negro folk songs as striking and characteristic as these. There are, too, songs that seem to be a step removed from the more primitive types: there is the maze-like medley "Bright Sparkles"; the Easter carol "Dust, Dust and Ashes"; the dirge "My Mother's Took Her Flight and Gone Home."

These represent a third step in the development of the slave song, of which "You May Bury Me in the East" is the first, and songs like "March On" and "Steal Away" are the second. The first is African music, the second Afro-American, while the third is a blending of Negro music with the music heard in the foster land. The result is still distinctively Negro and the method of blending original, but the elements are both Negro and Caucasian. One might go further and find a fourth step in this development, where the songs of white America have been distinctively influenced by the slave songs or have incorporated whole phrases of Negro melody, as "Old Folks at Home" and "Old Black Joe." Side by side with the growth has gone the debasement and imitation—the Negro minstrel songs, many of the gospel hymns and some of the contemporary "coon songs"—a mass of music in which the novice may easily lose himself and never find the real Negro melodies.

In these songs, I have said, the slave spoke to the world. Such a message is naturally veiled and half articulate. Words and music have lost each other, and new and cant phrases of a dimly understood theology have displaced the older sentiment. Once in a while we catch a strange word of an unknown tongue, as the "Mighty Myo," which figures as a river of death; more often slight words or mere doggerel are joined to music of singular sweetness. Purely secular songs are few in number, partly because many of them were turned into hymns by a change of words, partly because the frolics were seldom heard by the stranger, and the music less often caught. In nearly all the songs, however, the music is distinctly sorrowful.

The words that are left to us are not without interest, and, cleared of evident dross, they conceal much of real poetry and meaning beneath conventional theology and unmeaning rhapsody. Like all primitive folk, the slave stood near to Nature's heart. Life was a "rough and rolling sea" like the brown Atlantic of the Sea Islands; the "wilderness" was the home of God; and the "lonesome valley" led to the way of life. "Winter'll soon be over" was the picture of life and death to a tropical imagination. The sudden wild thunderstorms of the South awed and impressed the Negroes—at times the rumbling seemed to them mournful, at times imperious:

> My Lord calls me,
> He calls me by the thunder,
> The trumpet sounds it in my soul.

The monotonous toil and exposure are painted in many words. One sees the ploughman in the hot, moist furrow, singing:

> Dere's no rain to wet you,
> Dere's no sun to burn you,
> Oh, push along, believer,
> I want to go home.

The bowed and bent old man cries, with thrice-repeated wail:

> O Lord, keep me from sinking down,

and he rebukes the devil of doubt who can whisper:

> Jesus is dead and God's gone away.

Over the inner thoughts of the slaves and their relations one with another the shadow of fear ever hung, so that we get but glimpses here and there, and also, with them, eloquent omissions and silences. Mother and child are sung, but seldom father; fugitive and weary wanderer call for pity and affection, but there is little of wooing and wedding; the rocks and the mountains are well known, but home is unknown.

Love songs are scarce and fall into two categories—the frivolous and light, and the sad. Of deep, successful love there is ominous silence.

Of death the Negro showed little fear, but talked of it familiarly and even fondly as simply a crossing of the waters, perhaps—who knows?—back to his ancient forests again. Later days transfigured his fatalism, and amid the dust and dirt the toiler sang:

> Dust, dust and ashes, fly over my grave,
> But the Lord shall bear my spirit home.

The things evidently borrowed from the surrounding world undergo characteristic change when they enter the mouth of the slave. Especially is this true of Bible phrases. "Weep, O captive daughter of Zion," is quaintly turned into "Zion, weep-a-low," and the wheels of Ezekiel are turned every way in the mystic dreaming of the slave, till he says:

> There's a little wheel a-turnin' in-a-my heart.

Through all the sorrow of the sorrow songs there breathes a hope—a faith in the ultimate justice of things. The minor cadences of despair change often to triumph and calm confidence. Sometimes it is faith in life, sometimes a faith in death, sometimes assurance of boundless justice in some world beyond. But whichever it is, the meaning is always clear: that sometime, somewhere, men will judge men by their souls and not by their skins. Is such a hope justified? Do the sorrow songs sing true?

The silently growing assumption of this age is that the probation of races is past, and that the backward races of today are of proven inefficiency and not worth the saving. Such an assumption is the arrogance of peoples irreverent toward Time and ignorant of the deeds of men. A thousand years ago such an assumption, easily possible, would have made it difficult for the Teuton to prove his right to life. Two thousand years ago such dogmatism, readily welcome, would have scouted the idea of blond races ever leading civilization. So woefully unorganized is sociological knowledge that the meaning of progress, the meaning of "swift" and "slow" in human doing, and the limits of human perfectability, are veiled, unanswered sphinxes on the shores of science. Why should Aeschylus have sung 2,000 years before Shakespeare was born? Why has civilization flourished in Europe, and flickered, flamed and died in Africa? So long as the world stands meekly dumb before such questions, shall this nation proclaim its ignorance and unhallowed prejudices by denying freedom of opportunity to those who brought the sorrow songs to the Seats of the Mighty?

Your country? How came it yours? Before the Pilgrims landed we were here. Here we have brought our three gifts and mingled them with yours: a gift of story and song—soft, stirring melody in an ill-harmonized and unmelodious land; the gift of sweat and brawn to beat back the wilderness, conquer the soil, and lay the foundations of this vast economic empire 200 years earlier than your weak hands could have done it; the third, a gift of the spirit. Around us the history of the land has centered for thrice 100 years; out of the nation's heart we have called all that was best to throttle and subdue all that was worst; fire and blood, prayer and sacrifice, have billowed over this people, and they have found peace only in the altars of the God of Right. Nor has our gift of the spirit been merely passive. Actively, we have woven ourselves with the very warp and woof of this nation—we fought their battles, shared their sorrow, mingled our blood with theirs, and, generation after generation, have pleaded with a headstrong, careless people to despise not Justice, Mercy and Truth, lest the nation be smitten with a curse. Our song, our toil, our cheer and warning have been given to this nation in blood-brotherhood. Are not these gifts worth the giving? Is not this work and striving? Would America have been America without her Negro people?

Even so is the hope that sang in the songs of my fathers well sung. If somewhere in this whirl and chaos of things there dwells Eternal Good, pitiful yet masterful, then anon in His good time America shall rend the Veil and the prisoned shall go free. Free, free as the sunshine trickling down the morning into these high windows of mine, free as yonder fresh young voices welling up to me from the caverns of brick and mortar below—swelling with song, instinct with life, tremulous treble and darkening bass. My children, my little children, are singing to the sunshine, and thus they sing:

> Let us cheer the weary traveler
> Along the heavenly way.

And the traveler girds himself, sets his face toward the morning and goes his way.

—1902

# Spirituals and Neo-Spirituals

by Zora Neale Hurston

THE REAL spirituals are not really just songs. They are unceasing variations around a theme.

Contrary to popular belief, their creation is not confined to the slavery period. Like the folk-tales, the spirituals are being made and forgotten everyday. There is this difference: the makers of the songs of the present go about from town to town and church to church singing their songs. Some are printed and called ballads, and offered for sale after the services at 10 and 15 cents each. Other spirituals are merely sung in competition. The lifting of the collection is the time for the song battles. Quite a bit of rivalry develops.

These songs, even the printed ones, do not remain long in their original form. Every congregation that takes one up alters it considerably. For instance, "The Dying Bed-Maker," which is easily the most popular of the recent compositions, has been changed to "He's a Mind Regulator" by a Baptist church in New Orleans.

The idea that the whole body of spirituals are "sorrow songs" is ridiculous. They cover a wide range of subjects from a peeve at gossips to Death and Judgment.

The nearest thing to a description one can reach is that they are Negro religious songs, sung by a group, and a group bent on expression of feelings and not on sound effects.

There never has been a presentation of genuine Negro spirituals to any audience anywhere. What is being sung by the concert artists and glee clubs are the works of Negro composers or adapters *based* on the spirituals. Under this head come the works of Harry T. Burleigh, Rosamond Johnson, Lawrence Brown, Nathaniel Dett, Hall Johnson and Work. All good work and beautiful, but *not* the spirituals. These neo-spirituals are the outgrowth of the glee clubs. Fisk University boasts perhaps the oldest and certainly the most famous of these. They have spread their interpretation over America and Europe. Hampton and Tuskegee have not been unheard. But with all the glee clubs and soloists, there has not been one genuine spiritual presented.

To begin with, a Negro spiritual is not solo or quartet material. The jagged harmony is what makes it, and it ceases to be what it was when this is absent. Neither can any group be trained to reproduce it. Its truth dies under training like flowers under hot water. The harmony of the true spiritual is not regular. The dissonances are important and not to be ironed out by the trained musician. The various parts break in at any old time. Falsetto often takes the place of regular voices for short periods. Keys change. Moreover, each singing of the piece is a new creation. The congregation is bound by no rules. No two singings are alike, so that we must consider the rendition of a song not as a final thing, but as a mood. It won't be the same thing next Sunday.

*Negro songs to be heard truly must be sung by a group, and a group bent on expression of feelings and not on sound effects.*

Glee clubs and concert singers put on their tuxedos, bow prettily to the audience, get the pitch and burst into magnificent song—but not *Negro* song. The real Negro singer cares nothing about pitch. The first notes just burst out and the rest of the church join in—fired by the same inner urge. Every man trying to express himself through song. Every man for himself. Hence the harmony and disharmony, the shifting keys and broken time that make up the spiritual.

I have noticed that whenever an untampered-with congregation attempts the renovated spirituals, the people grow self-conscious. They sing sheepishly, in unison. None of the glorious individualistic flights that make up their own songs. Perhaps they feel on strange ground. Like the unlettered parent before his child just home from college. At any rate, they are not very popular.

This is no condemnation of the neo-spirituals. They are a valuable contribution to the music and literature of the world. But let no one imagine that they are the songs of the people, as sung by them.

The lack of dialect in the religious expression—particularly in the prayers—will seem irregular.

The truth is, that the religious service is a conscious art expression. The artist is consciously creating—carefully choosing every syllable and every breath. The dialect breaks through only when the speaker has reached the emotional pitch where he loses self-consciousness.

In the mouth of the Negro the English language loses its stiffness, yet conveys its meaning accurately. "The booming bounderries of this whirling world" conveys just as accurate a picture as mere "boundaries," and a little

music is gained besides. "The rim bones of nothing" is just as truthful as "limitless space."

Negro singing and formal speech are breathy. The audible breathing is part of the performance, and various devices are resorted to to adorn the breath taking. Even the lack of breath is embellished with syllables. This is, of course, the very antithesis of white vocal art. European singing is considered good when each syllable floats out on a column of air, seeming not to have any mechanics at all. Breathing must be hidden. Negro song ornaments both the song and the mechanics. It is said of a popular preacher, "He's got a good straining voice." I will make a parable to illustrate the difference between Negro and European.

A white man built a house. So he got it built and he told the man: "Plaster it good, so that nobody can see the beams and uprights." So he did. Then he had it papered with beautiful paper, and painted the outside. And a Negro built him a house. So when he got the beams and all in, he carved beautiful grotesques over all the sills and stanchions, and beams and rafters. So both went to live in their houses and were happy.

The well-known "ha!" of the Negro preacher is a breathing device. It is the tail end of the expulsion just before inhalation. Instead of permitting the breath to drain out, when the wind gets too low for words, the remnant is expelled violently. Example: (inhalation) "And oh!"; (full breath) "my Father and my wonder-working God"; (explosive exhalation) "ha!"

Chants and hums are not used indiscriminately, as it would appear to a casual listener. They have a definite place and time. They are used to "bear up" the speaker. As Mama Jane, of Second Zion Baptist Church, New Orleans, explained to me: "What point they come out on, you bear 'em up."

For instance, if the preacher should say:

"Jesus will lead us," the congregation would bear him up with: "I'm got my ha-hands in my Jesus' hands"; if, in prayer or sermon, the mention is made of nailing Christ to the cross: "Didn't Calvary tremble when they nailed Him down?"

There is no definite post-prayer chant. One may follow, however, because of intense emotion. A song immediately follows prayer. There is a pre-prayer hum which depends for its material upon the song just sung. It is usually a pianissimo continuation of the song without words. If some of the people use the words, it is done so indistinctly that they would be hard to catch by a person unfamiliar with the song.

As indefinite as hums sound, they also are formal and can be found unchanged all over the South. The Negroized white hymns are not exactly sung. They are converted into a barbaric chant that is not a chant. It is a sort of liquefying of words. These songs are always used at funerals and on any solemn occasion. The Negro has created no songs for death and burials, in spite of the sombre subject matter contained in some of the spirituals. Negro songs are one and all based on a dance-possible rhythm. The heavy interpretations have been added by the more cultured singers. So for funerals, fitting white hymns are used.

Beneath the seeming informality of religious worship, there is a set formality. Sermons, prayers, moans and testimonies have their definite forms. The individual may hang as many new ornaments upon the traditional form as he likes, but the audience would be disagreeably surprised if the form were abandoned. Any new and original elaboration is welcomed, however, and this brings out the fact that all religious expression among Negroes is regarded as art, and ability is recognized as definitely as in any other art. The beautiful prayer receives the accolade as well as the beautiful song. It is merely a form of expression which people generally are not accustomed to think of as art. Nothing outside of the Old Testament is as rich in figure as a Negro prayer. Some instances are unsurpassed anywhere in literature.

There is a lively rivalry in the technical artistry of all of these fields. It is a special honor to be called upon to pray over the Communion table, for the greatest prayer artist present is chosen by the pastor for this; a lively something spreads over the church as he kneels, and the "bearing up" hum precedes him. It continues sometimes through the introduction, but ceases as he makes the complimentary salutation to the Deity. This consists in giving God all the titles that form allows.

The introduction to the prayer usually consists of one or two verses of some well-known hymn. "O, That I Knew a Secret Place" seems to be the favorite. There is a definite pause after this, then follows an elaboration of all or parts of the Lord's Prayer. After that, follows what I call the setting, that is, the artist calling attention to the physical situation of himself and the church. After the dramatic setting, the action begins.

There are certain rhythmic breaks throughout the prayer, and the church "bears him up" at every one of these. There is in the body of the prayer an accelerando passage where the audience takes no part. It would be like applauding in the middle of a solo at the Metropolitan. It is here that the artist comes forth. He adorns the prayer with every sparkle of earth, water and sky, and nobody wants to miss a syllable. He comes down from this height to a slower tempo and is borne up again. The last few sentences are unaccompanied, for here again one listens to the individual's closing peroration. Several may join in the final amen. The best figure that I can think of is that the prayer is an obbligato over and above the harmony of the assembly.

—1933

Brock Peters (left), Leon Bibb (bottom left) and the late Josh White (bottom right) are modern bards of Negro folk songs.

# The Source

by Maud Cuney Hare

In A SERIOUS study of Negro music it is readily seen that there is a rhythmical relationship and melodic similarity between native African music and the Negro American folk song. As the Negro, first brought to the United States with the exploiters of Virginia in 1619, over 300 years ago, gradually became a product of American institutions in the making, and a new race was developed by a new environment and the fusion of Negro blood with that of the Indian native and white inhabitant, it is obvious that his folk music, brought with him from Africa, should have become a particular music absolutely his own.[1]

There is, of course, the universality of certain principles of design which are to be found in all folk music, but the ingenuity shown in the shifting of accent or addition of grace notes and embellishments to give contrast in different repetitions, in the manner of reiteration of the same figure or phrase at higher levels, and in the enhancement of tonal coloring given by intricate rhythmical clapping of hands and patting of feet—these qualities produce a folk musical contribution that is unique and apart. We may remember that the Irish, too, repeat their melodic phrases higher and higher, and that the Scotch and Italians employ the jerking figuration of an eighth (1/8) note to a quarter (1/4) note, or a sixteenth (1/16) towards an eighth, but in its entirety the Negro American folk song shows a well-developed sense of form and an original usage of familiar devices.

The African Negro was sufficiently advanced to invent musical instruments. As he was stripped of every form of birthright when brought to America, necessity forced him to fashion crude instruments from material at hand—trees, reeds and bones. Added to clapping and patting, one form of rhythm grew from the performers beating an improvised drum in such a manner as to bring the beat and words simultaneously together. The rhythmic patterns, never simple, were made to suit the verbal expression.

Intricacy of rhythm has added to the folklorist's difficulty in notating songs as heard sung. The meter is sometimes changed in the same song—such as passing from 4/4 to 2/4 or 4/4 to 3/4. There is a rarity of 3/4 time, in comparison with 4/4 or 2/4. A frequent change of bar time as practiced now by writers of "modern music" is in keeping with a custom followed in Russian and in southern French folk song. To these races the Negro is spiritually akin. Dalcroze, in *Eurhythmics, Art and Education,* states that "at present time, owing to Negro and Oriental rhythms, freedom has been restored to rhythmic successions; alternating unequal bars have become natural, and arbitrary accentuations no longer astonish anyone."

The layman speaks of the Negro folk song

as being in the minor mode. The fact is that the songs sound minor because they are in the old "Dorian" (arithmetic) mode—the oldest used in folk songs.

In the earliest Greek system the musical scale consisted of seven tones that corresponded to the seven "planets" of Moon, Mercury, Venus, Sun, Mars, Jupiter and Saturn. The seven colors of the rainbow corresponded to the tones of the scale, which gives a table for the new exponents of "color" in music. The African had no written musical system, but is it not possible that the Yorubans tuned their lyre to their five gods of protection—Hermes (lightning), Shango (thunder), Ifa (prophecy), Helios (sun) and Oshu (moon)? At least it is an amusingly interesting conjecture. The African *kissar* is tuned to a five-tone scale.

An imagery of poetic text found in the religious and sentimental songs was born of the Negro's innate gift of oratory and his transcendental reasoning. African folklore abounds with legends and proverbs, and the use of metaphor is very pronounced in the songs of the Negro. It is noticeable that the words of the songs are grouped in short phrases which are repeated over and over again, the first and third lines usually sung as the verse and the second and fourth as a refrain which is repeated after each stanza. In many songs the verse is varied only by the naming of each family relationship. Outside of the religious songs, the words are often difficult to understand.

It is not surprising that those Africans first brought as captives to America found it difficult to express themselves in the words of a newly heard language, and that the meaning of the words in a number of the oldest songs should be obscure. Language as spoken by their captors had to be acquired as a child learns to formulate the words of his parents' tongue.

African speech itself consists of many tongues. The English acquired by the illiterate slave became a means of communication among the early captives from various sections of the African coast.[2] In the Negro dialect as evolved in America all harsh letters, such as G, D, T and R, are softened or eliminated, while, as in Latin America, the V is blurred to B. David Guion, a musician who is interested in Negro song and in his own west Texas cowboy songs, said in an interview, "Half the beauty of the old, typical Negro music is in the quaint pronunciation of words and their still quainter and more charming mispronunciations. If these are altered, the value of the song is lowered by half. A proof of this lies in the fact that the Moody-and-Sankey-izing that has been done to much of Negro music has invariably been detrimental."[3]

There are about 800 folk songs recorded, but the spirituals, the songs in which the Negro expressed his faith in "a victory that overcometh the world," are the most commonly known of these melodies. Many of the hymns were known in the early period as "shouts." These were stirringly sung at camp meetings and are still to be heard in rural churches in the South. For example, in Alabama, the old song "Redeem, Redeem," expressed the thought which could not be spoken:

> Some go to church an' dey put on pretense
> Until de day ob grace is spent.
> Ef dey haven' been changed you'll know it well,
> When Gabriel blow, dey will go to hell.
> Sunday come, dey'll have Christian faith,
> Monday come, dey will lose deir grace;
> De Devil gets in, dey will roll up deir sleeve,
> Religion come out an' begin to leave.[4]

In this manner, even the religious songs were used as songs of satire, or as "taunts" such as are generously found in true African song. The hymns or shouts also did duty as rowing songs. The fine old spiritual "Michael, Row the Boat Ashore" was one of the songs employed interchangeably. John J. Niles' *Old Songs Hymnal* includes Negro spirituals characteristic of the highly emotional songs sung at revivals. A reprint in 1929 of the early collection of *Slave Songs of the United States,* by William Francis Allen, Charles Pickard Ware and Lucy McKim Garrison, who gathered the folk songs personally before 1867, places at hand the most valuable historic data relating to the shouts and other forms of folk melodies.

Referring to the singing, the authors give in this book an illuminating passage to describe the manner in which the songs were sung at Coffin's Point, St. Helena Island, off the coast of South Carolina. On a neighboring plantation, "The Negroes keep exquisite time in singing and do not suffer themselves to be daunted by any obstacle in the words. The most obstinate scripture phrases or snatches from hymns they will force to do duty with any tune they please and will dash heroically through trochaic tunes at the head of a column of iambics with wonderful skill."

Of the later day manner of shouting and the use of shout songs, James Weldon Johnson, in his *Book of American Negro Spirituals,* describes the ring shout as that of a late type which he saw danced in boyhood days in Florida. He speaks of it as a "survival of an African ceremony" such as he saw performed in Venezuela and in Haiti. He rightly adds that educated ministers and congregations discouraged the shouts. And yet, during the present year (1935), hysterical and ecstatic shouting was an excitable feature of "revivals" held in a Negro church in Boston.

A number of rare old songs in light vein were discovered on the island of St. Helena a few years ago by Natalie Curtis Burlin. In these parts, a section least influenced by white civilization, and in not far distant parts, the odd and peculiar dialect of the Geechee people, whom the author sought to hear speak and sing in Georgia, attests to the influence of the land of their forbears, that of Africa. In recent years, we have had a number of writers investigating and studying the speech and customs of the Geechees and Gullahs, who never came into close contact with Anglo-Saxons, as their forefathers were brought to this country shortly before the emancipation of the slaves. These last cargoes of native Africans came from the Congo and other sections [distant from West Africa]—hence a difference in dialects.

The plantation songs were used interchangeably—for revival shouts, for burial songs, for hymns of consolation and for signals, or means of communication. In planning secret meetings or plotting ways by which they might escape to the free North or to Canada, they used songs that had a double meaning. At St. Michael, Talbot County, Maryland, five young men, Henry and John Harris, Sandy Jenkins, Henry Bailey and Charles Roberts, plotted with young Frederick Douglass, in 1836, to find means of escaping to free territory. They repeatedly sang "O Canaan, Sweet Canaan, I Am Bound for the Land of Canaan," which meant they were determined to reach the North—their Canaan.

## NEGRO SPIRITUALS

The songs known as spirituals are the expression of a supreme belief in immortality that transcends mere religious creeds and theoretical dogma. Through them the paganism of African "spirit" songs is reborn and modified by Christian doctrines, and they are the musical expression of spiritual emotion created *by* the race and not *for it.*

"Swing Low, Sweet Chariot," an American "Negro spiritual" in the pentatonic scale, noted in *Fisk Jubilee Songs,* 1871, offers a key to this development. The variants of this song are "Good Old Chariot," "Swing Low, Sweet Chariot," (Hampton) and "The Danville Chariot." In the first movement of Dvořák's *New World Symphony,* in which this theme occurs, it is given out by the flute. William A. Fisher, who has given the melody a setting for solo voice and piano, tells an interesting story about the song, which was told to him by Bishop Frederick Fisher of Calcutta, India, who had recently returned from Central Africa. He relates:

> Bishop Fisher stated that in Rhodesia he had heard the natives sing a melody so closely resembling "Swing Low, Sweet Chariot" that he felt that he had found it in its original form; moreover, the subject was identical. The tribe of natives that inhabit the region near the great Victoria Falls have a custom from which the song arose. When one of their chiefs, in the old days, was about to die, he was placed in a great canoe, together with the trappings that marked his rank, and food for his journey. The canoe was set afloat in midstream headed toward the great falls and the vast column of mist that rises from them. Meanwhile, the tribe on the shore would sing its chant of farewell. The legend is that on one occasion the king was seen to rise in his canoe at the very brink of the falls and enter a chariot that, descending from the mists, bore him aloft. This incident gave rise to the words "Swing Low, Sweet Chariot," and the song, brought to America by African slaves long ago, became anglicized and modified by their Christian faith.[5]

In America, it is told that the song arose from an incident which happened to a woman sold from a Mississippi plantation to Tennessee. Rather than be separated from her child, she was about to drown herself and little one in the Cumberland River, when she was prevented by an old Negro woman, who exclaimed, "Wait, let de Chariot of de Lord swing low, and let me take de Lord's scroll and read it to you." The heartbroken mother became consoled and was reconciled to the parting. The song became known with the passing on of the story, which seems more legendary than real.[6]

Among these songs several others of unusual importance should be noted: "My Lord Delivered Daniel," in the major key of G, with a variant from Florida, "O Daniel," and another title of the original in Kentucky; "Wrestling Jacob," with variants—"My Lord, What a Morning," from Southeastern slave states, "I Want to Be Ready," from Kentucky, with

such variants as "Walk, Jerusalem, Jes' Like John" and "Walk into Jerusalem Jes' Like John"; and "Go Down, Moses," an interpretation of Hebrew history, with variants from Virginia and the Bahamas. As the Lord delivered the Jews so would He the Negroes.

Then there are two distinct types of slave songs, although there are but few songs using the practice of slavery as a theme in the text. Some of these are "Many Thousand Gone," "No More Auction Block for Me" and "Is Master Going to Sell Us Tomorrow?" Then there are such songs as "O'er the Crossing," from Virginia, with such variants as "My Body Racked wid Fever," from the Port Royal Islands.

There are striking examples of burial hymns developed from the custom of sitting up and singing over the dead. A fine funeral song is "I Know Moonrise," reported first from Georgia. Impressive also are "Graveyard" and "Lay This Body Down," first noted from Port Royal.

"I Know Moonrise" is the finest funeral song in all this folk material. It comes from St. Simon's Island, Georgia. Writing of this song in the *Atlantic Monthly* of June, 1867, Colonel Higginson said, "I was startled when first I came on such a flower of poetry in that dark soil." Never since man first lived and suffered was his infinite longing for peace uttered more plaintively than in that line, "I'll lie in the grave and stretch out my arms." A possible variant is the melody "Graveyard," which was sung on Captain John Tripp's plantation and also at Coffin's Point. The variant "Lay This Body Down," used as a rowing song, was noted in 1867 as coming from the Port Royal Islands. W. H. Russell of the London *Times* heard this song when on a midnight row from Pocotaligo to the Trescot estate on Barnwell Island. Termed a "barbaric sort of madrigal," it was given by a solo voice then sung by others in chorus. Of the refrain, Lieutenant Colonel Trowbridge

The origins of Negro spirituals and folk songs.

wrote, "It was sung at funerals in the night-time—one of the most solemn and characteristic of customs of the Negroes that originated at St. Simon's Island, Georgia."

> Oh, your soul! Oh, my soul!
> I'm going to the churchyard
> To lay this body down;
>
> Oh, my soul! Oh, your soul!
> We're going to the churchyard
> To lay this nigger down.

In the early study of Negro folk song, the Sea Island section receives more notice than any other one. Miss Elizabeth Putnam, a Boston lady of abolitionist inheritance, wrote of these parts as they were after a battle of the Civil War:

> Some of the plantations and city houses were deserted by their owners, and the slaves came into the Union camps. Then Governor Butler suggested a name for these refugees; he called them contrabands of war. Meantime the Sea Island region had become Union territory, the planters and their families having fled. Mr. Pierce was commissioned to get under way some method of managing the Negroes and starting a cotton crop for 1862. An Educational Commission for Freedmen was organized in Boston, New York and Philadelphia, and on March 3, 1862, there set sail for Port Royal a party of public-spirited men and women, with salaries of from $25 to $50 per month. With that goodly company of Northern white men and women went Charlotte Forten (afterwards Mrs. Francis Grimké). My friend, H. W., wrote from Port Royal of Miss Forten, who was of partly Negro blood: "She has one of the sweetest voices I ever heard. The Negroes knew the instant they saw her what she was, but she has been treated by them with universal respect. She is an educated lady." June 1, 1863, came the Emancipation Proclamation. Colonel Thomas Wentworth Higginson immediately organized a colored regiment. In June, 1863, Colonel Robert G. Shaw led his troops through Pemberton Square to the State House, and they followed the rest out into the South.

Colonel Higginson proved a sympathetic and willing listener to the singing of the contrabands of war, and the value of his contribution is incalculable—a thrice-told story.

When searching for Creole folk songs in Louisiana, the author heard the burial song "Pilgrim's Death" sung by an old woman in New Iberia. The author again came across the melody in west Texas. Some time later, while roaming the countryside of Americus, Georgia, folk song gathering, the author secured a similar song from a washerwoman, heard singing over her tubs in her back yard.[7] After some persuasion, she repeated her hymn:

> O what you goin' to do
> When Death comes stealin' in your room?
>   (three times)
> O my Lord, O my Lord,
> What shall I do?
>
> I'm goin' to *lay* my *head,*
> My head on Jesus' breast,
>   (three times)
> O my Lord, O my Lord,
> What shall I do?
>
> I'm goin' to breathe
> My life out sweetly there,
>   (three times)
> O my Lord, O my Lord,
> What shall I do?
>
> O I'm so glad,
> My soul got a hidin' place,
>   (three times)
> O my Lord, O my Lord,
> What shall I do?

There were seven verses to the song. As sung in Texas, additional lines were:

> We *are,* we *are,*
> The true born sons of Levi.
>
> We *are,* we *are,*
> The root and branch of-er David.
>
> Shining brighter-*er*
> Than any-er mornin' star.

In Americus, Georgia, the author heard a variant, "Go Back, Ol' Man," which was sung in the same manner—that of accenting the words that fell on the strong beats of the measures. There was the same striking glissando interpolation—"Welcome travelers, welcome home."

> Go back, ol' man. You dead too late; ol' Master Jesus locked der door, and carried de key on high.

The song of consolation, burdened by what it does *not* say, "Do Doan' Yer Weep for de

Baby," comes from Georgia—the heart of the South.

Two beautiful spirituals which are Christmas carols are the songs, "De New-Born Baby," and "Go Tell It on de Mountain." The first comes from South Carolina and is sung by the fishermen on the Atlantic Seaboard coast. The second was noted in *Religious Folk Songs of the Negro*. It is typical of songs extemporized at Christmas time on the plantations.

Seldom does one find extant songs of mother-love—of the parting, by death or ruthless fate, of an enslaved mother from her helpless child. What words or tones could express her agony?

## OTHER SONGS

Children's songs—lullabies, action songs and "rounds"—come from a later period than the spirituals and tell a story all their own. "Li'l Liza Jane" (taken to France by colored soldiers), and "Crickaney, Crickaney, Craney Crow," sung and played as a game by children as far south as Texas, are types of dance songs found in towns and on plantations. They are familiar to both white and black children.

Memory of childhood days in Texas brings before the writer the picture of a certain little girl in trailing white nightdress, striving to maintain her equilibrium as she stands upright in bed, calling out, "Here I stand, raggety and dirty, if you don't come kiss me, I'll run like a turkey." It was the signal for the morning kiss from an adoring and adored father—a ritual performed without thought that the nonsense words would ever rise to the dignity of being enclosed by quotation marks.

The first of two love songs, of which there are but few, is "Poor Rosy," a lament found in E minor and said to come from Maryland. Variants known as "I'm in Hopes to Pray My Sins Away," and "Before I Stay in Hell

One Day," are found in Florida and South Carolina. "O Suzanne," in D minor, probably came originally from the Southeastern states.

The custom of slavery, with its ruthless breaking of home ties, often caused unhappy separations between lovers, but it evidently did not destroy steadfastness of affection, according to this philosophy of the slave "Strappan," in *Slave Songs of the United States* (p. xxxvi):

> Arter you lub, you lub you know, boss. You can't broke lub. Man can't broke lub. Lub stan'—e ain't gwine broke—Man heb to be very smart fo' broke lub. Lub is a ting stan' just like tar, arter he stick, he stick, he ain't gwine move. He can't move less dan you burn him. Hab to kill all two arter he lub fo' you broke lub.

\* \* \* \* \* \*

The American Negro, like the Negro in Africa, found much pleasure and consolation in his music, both while at work and at play. In the fields, when cleaning rice, the workers were followed by singers who clapped their hands and stamped their feet as an accompaniment to their song.

The Negro's dance and song tunes and his work songs were produced just as were his spirituals, with the same modes and rhythms: "The Battle of Jericho" could easily become a fox-trot. A fine example of the type of religious hymn that was evolved into a labor song is one found in Calhoun's *Plantation Songs*, under the title "Hammering Judgment":

> Don't you hear God talking, hammering, etc.,
> He's talking to Moses, hammering, etc.,
> He's talking through thunder, hammering, etc.,
> Hammering judgment, hammering, etc.,
> Hammer keep a-ringing, hammering, etc.,
> God tol' Moses, hammering, etc.,
> Go down in Egyp', hammering, etc.,
> To tell ol' Pharoah, hammering, etc.,
> To loose His people, hammering, etc.,
> Ol' Pharaoh had a hard heart, hammering, etc.
> An' would not loose dem, hammering, etc.

The imitative ejaculations of *wham, whum, boum, bam, hunk* and *huh* are familiar descriptions given the songs of the laborers and the workers on the railroads and roadways.

"Water Boy," a convict song arranged by Avery Robinson, a white musician born in Louisville, Kentucky, is one of the modern secular songs widely known. A version as sung by a gang of Mississippi laborers reads:

Water boy, water boy,
Bring de water roun'.
If yo' don't like yo' job,
Set de bucket down.

The large body of work songs in the making, and the vulgar so-called social songs of the Negro underworld now interesting a group of educators and writers, play little part in Negro music. They are neither popular songs nor true folk songs.

\* \* \* \* \* \*

The type of folk song known as the chantey is the latest taken up by musicians, and these rollicking old songs have been introduced on the concert stage by soloists looking for novelties, as well as by groups such as the London Singers, who do them so successfully. Many English and American folk songs of the sea are of Negro origin. We find rowing songs in South Carolina, where fine old lyrics were used interchangeably as "shouts," chanteys sung on the old clipper ships that sailed to distant seas, and steamboat songs sung in the Southwest. The last were heard from the banks of the Ohio to the Rio Grande and are a part of chantey singing.[8]

The construction of the chantey is akin to that of the "corn songs" of the Negroes, and the method of singing it practically the same as that followed by the workers on land. The sailor songs were extemporized at sea by the chanteyman, who led the singing, and words and melody partake of the vernacular of the seafaring man.

The name of "chantey," or "shanty," is said not to have been used before 1869, but the folk song of the sea was known before that date. *The Sailor's Song Book* was published in 1842. Since then a number of sailor song anthologies have appeared. One of the best of these, *Roll and Go: Songs of American Sailormen,* edited by Joanna C. Colcord in 1924, gives a number of chanteys of the Negro. Miss Colcord brings forth the interesting supposition of Sir Richard Runciman Terry, who believes that the term was taken from the "shanties" of the humbler class of Negroes—shanties along the waterfront of Mobile, whence many of the old tunes came. The word "chantey" or "shanty" was thought to have been derived from the French word *chanter* [to sing].

But we rarely think of the French in connection with sailor songs, while Englishmen, particularly Cecil Sharp, have made us familiar with these songs. Miss Colcord, herself born on the sea, a daughter of a master mariner and skillful chanteyman, writes that while Englishmen or Irishmen "were admitted to rank ahead of the white Americans as chanteymen, they in turn were far outstripped by the American Negroes—the best singers that ever lifted a chantey aboard ship."

Since there is no complete record of life at sea as it existed during the period of 1812 to 1860, the chantey has a special value. At one time, the ships that were loaded and unloaded on the wharves at Baltimore carried what was called "chequered crews," that is, one half white and one half colored, and it is thought the white boys thus learned the Negro chanteys.

Sir Walter Runciman, who lived some years in the West Indies, names "Sally Brown" in his collection of chanteys. The musical form is that of a halliard chantey," [9] but was used for heaving the anchor. "Sally" seems to be the heroine of all chanteydom, for different versions appear in various American as well as English collections. The author's song, from New Orleans, reads, "Sally Brown is a Creole lady, Way O, roll and go. For seven long years I courted Sally, Way O, roll and go." But Sally marries a "Negro soldier," and the singer laments the fact that he has spent all his money on Sally Brown.

From London, Cecil Sharp quotes different verses, while one version, which is listed among windlass and capstan chanteys, bears these significant words: "Sally lives on the Old Plantation. She belongs to the Wild Goose Nation." The chanteyman who improvised these words probably placed "Sally Brown" as the progeny of the admixture of Negro and Indian blood which was so common in Louisiana as well as in the East. The "wild goose nation" often appears in British chanteys.

The pirate days of the West Indies, the American slave trade, the Irish emigration of the Fifties and the War of 1812 are some of the historic events recorded in the so-called "fo'c's'le songs," which rang out on the old clipper ships. A Negro chantey, "The Black Ball Line," a halliard chantey, perpetuates the name of the first and most famous line of American packet ships, which started its run between New York and Liverpool in 1816. There are a number of versions of this song.

Other popular chanteys of Negro American origin are: "He-Back, She-Back"; "Santa Anna"; "Mudder Dinah"; and "Haul Away, Jo," also called "Sing, Sally, O." One of the best windlass songs of the Negro is "Shanadore," of which there are six versions. It is thought that, in ignorance, a singer interpreted the name of a river for that of a person:

> You Shanadore, I long to hear you,
> Hurrah, you rollin' river,
> You Shanadore, I long to hear you,
> Oh, ho, you Shanadore.

As long ago as June 24, 1852, a Boston paper printed in its columns that the "Royal Mail liner *America* sails with full passenger list; the day of clipper packets seems about over." With the final passing of the beautiful old sailing vessels came the end of the making of the gay, ofttimes ribald, sea chantey.

The Negro of South Carolina and Georgia chanted rowing songs to religious texts, in sentiment quite unlike the rollicking chantey of the sailor.

Colonel Higginson, in *Army Life in a Black Regiment*, quotes a boat song which he heard in South Carolina that was sung in time to the tug of the oar. It was the spiritual "I Want to Go to Canaan," known also as "The Coming Day."

An equally fine boat song was that of "One More River":

> O, Jordan bank was a great old bank,
> Dere ain't but one more river to cross.

The Negro's custom of singing while rowing came from Africa. The author was told by a native African friend that it is customary for the rowers to join in song after listening a moment to a melody which is extemporized by one of the oarsmen. Each man sings a different part. Charles Pickard Ware explained that the rowing tunes were sung in South Carolina two measures to each stroke, the first measure being accented by the beginning of the stroke, the second by the rattle of the oars in the oarlocks. "Michael, Row the Boat Ashore" was used when the load was heavy or the tide against them.

Explorer James Barnes, in describing the harmony of African rowing songs, speaks thus of a paddling song which has similarities to Negro American song, "Some especially good singer booms out the melody, and it is sung with a sort of drone accompaniment . . . there is a countertenor part which maintains an antiphonal repetition of high F, E, D and C, with an effect almost Wagnerian."[10]

\* \* \* \* \* \*

In Mark Twain's entertaining book *Life on the Mississippi*, he tells of the romantic old days of steamboating from New Orleans to St. Louis and on the "upper river," between St. Louis and Cairo, where the Ohio enters. The departures of steamers from New Orleans between four and five o'clock in the afternoon were exciting and bustling moments:

> Every windlass connected with every fore-hatch, from one end of that long array of steamers to the other, was keeping up a whiz and whirr lowering freight into the hold, and the half crew of Negroes that worked them were roaring such songs as "De Las' Sack, De Las' Sack," inspired to unimaginable exultation by the chaos of turmoil and racket that was driving everyone else mad.

The same spirit is shown in the following stanza and chorus of "Down the Ohio," sung by the Negro minstrel companies in the Sixties. It is an admixture of dialect and English. The song was contributed to the Boston *Evening Transcript,* by E. W. F.:

> Oh, de massa am proud of de old broad-horn,
> For she brings him a-plenty of tin;
> De crew dey are darkies, de cargo am corn,
> An' de money comes tumblin' in.
>
> Dar is plenty on board for de darkies to eat,
> An' somethin' to drink an' to smoke;
> Dar's de banjo, de bones, an' de old
>    tambourine,
> Dars de clown an' de comic joke.
>
> *Chorus*
> Oh, de river is up,
> An' de channel is deep,
> An' de wind blows steady an' strong,
> Let de splash of your oars
> De measure keep,
> As we row de old [boat] along,
> Down de river, down de river,
> Down—de—O-hi—O!

This chantey was sung on the flat boats of the Ohio River:

> Oh, the river is up, the channel is deep,
> The wind blows steady and strong,
> A-splashing their oars the mariners keep
> As they row their boats along.
> Down the river,
> Down the river,
> Down the O-H-I-O.

"If we could divest ourselves of prejudice," says Haweis in *Music and Morals,* "the songs that float down the Ohio River are one in feeling and character with the songs of the Hebrew captives by the waters of Babylon. We find in them the same tale of bereavement and separation, the same irreparable sorrow, the same simple faith and childish adoration, the same wild tenderness and passionate sweetness, like music in the night."

A Texas-Louisiana chantey noted by M. R. Delany, the colored author of *Blake: Or the Huts of America* (published in 1859), is a song of the black firemen, which they chanted "when the boat glided steadily upstream, seemingly in unison with the lively, though rude and sorrowful, song":

> I'm a-goin' to Texas, O! O! O! O!—
> I'm goin' to Texas, O! O! O! O!

Slave songs were heard on the river in 1823, and of these laments Delany wrote, "They were sung to words . . . as if in unison with the restless current of the great river upon which they were compelled to toil. In the capacity of leader, one poor fellow sang a lament":

> Way down upon the Mobile River,
>    Close to Mobile Bay,
> There's where my thoughts is running ever,
>    All thro' the live-long day.
> There I've got a good and fond old mother,
>    Tho' she is a slave,
> There I've got a sister and a brother,
>    Lying in their peaceful grave.
> O, could I somehow a'nother
>    Drive these tears away;
> When I think about my poor old mother
>    Down upon Mobile Bay.

"In the distance," continues Delany, "on the levee and in the harbor among the steamers, the songs of the boatmen were incessant. Every few hours, landing, loading and unloading, the glee of these men of sorrow was touchingly appropriate and impressive. . . . If there is any class of men anywhere to be found whose sentiments of song and words of lament are made to reach the sympathies of others, the black slave-boatmen on the Mississippi River are that class . . . they are seemingly contented by soothing their sorrows with songs apparently cheerful, but in reality wailing lamentations."

\* \* \* \* \* \*

Apart from the groups of self-taught, gifted musicians who were accustomed to play for

# The Age of Minstrelsy

**by Alain Locke**

## FIRST AGE OF MINSTRELSY: 1850–1875

*M*INSTRELSY—*what is it?* One may well ask, especially if we give it an important place in the history of American and Negro music. For it was not primarily music: the early minstrel, black or white, was no lyric troubadour but an improvising clown. Music was in the bottom of his bag of tricks; his main show was antics, capers and eccentric dancing. And stage minstrelsy preceded the musical age of minstrelsy by 15 or 20 years, just as plantation minstrelsy had preceded it for generations. However, the tradition which gave American music "Dixie" (Dan Emmett, its author, was a minstrel), "The Old Folks at Home" (Stephen Foster was a minstrel's bard) and "Carry Me Back to Old Virginny" (James Bland, its Negro composer, was a minstrel), commands the attention of the musical historian and, in addition, the music-lover.

*Minstrelsy's origin.* Minstrelsy originated on the slave plantations of the South. James Weldon Johnson tells us:

> Every plantation had its talented band that could crack Negro jokes, and sing and dance to the accompaniment of the banjo and the bones —the bones being the actual ribs of a sheep or other small animal, cut the proper length, scraped clean and bleached in the sun. When the planter wished to entertain his guests, he needed only to call his troupe of black minstrels.

At times these bands became semi-professional and traveled around a circuit, but the limitations of chattel slavery set definite bounds to that.

Negro minstrelsy came to the American stage, however, in a counterfeit imitation of this by white actors, who began comic Negro impersonations as "blackface" acts before 1830. But in that year, in Louisville, T. D. Rice, the father of stage minstrelsy, put on an act copied from a Negro stable hand—named Crow, reputedly—which was such a success that it was introduced at the Bowery Theatre in New York, November 12, 1832, to begin formally what was to be the entertainment vogue of two generations of the comic American stage and what has been correctly called "one of the most completely original contributions America has made to the theatre." But, as a stage tradition, minstrelsy was and remained a caricature of Negro life and ways, and when Negroes themselves came into stage minstrelsy, the mold was too set to be radically changed. They had to accept "almost wholly the performance pattern as it had been worked out and laid down by the white minstrels during the preceding 25 years, even to blacking their faces, an expedient which, of course, never entered the minds of the original plantation artists" (Johnson). However, they not only brought to the fore a more genuine and cleaner humor and a new vivacity, but, in addition, they brought expertness on many instruments besides the banjo, to add to the main attractions and appeals of orthodox minstrelsy. But before that, in 1843, a quartet of white men had appeared in New York City as the Virginia Minstrels; their tenor was Dan Emmett, the composer of "Dixie," which ironically enough was Negro before it was "Confederate." Its first official title was: "Dixie-Land: Ethiopian Walk 'Round."

Minstrelsy was instantly popular and profitable. Rice was not only the box-office success of his day, but spread the minstrel vogue by several trips abroad. In 1833, he introduced Joseph Jefferson at the age of four to the stage as a co-minstrel singing the same "Jim Crow." Even the elder Booth at the time was not above Negro character parts. He appeared in several with his lifelong friend and associate Rice, who died in 1860. Despite the fact that "this first native form of stage entertainment" was launched by white comedians and that where the "white man began by imitating the Negro, the Negro began by imitating him in turn," the first Negro troupes brought a real contribution to the minstrel show. The two really great Negro minstrel troupes of those days were Lew Johnson's Plantation Minstrel Company and the Georgia Minstrels. The latter was the first successful all-Negro group and was founded in 1865 by Charles Hicks, a native Georgian. This company, with many changes of management, name and personnel, made extraordinary contributions to the American stage and American music. Reorganized first under a white manager, it was known until 1878 as Callender's Original Georgia Minstrels; then, bought by Jack Haverly, it was managed by Gustav Frohman as Haverly's European Minstrels, and finally, in 1882, reorganized by Charles Frohman as Callender's Consolidated Minstrels. Three series of European tours, in 1876, 1880 and 1882, made this troupe of minstrels world famous.

But celebrated managers were matched by celebrated comedians, singers, dancers and instrumentalists. The greatest of the early Negro comedians, Billy Kersands and Sam Lucas, were members of this troupe. James Bland, the composer of "Carry Me Back to Old Virginny" and other less known but really important melodies, was a star performer in the Haverly period. The celebrated Bohee Brothers, perhaps the most sensational banjoists in generations, were instrumentalists in this troupe. At the height of their success, about 1876, the Georgia Minstrels were an aggregation of 21 performers, most of them trained musicians, who really so dignified the tradition that they played in concert halls and attracted the attention of the cultivated musical public. They introduced serious music on their programs, to the best of their ability to work it in with the stereotype of minstrelsy, and were recognized for their contrast with the slapstick school of minstrels. In fact, it may be said that minstrelsy was born in the slapstick of burlesque and died in the straw of the circus. There was a period in between when it rose to a sturdy, healthy prime of clean comedy and pleasantly diluted folk music. This was its romantic period, and it was minstrelsy's musical heyday, as distinguished from its vaudeville phase. There were two stellar geniuses of this romantic period, one white, one Negro—Stephen Collins Foster and James Bland.

*Foster, the troubadour.* A native of Pittsburgh, Stephen Foster was by main intention a maker of drawing-room ballads suited to the sentimental taste of the 1850's. But his sensitive musical genius was caught by an idealized fascination for the plantation. Son of a former mayor of Pittsburgh, he saw more of the stage Negro than the genuine article. It has been said: "Strangely, the man who wrote the greatest songs of the Southland was not a Southerner. He stood afar off and caught the spirit of the cane field and cabin, the porticoed mansion and the white seas of cotton." It is just as ironical that Foster was not a Negro, for his real success and lasting fame came not through the balladry by which he set such store, but through the Negroid folk ballads which came out of his curious fascination with a romantic and half-mythical South. In fact, "Old Folks at Home" was the title of America's most famous song, which he wrote in 1851, but everyone knows it as "Swanee River" or "Way Down upon the Swanee River." Foster had to ask his brother to look up in the atlas a "good two-syllable name" for a Southern river. But Foster had gone at an impressionable period to Cincinnati, just across the river from the Kentucky he made famous later in "Old Black Joe," "My Old Kentucky Home" and "Away Down Souf." And the Negro influence registered deeply.

Foster evidently came into first-hand contact with Negro plantation singing. It was known that he visited out from Cincinnati, especially at the old Kentucky manor house of his kinsfolk, the Rowan family, at Bardstown. At any rate, he caught enough of the unique flavor of Negro folk song to give vitality and deep sentimental appeal to his music, yet had enough of the fashionable style of his day to give his songs immediate vogue and popularity. In this respect his relation to Negro folk song is very like Joel Chandler Harris' relation to Negro folklore. Both watered the original down just enough to give it the touch of universality, and yet not enough to destroy entirely its unique folk flavor. But neither service, as we shall soon see, was an unmixed blessing.

In the straight vein of the sentimental ballad without Negro elements, there is scarcely a song of Foster's long list of 160 that has survived in more than the title. No one hears them, except for "Come Where My Love Lies Dreaming" and "Jeanie with the Light-Brown Hair." "Ah! May the Red Rose Live Alway," and the like, are scarcely known. But "Old

Uncle Ned," "De Camptown Races," "Swanee River" ["Old Folks at Home"]—written, in fact, for the Christy Minstrels—"Massa's in de Cold, Cold Ground," "My Old Kentucky Home" and "Old Black Joe" are known and will be known as long as American popular music has admirers. His biographer says: "Without the minstrels, Foster would probably have died keeping books for his father's business." With the vogue of these songs, the sentimental side of the plantation legend wormed its way into the heart of America for better or worse, mostly worse. For with its shallow sentiment and crocodile tears went an unfortunate and undeserved glorification of the slave regime. Only recently has anyone dared question, musically or otherwise, "Is It True What They Say about Dixie?" Foster and his music did more to clinch this tradition than all the Southern colonels and novelists put together, ironically enough—a tribute to the power of music in general and a tribute to the power of Negro folk song idioms in particular.

*James Bland*. A little later, in the Seventies, when the minstrel style was turning from melody to jig rhythm, a last brilliant strain of romantic music poured from the prodigal and careless genius of James Bland. His life was as tragic as Foster's; both were reckless and irresponsible troubadours. Neither was a Southerner; Bland was born on Long Island, of mixed Negro, Indian and white parentage, and, after several years at Howard University, ran away, as Will Marion Cook puts it: "banjo under arm, to join Callender's Minstrels and to become, at the height of his fame in the United States, London and Paris, the brightest and most versatile star of the heyday of minstrelsy." Research about Bland's career and revival of his music ought to be one of the major projects in the history of Negro music. He was far more than a great songwriter. However, it is as the composer of "In the Morning by the Brightlight," "In the Evening by the Moonlight," "Oh, Dem Golden Slippers" and "Carry Me Back to Old Virginny" that he will be best remembered. His contemporaries testify to his great composing talent as well as his extraordinary musicianship, especially to his way of playing these songs so differently from their now popular versions that to these men they are "scarcely the same songs." This is so often the case with the work of Negro musicians. It results from the sad fact that so many of them were careless, extemporizing talents who let their publishers rob and edit them, and from the fact that many of the virtuoso tricks of Negro musicians cannot be put down in black and white notation. For years, Foster's "Swanee River" [sic] was passed off as a composition of Edwin Christy's (the minstrel magnate); how much of Jim Bland's music has been filched or lost will never be known.

It is interesting to note, even as early as the minstrel period, the double strand in Negro music which today divides it as "sweet jazz" and "hot jazz." Then it was the twanging, swift "banjo music" and the more stately, sugary "guitar music." As the minstrel tradition drew toward its close, the burlesque motive dominated and the banjo-picker was in the ascendant; but Foster and Bland were the sweet minstrels responsible for the romantic Southern legend and the sentimental ballad that for two generations dominated American song. Tracing its derivation, Isaac Goldberg says:

> Traveling southwards, along the banks of the great river and its tributaries (the Mississippi), we encounter a decidedly new and more melancholy and refined musical element—its sadness blended with the strains of the English ballads of 50 or 60 years ago, and reproduced, with a certain indescribable charm, in one or two of the more ancient Christy Minstrels ditties. The element we speak of proceeds doubtless from the Creole stock in Louisiana, and is, perhaps, mixed with the tango of the Cuban Negro.

To say that one of these strands is more Negro than the other is entirely out of place,

even though the melodic vein may have fused with the seventeenth- and eighteenth-century tunes transplanted by the colonists. Because, when the Negro fusion came, it brought a glow and emotional warmth that is easily recognized as different and more compelling. Even after its heyday, it has re-echoed powerfully through later American music in the lullaby and the "pickaninny croon," suffering usually from atrociously sentimental and silly ditties for words, whereas most of the original renditions were wordless croons and humming phrases.

Although this more melodic and melancholy element in Negro song is nowadays associated with the deeper South, particularly Louisiana, Foster and Bland prove that it was just as native to Kentucky and Virginia. Without it, we would never have had such art songs as the later "Go to Sleep, My Little Pickaninny," "Li'l Gal," or even "Mighty Lak' a Rose." Isaac Goldberg rightly comments that there are two strands in Negro music—"music of the heels" and "music of the heart," as he calls them. He is also right in tracing the sentimental strain in American popular song to a Negro main source, long before the vogue of the Irish sentimental ballad. He quotes Gus Kahn as thus explaining the vogue of the romantic South in our popular music: "The South is the romantic home of our Negro; he made it a symbol of longing that we, half in profiteering cold blood, but half in surrender to the poetry of the black, carried over into our American song." Much, therefore, that is typically American in mood and sentiment was precipitated in the minstrel period and by the minstrel tradition.

## SECOND AGE OF MINSTRELSY: 1875–1895

*Copper and brass.* The period following the golden age of minstrelsy can barely be described as silver; it was an age of copper and brass. Musical taste generally was not high in America before 1875, but the cheapening effect of commercialism had not yet touched what music there was. But 1875–95 was the circus age in American life, and music was hitched to the circus chariot; it became gaudy and cheap. There is no wonder that in those days there was such a bitter feud between popular and classical music. But for the triumphant vindication of real folk music by the rediscovery of the spirituals through the work of the Fisk Jubilee Singers, true Negro music would have been extinguished. Thus, the best Negro musicians of this period had to make common cause with "classical music" in self-defense. The music thought representative of the Negro by the general public was the "jig," the "clog" (a terrible hybrid of Negro and Irish dance figures), the "double shuffle" and the "pigeon wing," together with their musical companions, the "minstrel ballad" (usually a slapstick topical ditty) and the "coon song." The minstrel tradition dwindled down to a long twilight of burlesque and buffoonery, in spite of carrying along with it considerable talent—whose brilliance it seriously dimmed.

*An age of caricature.* From 1875 to 1895, then, was a period of artistic decline even in the midst of an increasing popularity of the minstrel tradition. Note that it was an age of slapstick caricature, and that the burlesque spirit, once the vogue began, spread from the Negro folk types to the Irish and the Jewish in quick succession. Music declined in quality with this cheapening of the content of the stage. Oddly enough, as the emphasis on Negro mannerisms and traits grew stronger, the actual racial characteristics in song, dance and speech idiom were lost sight of and caricature versions substituted. Much of the minstrel stock in trade had its Negro, Irish and Jewish versions that underneath separate false dialects were pretty much the same. Dr. Goldberg is right when he says that:

The old minstrel show, truth to tell, for all the sentimental memories that are linked to it, must have been a pretty dull affair. Its wheezes were old when Cleopatra was a child. Read them, if you have the courage, in the sere chapbooks. Its tunes were undistinguished, though they had the country by the ears. The words of its ditties chiefly served to fill space. And yet it is from the minstrel show that we get our patterns of modern popular song. And if, even today, an Al Jolson or an Eddie Cantor seems somehow not himself without the blackface make-up, it is because he got his start in these troupes of pseudo-minstrels. Almost every song-and-dance man of note, from the times of Harrigan and Hart down to our own sophisticated day, began behind the burnt cork.

*Pseudo-Negroes.* "Pseudo-Negroes" is an inspired term. Not only were these latter-day minstrels predominantly white performers in make-up, but they were pseudo-Negroes spiritually. Even the real Negro minstrels were, too, in the psychological sense. Superficially, they reflected some of the characteristic traits of the Negro, but instead of his real peasant humor, his real folk farce, his amazing ribaldry, the minstrels made a decoction of their own of slapstick, caricature and asininity. It was this period that fixed the unfortunate stereotype of the Negro as "an irresponsible, happy-go-lucky, wide-grinning, loud-laughing, shuffling, banjo-picking, dancing sort of being." It should be noted how different the Negro types of the Foster era were in mood, traits and sentiments. If anything, the Negroes of the first age of minstrelsy were too pathetic and romantic and too serious, just as those of the second period were too comic and over-ridiculous. Eventually, the full blast of the circus tradition struck the minstrels, and there was little difference: everything was freakishly exaggerated; squeaky music and falsetto singing were almost standard; fat men impersonated colored cook-ladies; horse-play was more and more emphasized; and if there had been good music, it would have been drowned out in continuous convulsions and explosions of laughter. Certain musical interludes were provided, usually barber-shop quartets, equally unrepresentative of the Negro folk singing they were supposed to derive from.

So pseudo-Negro characterization led to misrepresentative music. In this interval between the old-time ballads which, in their way, had folk flavor, and ragtime, which was even more folky and genuine, the popular types of Negro music and song were bad and superficial. Even serious singing took on the trite form of the barber-shop quartet; Negro harmony was supposed to be the "barber-shop chord," and you could make any song Negro by sprinkling it with Negro dialect. Negro musical taste itself became seriously corrupted as the common notions prevailed. We took to the melodeon organ and the piano, instruments not suited to folk music, as well as the banjo and the guitar. Not until the jazz age did genuine Negro harmony and rhythm conquer the piano, or Negro techniques of singing and playing reappear. For a long time, then, Negroes played and sang not as they had originally done but as they were supposed to. This was inevitably a period of decadence for both Negro music and American music. For when popular music becomes cut off from sound roots in folk music, and good music has to wall itself about to keep from being contaminated by popular music, music is in a precarious condition all round. This was the situation in American music, with few exceptions, in the period between 1875 and 1895.

But underground there were streams, or rather reservoirs, of pure folk music waiting to be tapped. In the very midst of this musical drought the gusher of the spirituals was unexpectedly "brought in." A considerable time would elapse before it would creatively kindle native American musical composition, but in the meantime it received, as we have seen, immediate acceptance from the serious musical public. Then from another source came the quickening tradition of the waltz and the waltz ballad, in the early Nineties, to found the fame and fortune of early Tin Pan Alley, with the hits of Charles K. Harris, composer of "After the Ball Is Over," Von Tilzer and Victor Herbert. It is interesting to note that Tin Pan Alley's second ride to fortune was to be in the wake of the Negro cakewalk and on the rising tide of ragtime, and that exactly what the genius of Victor Herbert did with the dying tradition of the Irish comedy song of the Chauncey Olcott ballad, the next generation of Negro musicians did with the stiff minstrel cakewalks and the sentimental ditties first called "coon songs."

In the second period of minstrelsy, Negro music was doing little besides marking time and tuning up its audience. Meanwhile, from Christy to Weber and Fields, "Bones," "Tambo," "Interlocutor" and the minstrel formula were dominating popular entertainment and laying the basis for the great American vogues of burlesque, vaudeville and musical comedy.

—1936

## Post-Minstrel

Will Marion Cook

# Negro Songmakers

by James Weldon Johnson

TOWARDS the close of the minstrel era and during the middle theatrical period, the Negro in New York gained an important place among the makers of the nation's songs. For a century or more, the Negro in America had been a folk-song maker. Blackface minstrelsy, in its beginnings, depended for its songs almost entirely on the Negro plantation jingles. In the earliest attempts to write songs for the minstrel stage, there was merely slavish imitation or outright appropriation of this folk material. It is plain that even so great a songwriter as Stephen Foster, who wrote his best songs when he lived in Cincinnati, just across the river from Kentucky, was greatly indebted to the enormous supply of Negro folk-song material at hand. But, quite early, the Negro emerged as an individual songmaker. Foster, America's first real songwriter, was at his height in the Fifties; and, in 1855, there appeared a song which became as popular and remains as lasting as any song he wrote, with the exception, perhaps, of "My Old Kentucky Home," "Old Folks at Home" and "Old Black Joe." In Philadelphia there lived a colored barber named Richard Milburn, who worked in his father's shop on Lombard Street near Sixth. He was a guitar player and a marvelous whistler, and it was he who originated the melody, and at least the title, of "Listen to the Mocking Bird." Credit for this song is given to Septimus Winner (or to Alice Hawthorne,

which was his mother's name, under which he published some of his compositions), but the truth is that Winner only set down the melody and arranged it after it had been played and whistled and sung over to him by Milburn. Winner or someone else may have furnished most or all of the words, but the life of the song springs from the melody. Old colored residents of Philadelphia used to relate that, before the song was ever published, Milburn played and whistled it at several gatherings, notably at a concert that was given at St. Thomas' Church, the colored Episcopal church in Philadelphia. But the incontrovertible proof of Milburn's part in the making of the song is shown by its title page as originally published by Winner and Shuster, under the copyright date of 1855, which reads: "Sentimental Ethiopian Ballad —'Listen to the Mocking Bird'—Melody by Richard Milburn—Written and arranged by Alice Hawthorne." The title page of the song as published by Lee and Walker, under the copyright date of 1856, reads: " 'Listen to the Mocking Bird'—As sung by Rose Merrifield—Written and Arranged by Alice Hawthorne." Richard Milburn's name has not since appeared on the song.

One of the most popular of the minstrel songs of the Seventies was "Carve Dat 'Possum," written by Sam Lucas. Then from the ranks of the Negro minstrels there rose a great songwriter in James Bland, who wrote a long list of songs, of which four, at least, possess the qualities that entitle him to a place in the front rank of American song-writers. They are: "Carry Me Back to Old Virginny," "Oh, Dem Golden Slippers," "In the Morning by the Brightlight" and "In the Evening by the Moonlight." Frequently, "Carry Me Back to Old Virginny" is used in lieu of a state song. All of Bland's songs hark back to the South—a South of tender-ness and beauty.

Following him came Gussie L. Davis, a writer of popular ballads. Among many other songs, he wrote: "Down in Poverty Row," "The Fatal Wedding" and "In the Baggage Coach Ahead."

The close of the Nineties and the following decade was the high-water mark of the colored writers of popular songs. Let those with an interest in the old songs muse for a moment over the following bit of cataloguing: Ernest Hogan wrote one song that swept this and other countries, a song which he later in life expressed regret at ever having written; it was "All Coons Look Alike to Me." The melody of the song was beautiful, and the words quite innocuous, but the title became a byword and an epithet of derision. Another writer of a single hit with a title that became a catch phrase was Al Johns, who wrote "Go 'Way Back and Sit Down." James Tim Brymn, with R. C. McPherson, wrote "Please Go 'Way and Let Me Sleep" and "Josephine, My Jo." The Cole and Johnson combination, through their collaboration on Broadway musical plays, wrote a string of popular hits. Among them were: "Under the Bamboo Tree"; "The Maiden with the Dreamy Eyes"; and "My Castle on the Nile." The Cole and Johnson songs were sung by the most popular musical comedy stars of the day: May Irwin; Marie Cahill; Fay Templeton; Lillian Russell; Anna Held; Virginia Earle; Mabelle Gilman. Will Marion Cook wrote "Exhortation," "Rain Song" and "Bon Bon Buddy." Bert

Williams, with Rogers, wrote "Nobody." There were also several writers of popular instrumental music, the outstanding one being Will Tyers, who wrote "La Trocha," "La Mariposa" and "Maori." This list of writers could be extended, as could the lists of songs by the several writers; but here is enough to indicate how important the Negro in New York came to be in the making of popular songs for the American people.

In the meantime, Harry T. Burleigh was writing songs which were to give him his place among American composers. In the work of writing the more musicianly songs, J. Rosamond Johnson and Will Marion Cook also took part. These three men, unlike the other songwriters named, were thoroughly trained musicians. Mr. Burleigh was a stu-dent at the National Conservatory of Music in New York while Anton Dvořák was direc-tor. It was he who called to the attention of the Bohemian composer the Negro spirituals and is therefore in that degree responsible for the part they play in the *New World Symphony.* In 1894, he had the unique dis-tinction of being made baritone soloist at St. George's Church. Regarding this revolu-tionary innovation, Dr. William S. Rainsford, then rector of St. George's, says in his auto-biography:

> I broke the news to them [the St. George's choir] that I was going to have for soloist a Negro, Harry Burleigh. Then division, con-sternation, confusion, and protest reigned for a time. I never knew how the troubled waters settled down. Indeed, I carefully avoided knowing who was for and who against my revolutionary arrangement. Nothing like it had even been known in the church's musical history. The thing was arranged and I gave no opportunity for its discussion.

The troubled waters did settle down, and Mr. Burleigh has held his position now for 36 years. In 1900, he became a member of the choir of Temple Emanu-El. He has written more than 100 songs, in addition to his ar-rangements of the spirituals. Among them

Basile Barés

James Reese Europe

Abbie Mitchell

Harry T. Burleigh

are "Jean"; "Little Mother of Mine"; and "The Glory of the Day Was in Her Face."

Mr. Johnson received his training at the New England Conservatory of Music, Boston. Mr. Cook studied at the Hochschule in Berlin, and took violin with Joachim. These two men have worked in both the popular and the classical fields, but their reputations have been gained chiefly in the former. Mr. Burleigh, on the other hand, has consistently stuck to the latter. Mr. Johnson has had a varied musical career and has shown great versatility. He has written the music for Negro musical comedies; he has written scores for white Broadway musical comedies; he was the supervisor of music at the London Opera House, Oscar Hammerstein's venture in the English metropolis; and when Messrs. Harris and Lasky attempted to give New York something more Parisian than anything in the French capital in *Hello, Paris,* he wrote the music, trained the company and conducted the orchestra—this being, it seems, the only time a Negro has conducted a white orchestra in a New York theatre for a play with a white cast. He has written songs of every description, from a Mississippi roustabout frolic like "Roll Dem Cotton Bales" to a delicate love song like "Three Questions." But his most widely sung composition is "Lift Ev'ry Voice and Sing," a song that is used as a national hymn in colored schools and churches and at Negro gatherings all over the country.

In the midst of the period we are now considering, another shift in the Negro population took place, and by 1900 there was a new center established in West 53rd Street. In this new center there sprang up a new phase of life among colored New Yorkers. Two well-appointed hotels, the Marshall and the Maceo, run by colored men, were opened in the street and became the centers of a fashionable sort of life that hitherto had not existed. These hotels served dinner to music and attracted crowds of well-dressed people. On Sunday evenings, the crowd became a crush, and to be sure of service one had to book a table in advance. This new center also brought about a revolutionary change in Negro artistic life. Those engaged in artistic effort deserted almost completely the old clubs farther downtown, and the Marshall, run by Jimmie Marshall, an accomplished Boniface, became famous as the headquarters of Negro talent. There gathered the actors, the musicians, the composers, the writers and the better-paid vaudevillians; and there one went to get a close-up of Cole and Johnson, Williams and Walker, Ernest Hogan, Will Marion Cook, Jim Europe, Ada Overton, Abbie Mitchell, Al Johns, Theodore Drury, Will Dixon and Ford Dabney. Paul Laurence Dunbar was often there. A good many white actors and musicians also frequented the Marshall, and it was no unusual thing for some among the biggest Broadway stars to run up there for an evening. So there were always present numbers of those who love to be in the light reflected from celebrities. Indeed, the Marshall for nearly 10 years was one of the sights of New York, for it was gay, entertaining, and interesting. To be a visitor there, without at the same time being a rank outsider, was a distinction.

In the brightest days of the Marshall, the temporary blight had not yet fallen on the Negro in the theatre. Williams and Walker and Cole and Johnson were at their height; there were several good Negro road companies touring the country, and a considerable number of colored performers were on the big time in vaudeville. In the early 1900's there came to the Marshall two young fellows, Ford Dabney and James Reese Europe, both of them from Washington, who were to play an important part in the artistic development of the Negro in a field that was, in a sense, new. It was they who first formed the colored New York entertainers who played instruments into trained, organized bands, and thereby became not only the daddies of the Negro jazz orchestras, but the grand-daddies of the countless jazz orchestras that have followed. Ford Dabney organized and directed a jazz orchestra which for a number of years was a feature of Florenz Ziegfeld's roof garden shows. Jim Europe organized the Clef Club.

How long Negro jazz bands throughout the country had been playing jazz at dances and in honky-tonks cannot be precisely stated, but the first modern jazz band ever heard on a New York stage, and probably on any other stage, was organized at the Marshall and made its debut at Proctor's 23rd Street Theatre in the early spring of 1905. It was a playing–singing–dancing orchestra, making dominant use of banjos, mandolins, guitars, saxophones and drums in combination, and was called the Memphis Students—a very good name, overlooking the fact that the performers were not students and were not from Memphis. There were also a violin, a couple of brass instruments and a double bass. The band was made up of about 20 of the best performers on the instruments mentioned above that could be got together in New York. They had all been musicians and entertainers for private parties. Will Marion Cook gave a hand in whipping them into shape for their opening. They scored an immediate success. After the Proctor engagement they went to Hammerstein's Victoria, playing on the vaudeville bill in the day, and on the roof garden at night. In the latter part of the same year they opened at Olympia in Paris; from Paris they went to the Palace Theatre in London, and then to the Schumann Circus in Berlin. They played all the important cities of Europe and were abroad a year.

At the opening in New York, the performers who were being counted on to carry the stellar honors were: Ernest Hogan, comedian; Abbie Mitchell, soprano; and Ida Forsyne, dancer. But while they made good, the band proved to be the thing. The instrumentalists were the novelty. There was one thing they did quite unconsciously which, however, caused musicians who heard them to marvel at the feat. When the band played and sang, there were men who played one part while singing another. That is, for example, some of them, while playing the lead, sang bass, and some while playing an alto part sang tenor. The Memphis Students were the beginners of several things that still persist as jazz-band features. They introduced the dancing conductor. Will Dixon, himself a composer of some note, conducted the band here and on its European tour. All through a number he would keep his men together by dancing out the rhythm, generally in graceful, sometimes in grotesque, steps. Often an easy shuffle would take him across the whole front of the band. This style of directing not only got the fullest possible response from the men, but kept them in just the right humor for the sort of music they were playing. Another innovation they introduced was the trick trap-drummer. "Buddy" Gilmore was the drummer with the band, and it is doubtful if he has been surpassed as a performer of juggling and acrobatic stunts while manipulating a dozen noise-making devices aside from the drums. He made this style of drumming so popular that not only was it adopted by white professionals, but many white amateurs undertook to learn it as a social accomplishment, just as they might learn to do card tricks. The whole band, with the exception, of course, of the players on wind instruments, was a singing band; and it seems safe to say that they introduced the singing band—that is, a band singing in four-part harmony and playing at the same time.

One of the original members of the Memphis Students was Jim Europe. Afterwards, he went for a season or two as the musical director with the Cole and Johnson shows, and then in the same capacity with Bert Williams' *Mr. Lode of Koal.* In 1910, he carried out an idea he had, an idea that had a business as well as an artistic reason behind it, and organized the Clef Club. He gathered all the colored professional instrumental musicians into a chartered organization and systematized the whole business of "entertaining" private parties and furnishing music for the dance craze, which was then just beginning to sweep the country.

Later, Jim Europe, with his orchestra, helped to make Vernon and Irene Castle famous. When the World War came, he assembled the men for the band of New York's noted Negro regiment. He was with this band, giving a concert in a Boston theatre after their return from the War, when he met his tragic end.

In 1912, there came out of the South a new genre of Negro songs, one that was to have an immediate and lasting effect upon American popular music: namely, the blues. These songs are as truly folk songs as the spirituals, or as the original plantation songs, levee songs and ragtime songs that had already been made the foundation of our national popular music. The blues were first set down and published by William C. Handy, a colored composer, and for a while a bandleader in Memphis, Tennessee. He put out the famous "Memphis Blues" and the still more famous "St. Louis Blues," and followed them by blues of many localities and kinds. It was not long before the New York songwriters were turning out blues of every variety and every shade. Handy followed the blues to New York and has lived in Harlem ever since, where he is known as the Father of the Blues. It is from the blues that all that may be called *American music* derives its most distinctive characteristics.

It was during the period we have just been discussing that the earliest attempt at rendering opera was made by Negroes in New York. Beginning in the first half of the decade 1900–10, and continuing for four or five years, the Theodore Drury Opera Company gave annually one night of grand opera at the Lexington Opera House. In September, 1928, H. Lawrence Freeman, a Negro musician and composer of six grand operas, produced his opera *Voodoo* at the 52nd Street Theatre. Mr. Freeman's operas are *The Martyr, The Prophecy, The Octoroon, Plantation, Vendetta* and *Voodoo.* In the spring of the present year he presented scenes from various of his works in Steinway Hall. He was the winner of the 1929 Harmon Award.

—1930

# *Ragtime*

# Negro Producers of Ragtime

by Sterling A. Brown

Explaining why English ragtime writers were not more numerous, in spite of English enthusiasm for the fad, Edward B. Marks writes:

> Perhaps the entirely Caucasian make-up of the group slowed them up. For in the United States colored composers were turning out an important part of the song crop. To me, at least, their songs rang a little truer than the rest.

So many of these colored composers submitted their songs with the added blandishments of singing and "hoofing," that Marks and his partner Stern wondered whether they "were running a publishing house or a vaudeville theatre." The quartet harmonizing made even a poor song sound like a hit. Since, according to Marks, the more dignified publishing houses in the Nineties did not welcome Negro composers, his own sympathy resulted in a large pile of unusable manuscripts "which white smiles and mellow voices had cajoled us into buying."

Nevertheless, Negro composers did well for their publishers and fairly well for themselves. In 1895, Ernest Hogan, one of the best comedians of the day, composed "Pas-Ma-La," a dance song. The following year he first sang "All Coons Look Alike to Me." The melody was catching; the words merely amounted to a rejection of an old lover for a new beau who "spends his money free." But the refrain incited fights whenever sung by a white man in the hearing of a Negro, and Ernest Hogan is supposed to have regretted this song to the day of his death. Rosamond Johnson remembers seeing two men thrown off a ferryboat in a row caused by the refrain. A sequel by two white composers, "Coon, Coon, Coon, How I Wish My Color Would Fade," caused street fights to break out anew.

In spite of the objections to the word "coon," however, which made Hogan "an object of censure among the Civil Service intelligentsia, and . . . haunted by the awful crime . . . unwittingly committed against the race," a group of ragtime songs known as "coon songs" soon flourished. Hogan continued putting songs over; his second hit, composed for him by Barney Fagan (a white writer), was "My Gal's a High-Born Lady" (1896), and his best song was called "Lamb, Lamb, Lamb" (1900). Perhaps the resentment rose from the fact that Hogan's phrasing could be used so patly to express the white man's refusal to differentiate between Negroes, always a sore point with the Negro bourgeoisie. The mere use of "coon" did not bring down censure; as will be seen, Bert Williams, George Walker, Will Marion Cook and many others used it without grave consequences. Irving T. Jones, a New York Negro, but remembered as "one of the most typically comic-strip darkies of the lot," wrote "Take Your Clothes and Go" (1897); "I'm Living Easy"; "You Ain't Landlord No More"; and

"When a Coon Sits in the Presidential Chair."

Gussie Davis is generally credited with only sentimental songs, but he also wrote a comic Negro song "When I Do de Hoochy-Koochy in de Sky" (1896). Fred Stone's "Ma Ragtime Baby" is one of the earliest ragtime pieces.

Chris Smith is, together with R. C. McPherson, the composer of "Good Morning Carrie!" (1901); with McPherson, of "The Right Church, but the Wrong Pew" (1908), written for Bert Williams.

Marks writes that "not many of those first ragtime colored composers read music. They played right out of their head, and an arranger took down the notes as they played." Irving Jones, for instance, was called "a musical illiterate." A notable exception, however, was Scott Joplin, a Texas Negro, whose "Maple Leaf Rag" (1899) "created a distinct piano technic."

> Instrumentally, and in particular pianistically, most [ragtime] was backward; the air was the whole thing, the accompaniment merely strummed. The piano was in line for rescue, however, from its lowly condition, and again it was by a Negro, the gifted and unfortunate Scott Joplin . . . that a new order was ushered in: that of the brilliant and difficult instrumental exercises, the "rags," such as Joplin's own "Maple Leaf."

J. Rosamond Johnson describes the playing of Scott Joplin and similar musicians:

> As restless as a rolling stone, the dance-hall musicians reeled and rocked from one end of the keyboard to the other, inserting new idioms as the dancers rolled along.

Chris Smith, a veteran of ragtime, says of "Maple Leaf Rag": "Ain't nobody can play it, but lots likes to play *at* it." Other numbers by Joplin are "Scott Joplin's Rag," "Palm Leaf Rag," "Gladiolus Rag" and *Treemonisha,* an opera in ragtime (1911). As his work became more and more intricate, approaching that of "a Jazz Bach," Joplin used to say to his fellows: "When I'm dead 25 years, people are only going to begin to recognize me." His prophecy is coming true; the "unjustly forgotten precursor of ragtime" is now being recognized by many of the best analysts of jazz.

Another pioneer of ragtime was Thomas Million Turpin of St. Louis, whom Handy once called "the real father of jazz." Tom Turpin was undisputed king of the piano in a city where there were such fine piano players as Joe Jordan, Louis Chauvin and Gertrude "Sweety" Bell. Turpin had received a thoroughgoing musical foundation from a German teacher in St. Louis (Turpin's father had been a politician in Reconstruction Georgia and Mississippi and was well off), and he played the classics as easily as ragtime. In 1896, he published the "Harlem Rag." He wrote other compositions—"Bowery Buck," "St. Louis Rag," "The Buffalo" and, during the First World War, "When Sambo Goes to France." It is alleged that Scott Joplin came to St. Louis to learn from him. Taken with Joplin and Fred Stone, Tom Turpin is a proof of Marks's statement that "the tide of tintinnabulation flowed from West to East."

—1940

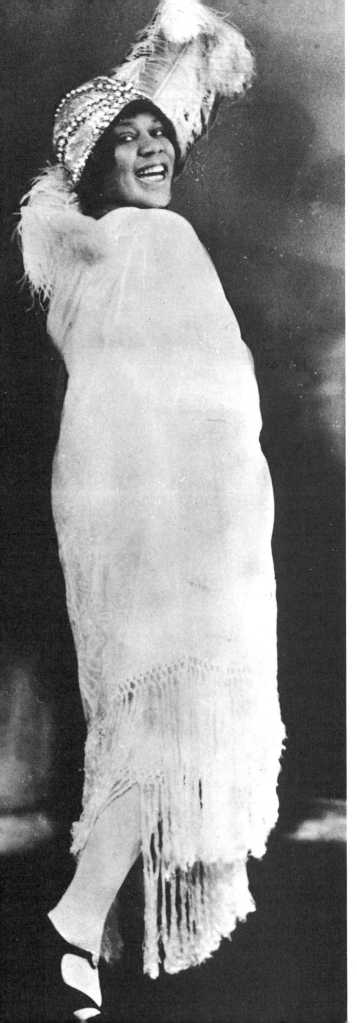

Bessie Smith

*Blues*

Ma Rainey and the Georgia Band

Sara Martin and Clarence Williams

Mamie Smith

Ethel Waters

# The Blues

### by E. Simms Campbell

FIRST let me say that I am no music critic, neither do I look upon myself as a fumbling layman—appreciating the blues form in American music from the pew of an enthusiastic but incoherent follower of *le Jazz Hot,* that strange hybrid that has ripened in France under the aegis of Monsieur Hugues Panassié, who has an ear to the ground as well as an ear for *le Jazz Hot.* Not that M. Panassié is insincere; neither are "jitterbugs" insincere. But an intellectual approach to blues that borders on the ridiculous, with the attendant erudite mumbo-jumbo, is doing one of the purest forms of American music much more harm than good.

It is not necessary to form a cult, to read hidden meanings and mystical expressions, as well as pretentious symbolism, into something as elemental as blues.

Books, essays and reams of scholarly European treatises have been written extolling jazz, the blues and all of the music that American Negroes have written and played—and it can only be forgiven because of the grossest ignorance on the part of intellectuals who delight in faddism.

There was in this country a "Negro Renaissance," as they called it—when every Negro who was literate was looked upon as a "find." New York in 1925 and 1926 was the hotbed of intellectual parties where Negroes who were in the theatre were looked upon as social plums, and the dumbest and most illiterate were fawned on by Park Avenue.

\* \* \* \* \* \*

The blues are simple, elemental. They have the profound depth of feeling that is found in any race that has known slavery, and the American Negro is no stranger to suffering. Out of the work songs and spirituals that he sang sprang this melancholic note, rising in a higher key because of its intensity, and enveloping the spirituals because of its very earthiness. One cannot continually ride in chariots to God when the impact of slavery is so ever-present and real.

"Some day ah'm gonna lay down dis heavy load . . . gonna grab me a train, gonna clam aboh'd . . . gonna go up No'th, gonna ease mah pain—Yessuh, Lord, gonna catch dat train"—this isn't mystical. It was the cry of a human being under the lash of slavery—of doubts, of fears, of the tearing apart of families, of the caprices of plantation owners—these hardships of slavery all fusing themselves together to burn into the Negro this blue flame of misery.

And yet it was never a wail, but a steady throbbing undertone of hope. "Times is bad, but dey won't be bad always," is the lyric carried in a score of blues songs: times are tough, but somehow, somewhere, they'll get better.

"Gotta git better 'cause dey caint git w'us" —stevedores toiling on the levee, chain gangs in Georgia, cotton pickers in Tennessee, sugar cane workers in Louisiana, field hands in Texas, all bending beneath the heel of Southern white aristocracy, the beautiful "befo' de Wa'h" South of the crinoline days.

One might as well be realistic about slavery. The South was as cruel as any Caesar to its slaves, and many slaves were as vindictive as any Richelieu to their masters, but both sides have profited. Without pain and suffering there would have been no blues, and without an understanding white America there would have been no expression for them.

\* \* \* \* \* \*

When Ma Rainey
Comes to town,
Folks from anyplace
Miles aroun',
From Cape Girardeau,
Poplar Bluff,
Flocks in to hear
Ma do her stuff;
Comes flivverin' in,
Or ridin' mules,
Or packed in trains,
Picnickin' fools. . . .
That's what it's like,
Fo' miles on down,
To New Orleans delta
An' Mobile town,
When Ma hits
Anywheres aroun'.

Dey comes to hear Ma Rainey from de little river settlements,
From blackbottom cornrows and from lumber camps;
Dey stumble in de hall, jes' a-laughin' an' a-cacklin',
Cheerin' lak roarin' water, lak wind in river swamps.

An' some jokers keeps deir laughs a-goin' in de crowded aisles,
An' some folks sits dere waitin' wid deir aches an' miseries,
Till Ma comes out before dem, a-smilin' gold-toofed smiles
An' Long Boy ripples minors on de black an' yellow keys.

O Ma Rainey,
Sing yo' song;
Now you's back
Whah you belong,

Git way inside us,
Keep us strong. . . .
O Ma Rainey,
Li'l an' low;
Sing us 'bout de hard luck
Roun' our do';
Sing us 'bout de lonesome road
We mus' go. . . .

I talked to a fellow, an' de fellow say,
"She jes' catch hold of us, somekindaway.
She sang 'Backwater Blues' one day:

*It rained fo' days an' de skies was dark as night,*
*Trouble takin' place in de lowlands at night.*

*Thundered an' lightened an' de storm begin to roll,*
*Thousan's of people ain't got no place to go.*

*Den I went an' stood upon some high ol' lonesome hill,*
*An' looked down on de place where I used to live.*

"An' den de folks, dey natchally bowed dey heads an' cried,
Bowed dey heavy heads, shet dey moufs up tight an' cried,
An' Ma lef' de stage, an' followed some de folks outside."

Dere wasn't much more de fellow say:
She jes' gits hold of us dataway.
(Sterling A. Brown: "Ma Rainey")

And now, what are the blues and into what category of music do they fit? They are not spirituals and they are not work songs, nor do they fit into the pattern described by many music critics as folk music in a lighter vein.

To me, they are filled with the deepest emotions of a race. They are songs of sorrow charged with satire, with that potent quality of ironic verse clothed in the raiment of the buffoon. They were more than releases, temporary releases, from servitude. The blues were the gateway to freedom for all American Negroes. In song, the Negro expressed his true feelings, his hopes, aspirations and ideals, and illiterate though many of them were, there was always a spiritual and ennobling quality to all of the music. True, many of the blues lyrics are downright vulgar, and the suggestive quality has crept in with the passing years—understandable enough when you realize that many audiences, both white and colored, wished to find such meanings in them. As paid entertainers, Negroes were only catering to popular taste—and the taste of the American public in the Mauve Decade was decidedly that of a slumming party toward any reception of blues.

They did not wish to hear lamentations in any form. They wanted something "hot." Knowing nothing of blues, other than that they were "dirty," they received what they expected. As court jester, the Negro had long since learned that his very existence depended upon his ability to please the white man. One was either a "good nigger," one who acquiesced to the wishes of the plantation owner or overseer and lived, or a "bad nigger," one who had decided ideas about what he would or wouldn't do, and who usually died.

This heritage and birthright of fear ground into the smallest Negro child a chameleon attitude toward life, and Negro musicians and entertainers were well schooled and versed in this pattern. As long as the field hands were singing on a plantation, the "boss man" would go into town; he had no fear of any uprising or discontent. A singing darky was a good darky. All Negroes knew this.

Picture the long fields of sugar cane in Louisiana, glinting in the sun, and rows of workers, acres across, all singing their work songs as they rhythmically cut cane; fields of cotton in Georgia; sweating stevedores in Memphis and St. Louis, stripped to the waist while they swung 200 pound bales of cotton; chain gang workers and railroad tampers, pile drivers on the Southern tracks—a race of black people singing as they worked, and it was hard physical work. There is little creative scope in work that requires dexterous hands and strong backs; there is only rhythm and timing, and these songs which they sang lightened that burden. "Ah'm

gonna swing my pick, gonna throw dis hammer—uh yes, Lord—gonna throw dat hammer—uh yes, Lord." The punctuation of "Yes, Lord," that occurs throughout many blues was the sigh, the sigh of physical exertion, the brief fraction of a second of suspended effort before the task was accomplished. As the *combite* works today in Haiti, carried over from the *combites* of Africa, in which large communal groups of Negroes work a field together, working to the rhythmic thumping of a drum and singing in time with it—just so did the American Negroes work on the plantations.

They worked and sang together, and many of these songs carried a meaning only to Negroes. To the white mind, it was perfect peace and contentment among the blacks, but to Negroes it was often a means of communication.

"Ya bettah breeze on down dat road—son—ya bettah breeze on down dat road. Mistuh Charlie from town ain't feelin' good—ya better lighten dat heavy load"; from one to another, the song was taken up and passed along the field. It simply meant that there was a white man from a different town who had arrived on the plantation, and the young Negro who was working among them, guarded zealously from the whites "at de big house," had better leave town. Negroes frequently hid one of their own who had sought refuge among them, and they were telling him in code that he had better leave the plantation that night.

A race that has been continually on the defensive for so many years has developed a keen sense of impending danger, and the blues grew out of this form of protection. Melancholy though they were, they could be interpreted a hundred ways, but the circumstances under which they were sung had everything to do with their proper interpretation.

Basically, the blues are similar to spirituals,

and it is important to note that the musical bars are of practically the same length. For those musically minded, take the song "Minnie the Moocher," or "St. James Infirmary." The spiritual "Hold On, Keep Your Hands on the Plow" is identical with them, and it was written more than 40 years ago.

This background of the "why" of the blues is essential to understanding them properly and to getting a fuller understanding of their true meaning. None of them was ever written to music before the 1890's, because the majority of Negroes had had no musical education, and the flood of ragtime pieces that immediately followed, in the early 1900's, consisted merely of melodies that have followed the blues pattern these many years. There is a definite pattern to the blues, just as there is for poetry and other forms of creative expression that have survived the centuries.

The blues always consist of 12 bars—the C seventh after the first four bars; the F chord and the remainder of the piece are essentially the same. An original blues composition must be original in the first four bars; the next four bars are merely relief, and then one returns to the major chords.

Often one hears pieces on the radio termed "blues," which are merely bastard products, because some well-known orchestra insists on stepping up 12 bars to 24, or even 32. This is "swing" as we know it today, but it has nothing in common with the blues, and, as Clarence Williams told me: "The flavor and color are taken from the blues when one tries variations and liberties with their original form."

Clarence Williams is now a music publisher in New York who has written hundreds of blues and who, I think, as do many of America's finest musicians, is the greatest living blues writer. If you know blues at all, I'll give you a few of his compositions, and then perhaps you'll know this man better. He wrote "Sister Kate"; "Royal Garden Blues";

"Gulf Coast Blues"; "You Don't Know My Mind"; "West End Blues"; "I Can't Dance, I've Got Ants in My Pants"; and that greatest of all blues (unless of course you are a "St. Louis Blues" fanatic), "Baby, Won't You Please Come Home?" The list is endless, and he's still writing.

When he was 14 (he told me one day), he wrote the "Michigan Water Blues":

Michigan water—taste like champagne wine,
Michigan water—taste like champagne wine,
Ah'm going back to Michigan
To see that gal of mine.

Ah believe to my soul—mah baby's got a black
cat born,
Ah believe to my soul—mah baby's got a black
cat born,
'Cause every time ah leave
Ah got to crawl back home.

This naturally led us into a discussion of the fact that blues, as we know them today, are always written about love, someone's baby leaving them, hard luck dogging one's trail, and the "misery 'roun yo' door." "It's the mood," he exclaimed. "That's the carry-over from slavery—nothing but trouble in sight for everyone. There was no need to hitch your wagon to a star, because there weren't any stars. You got only what you fought for. Spirituals were the natural release—'Times gonna git better in de promised lan' '—but many a stevedore knew only too well that his fate was definitely tied up in his own hands. If he was clever and strong, and didn't mind dying, he came through; the weak ones always died. A blue mood—since prayers often seemed futile, the words were made to fit present situations that were much more real and certainly more urgent."

"Ef ah kin jes grab me a handfulla freight train—ah'll be set. . . ." Always the urge to leave, to go to a distant town, a far city, to leave the prejudices and cruelty of the South. Superstition played its part, too, a large part —black cats, black women, conjures, charms, sudden death—working in steel mills or cot-

Sara Martin

Meade Lux Lewis

Albert Ammons

Ida Cox

ton fields, loving women, fighting over women: all of the most intimate and earthy pursuits. As I talked with Clarence Williams, his eyes brightened. "Tell you what I'll do." He pressed a buzzer near his desk and whispered a hurried message into the phone.

"I'm canceling all appointments for today. We'll just talk about blues. You ask the questions and I'll try and answer them if I can," he said, as he pushed a large sheaf of letters aside.

I only asked one question and that question started a discussion that ended when the neons began to blink over Broadway and 45th Street, and the taxi horns aroused us from a bygone period. I started: "Mr. Williams, if you were a white man, you'd probably be worth $1,000,000 today, wouldn't you? Because the radio and motion picture rights, as well as all mechanical rights, to all of your songs would be copyrighted. You'd have a staff of smart boys working for you, ferreting out tunes and buying them for a song from colored fellows who had no musical education, and you'd never have a material care in this world. Think hard now: wouldn't you have rather been born a white man?"

He laughed out loud, uproariously, and replied, "Why, I'd never have written blues if I had been white. You don't study to write blues, you *feel* them. It's the mood you're in. Sometimes it's a rainy day—cloud, mist—just like the time I lay for hours and hours in a swamp in Louisiana, Spanish moss dripping everywhere (but that's another story—it's a mood, though), white men were looking for me with guns; I wasn't scared: just sorry I didn't have a gun. I began to hum a tune, a little sighing kinda tune—you know, like this. . . ."

Clarence Williams was seated at the piano, and his large, muscular fingers caressed the keys. Eerie chords rumbled along. He sang: "Jes' as blue as a tree, an old willow tree, nobody 'roun' here, jes' nobody but me"—the

melody trailed off. "Never wrote that down; never published it either. I don't know why I'm playing it now."

I didn't intrude on his thoughts. "You never knew Tony Jackson, did you? No, of course not. You were too young." Williams was not conscious of my presence in the room. He talked and played. I listened.

Tony Jackson was probably the greatest blues pianist that ever lived. He was great because he was original in all of his improvisations—a creator, a supreme stylist. This all happened 30 years ago, when the wine rooms flourished.

These were nothing more nor less than sedate saloons, with a family entrance for ladies, and potted palms, and the usual ornate bric-a-brac in every corner. There was the inevitable three- or four-piece orchestra, with the diva belching out ballads, trailing her ostrich plumes as she coyly made her exit, and the mustached dons of the period keeping a sharp eye out for a well-turned ankle. Informality was the keynote, and any of the patrons who wished could render a song, vocal or otherwise, provided of course that they weren't too terrible. Booing was much too mild for a poor performance in those days. Negroes had their wine rooms, patterned as nearly as possible after the white ones, but they were necessarily less pretentious in every way. Often their wine rooms were combination billiard and pool parlor, saloon and clubroom for the tougher gentry. There were no paid entertainers, no orchestra, and the only music provided was that played and composed on the spot by these ragtime and blues piano players.

New Orleans was the focal point for Negro musicians, all of them coming down from the various river towns, but particularly from Memphis and St. Louis, on the many boat excursions that would wind up in the Delta. Blues was looked upon as "low music" 40 years ago, because its greatest exponents were hustlers and sports—itinerant musicians who played in river joints and dives because these were the only places sympathetic to their type of playing. Negroes have always loved the blues, but, in attempting to imitate the white man, many of them were trying to stamp out of their consciousness this natural emotional tie, because of its background of slavery.

Being ashamed of one's heritage is usually predominant in minority groups, and, in imitating the music of white America, many Negroes were contributing nothing worthwhile to American music. The blues musicians were the pioneers, those who refused to compromise with their music; and they were creating and forming the basis for present-day American music. Gershwin's *American in Paris* as well as his *Rhapsody in Blue* are outstanding examples of blues harmonies—you don't think he pulled them out of the air, do you?

Cities and towns figure in the names of so many blues because the writers of these pieces were definitely associated with the towns. In these early "jam sessions"—many of them held in these wine rooms in New Orleans—individual musicians would compete with one another. They came from the length and breadth of the Mississippi, and their styles of playing were as different as the sections of the country from which they came. Boogie-woogie piano playing originated in the lumber and turpentine camps of Texas and in the sporting houses of that state—a fast, rolling bass, giving the piece an undercurrent of tremendous power: power piano playing.

Not Pinetop Smith, not Meade Lux Lewis nor Albert Ammons originated that style of playing; they are merely the exponents of it.

In Houston, Dallas and Galveston, all Negro piano players played that way. This style was often referred to as a "fast western" or "fast blues," as differentiated from the "slow blues" of New Orleans and St. Louis. At these gatherings, the ragtime and blues boys could easily tell from what section of the country a man came, even going so far as to name the town, by his interpretation of a piece.

Even today, the finest clarinet players in the world usually come from New Orleans, and this is because of the French influence. France has always led the world in the making of reed instruments, and the first musical instrument that many of these Negroes owned was the clarinet. It is simple to trace this influence in the formation of blues as we know them today. The West Indies, Martinique in particular, always used the clarinet and bass viol in the béguine and in all of their other folk dances.

Clarinets were handed down from one generation to the next in New Orleans, and almost any young boy who showed any musical aptitude at all could play a reed instrument.

I would say that, through New Orleans, the Spanish and French rhythms were interjected into the blues. The late Chick Webb had it with his drumming, as does Zutty Singleton. Gene Krupa, the great white drummer, is another who acquired it.

St. Louis and Kansas City were noted for their piano players as well as their honky-tonk joints. To the Southerner, St. Louis and Kansas City were looked upon as northern cities, and a great many Southerners, both black and white, settled there. The Negroes that came brought with them the blues of the cotton fields and plantations of the deep South, not influenced in any fashion by the Spanish or French. That is why musicians often feel that the purest blues and the real "low-down blues," as they frequently call them, were born in these cities. New Orleans gave a lilt to the blues. The other cities gave them their solidity. Having been born in St. Louis, and intensely interested in blues, I was on

Joe Williams (left) and Jimmy Rushing (below) still carry on in the tradition of the early blues shouters.

many a boat excursion that carried these early Negro bands—and none of them ever played any other type of music. Jelly Roll Morton, from Kansas City, had probably the greatest blues band—there was Fletcher Henderson, Charlie Creath, Fate Marable and Bennie Moten. I could go on by the hour. All of these men, however, were preceded by Tom Turpin, Scott Joplin and Louis Chauvin, a great natural piano player. In 1896, Tom Turpin of St. Louis (his full name was Thomas Million Turner) had published "The Harlem Rag," "The Bowery Buck" and "The Buffalo," and Scott Joplin had just written "Maple Leaf Rag." This was white America's first introduction to ragtime, which was patterned after the blues. The blues were so essentially a part of Negro life that many musical pioneers rightly felt that America would not accept them, thus this offshoot, ragtime, which did happen to strike the public's fancy. It was gayer and was more in keeping with the mood of the American white man. Blues were always played among Negroes, seldom among white audiences, and when they were played, they were set apart as the pièce de résistance of the evening.

The first blues singer on a record was Mamie Smith, and the first band to play blues on a record was the white Dixieland Jazz Band, an aggregation of young men who came up North from New Orleans in 1916. The boom years for the blues were from 1919 through the Twenties. The five Smiths were among the greatest single artists to interpret the blues for the country. They were all Negro women, and were not related in any manner, neither by family nor by their varied vocal interpretations. Mamie, Bessie, Laura, Clara and Trixie were their names; today, among musicians and lovers of the blues, the hottest type of argument may be started over the respective merits of each. Bessie Smith is usually given credit for being the greatest, but to single any one out for that honor would not be fair. As I have mentioned before, style was important, and whereas Bessie Smith would sing certain numbers with all of the pathos and feeling that a certain blues number required, and would wring the song dry, as it were, Mamie Smith could do certain blues numbers much better in her own style. Bessie Smith was the depressed, mournful type; her blues were eloquent masterpieces of human misery bordering on the spirituals. She was blues personified.

She had a powerful voice and she sent her music in great waves of misery over audiences. Her "Empty Bed Blues" and "Backwater Blues" will forever remain classics.

Mamie Smith, and this is purely a personal opinion, had much more music in her voice. In her rendition of certain numbers, she might be compared today with Ella Fitzgerald.

Another great blues star was Sara Martin, who had a great flair for the dramatic. In a darkened theatre, with only candles on the stage, she would begin to wail in a low moan: "Man done gone—got nowhere to go." She literally surged across the stage, clutched the curtains in the wings, rolled on the floor, and when she had finished, the audience was as wilted as she. There are too many names to give them all: Ida Cox, Virginia Liston, Eva Taylor. Most of the greatest vocalists were women with rich contralto voices. When blues were sung by a woman the voice, that is, the female voice, carried tragic implications— the rich overtones of the cello; the man always imparted background on a guitar or piano. She was the hub of the family—black America crying out to her sons and her daughters.

The great Ethel Waters started her career as a blues singer, as did most of the greatest Negro dramatic actresses.

It is interesting to note that many who are still living are finishing their careers in church work. Virginia Liston and Sara Martin at this writing are both singing spirituals in churches. There is no doubt that blues and spirituals are closely interwoven.

As I started this article, I wished to tell of the St. Louis, Kansas City and Chicago periods of the blues:

When Earl Hines and Louis Armstrong were going strong, and Jimmy Noone, the great clarinetist who wrote "Four or Five Times," was hitting those high notes at the old Nest and Apex Club. The night I was there when Nora Holt, a celebrated Negro entertainer, just returned from China, handed me an autographed copy of George Gershwin's latest piece—" 'Swonderful"—and she played it for us.

The night I had my overcoat, as well as hat, gloves and my first silk neck-scarf stolen, as did 10 other fellows at the old Warwick Hall in Chicago, because we were gazing open-mouthed, watching beads of perspiration pour off the head of a trumpet player by the name of Louis Armstrong while he played a new piece called the "Heebie Jeebies."

The night King Oliver started his famous talking on a trumpet, actually preaching a sermon with it. Johnny Dunn was later to do the same thing, and play it on a record, so that America was soon to hear amazing things from the instruments it thought were finished as to technical virtuosity.

I wished to tell about the old Vendome Theatre in Chicago, with Weatherford at the piano, playing his eccentric solos.

The night there was that great fight on the steamer *St. Paul,* an old paddle-wheeler out of St. Louis, with Fate Marable's band playing. Five miles downstream a knife fight started, and the boat wheeled around to put ashore. The band continued to play; as I climbed up on the bandstand to get a better view of the proceedings, I soon found myself atop the old upright piano. The fight was overflowing to the bandstand. How those fellows continued to play, I'll never know, but they played as if everything was serenely

quiet on the old Mississippi. The boat did not come into the wharf but hung out in midstream until the "Black Anny," as we called the patrol wagons, had lined up on the dock.

Then we landed, and three loads of celebrants were carted away, and not once do I remember Marable's band stopping. He played blues after blues, and they sounded grand, too. All of the musicians who played on the boats and the river front were inured to fisticuffs of all sorts. As one musician told me: "I don't care what they do as long as they don't break this snare. It set me back 30 bucks." Of such stuff are musicians made. They had come up in the toughest of all schools. They had played the levee front from one end to the other. Night life, sporting houses, gamblers—they knew them all.

". . . And today," broke in Clarence Williams, "their music is played in Carnegie Hall before a select group; one sees many a full dress, high hat, ermine wrap there, you know." We had been exchanging experiences, talking nothing but the blues for over five hours, and the lights of Broadway were beginning to flash. I made another false start to leave, although I really didn't want to leave, when the door was quietly opened and a straight, elderly, copper-colored man walked in.

"Didn't knock, Clarence. Knew you'd be here. Just dropped in for a chat," he said, as he sat down in an overstuffed chair and deposited a briefcase on the desk.

I got up and was about to make my departure for good, when the amiable Williams stayed me.

"I'd like you to know Reese D'Pree," he said. I shook hands with the man, and I could see a look of resignation in his face. He seemed very tired and worn. Williams went on, "Reese D'Pree wrote a number about 43 years ago, wrote it in Georgia, Bibb County to be exact. Will you tell Campbell about that piece, Reese?" In simple language he told me of the number he had written and sung. He made money on a ship in 1905, wearing a chef's cap and apron and singing his song. He used to sing it at pound parties in the South. Pound parties were community affairs, given by Negroes at that time, where one would bring a pound of "vittles" of any kind—a pound of chitterlings, of pig's feet, of hog maw, barbecue, butter—anything that contributed to the feast. It was a simple little piece, but everywhere he went they wanted him to sing it. At present, he is having copyright trouble. D'Pree did not impress me as being a wealthy man, but the song must have earned over $1,000,000 for someone. Possibly you've heard it, too. It's called "Shortnin' Bread." Reese D'Pree loves the blues as much as Clarence Williams. I will always remember what that man told me the blues meant to him, as I left the office.

"Son," he said, "the blues regenerates a man."

—1939

The singing of
the late Dinah Washington
was often compared
to that of Bessie Smith.

# Memphis Blues: A Bungled Bargain

**by W. C. Handy**

I NEEDED a commercial outlet for my tune. That's where the misery began. Every reputable American publisher of popular music gave the "Memphis Blues" the go-by. The 12-bar strains, where there should be 16, to them lacked completeness. It's amusing to think about that now, but in those days, when I was featuring their hits and comparing them with my own work, I felt that someone was overlooking a good bet. At any rate, in the late summer of 1912, I decided that I wanted to publish the "Memphis Blues."

I had published nothing before, so I shopped around for some advice. I obtained it from a white man, whom I shall call X——, who was then employed by Bry's department store. Bry's music department was separately organized as the Southern Music Company. X—— (acting as an individual and not for his employers)' offered to arrange for the printing and copyrighting, and to put the piece on sale at Bry's. I accepted. It was agreed between us that the engraving and printing was to be done by Otto Zimmerman & Son, of Cincinnati, at my expense, and that the first printing should be of just 1,000 copies (that figure is important, as will be seen). I accordingly prepared and furnished X—— with my manuscript of the piece in early September, and a little later I went there and corrected the proof.

Another white man, whom I am calling Z——, had a music publishing company and also a store of his own in a Western city. He traveled extensively for his business, visiting retailers such as Bry's, with whom he made local headquarters, and spending weeks at a time with them, busily demonstrating his music to their customers by both piano and voice. I also had been a frequent caller at Bry's since October, 1909, when my band (playing on the steamer *Pattona,* as it escorted President Taft's vessel into Memphis on a river trip to encourage a deep Chicago–Gulf waterway) had plugged a tune of X——'s written for the same occasion along with my own blues. Through X——, I myself had occasionally met Z——, and he knew something about my work. And now, while I was dealing with X—— about the "Memphis Blues," Z—— appeared on one of his visits. On hearing of our plans and coming with X—— to rehear my tune at a Second Street dance hall, he persuaded me that with his out-of-town connections he could give the piece a wider circulation than I could, and without surrendering my ownership rights I consented to make him my sales representative.

On Friday afternoon, September 27, word came to me from X—— that the shipment of "Memphis Blues" had arrived and that if I would come over next morning I could see it opened up and put on sale. I was early at Bry's, where I met both X—— and Z——, and was shown, in the music stockroom, a fascinating package which we opened, revealing the 1,000 copies in their blue jackets. I took out 100 to try to place in other stores; X—— took more, and we proceeded to the music counter where I watched them put on sale. I paid out about $32.50 to X—— to cover the engraving and printing cost as reported by him, and an extra dollar for the copyright fee, and I left with the promise of an advertisement in Bry's newspaper space for Sunday.

My first hopes did not survive long. I found no such reception at the other Memphis stores as I had at Bry's. Even my friends, the O. K. Houck Piano Company on Main Street, shied away at first. Mr. Houck's attitude puzzled me, for at the time I approached him his windows were displaying "At the Ball," by J. Leubrie Hill, a colored composer who had gone to New York from Memphis some time earlier. Around it were grouped copies of recent successes by such Negro composers as Cole and Johnson and Scott Joplin, and the Williams and Walker musicals. So when he suggested that his trade wouldn't stand for his selling my work, I pointed out as tactfully as I could that the majority of his musical hits of the moment had come from the Gotham-Attucks Company, a firm of Negro publishers in New York.

I'll never forget his smile.

"Yes," he said pleasantly. "I know that—but my customers don't."

He turned me down, and I fared no better in other stores. Considerably later, I hasten to add, he more than made up for it; but meanwhile I had to take my copies back to Bry's.

The blows continued to fall. From day to day I asked X—— or Z—— what was happening, but their answer remained the same: the customers said the piece was too hard to play, and there were practically no sales. It was hard to believe that Memphis, which had loved its blues in the dance halls these two years, would now have none of it. But there lay the unsold copies as proof that my publishing venture was a failure. I was thoroughly discouraged, and when Z—— made me a proposal that would give me back my costs, with perhaps a tiny profit, I gave up and accepted.

I gave him a bill of sale of my music plates and my tune itself—saving authorship credit—free of royalties. For this I received $50 cash, and also the nearly 1,000 unsold copies left from my own original edition, as Z—— planned to republish under his own imprint and to try the tune out in New York and elsewhere. Z—— called it that I was selling for $100, rather than only $50, since the copies on hand had been carried at five cents apiece wholesale; and for years I accepted this theory myself, because $100 sounded better. Of course the flaw in this comforting theory was that I had paid for the whole edition in the first place. At any rate, I was through. Z—— left for New York, and my prospect of ever making any more from the "Memphis Blues" depended upon my surviving the next 28 years, till I became entitled to the author's copyright renewal privilege under the law.

Back in New York, Z—— started talking up an "unusual band" he had heard in Memphis and an "unusual tune" he had bought there. He himself met with difficulty for a little while, for my strains were still unorthodox, but he made some headway. I now know that he ordered 10,000 copies from Zimmerman's in October, 1912, of which 4,800 went to Memphis and the rest to Denver, Omaha and New York. He ordered another 10,000 the following March, after which he took the plates out of their hands. Then the white fiddler Waiman played the piece, and his full-length picture went on the cover. On September 20, 1913, Z—— wrote me (on a letterhead which named X—— as his wholesale manager) that he had sold 50,000 copies, that George Evans' "Honey Boy" Minstrels had taken it up and that he was about to publish a new vocal edition, with words all about my band. I quote from other parts of the same letter:

> I am convinced that this number will sell several hundred thousand copies, as a result of the advertising I am giving it. I have confidence in the number or I would not spend the large amount of money I am putting in it. I also believe in your ability as being the greatest ragtime writer of the day. . . . You will realize that you are about to land on the Honor Roll of hit writers.
>
> Once I get you landed there, you will have a demand from all other big publishers for numbers. You will have to retire to the field of composition and work some more wonderful melodies like "Memphis Blues." You may write some numbers just as good; but you will have to work to write some any better. Even at that I believe that you have the ability to do it.

The new vocal version omitted my entire first strain, but at least its lyric was a useful compliment. It was written by George A. Norton (who with Ernie Burnett and Maybelle Watson wrote "Come to Me, My Melancholy Baby"), and Norton's words were all about that band of ours that Z—— had heard playing the blues in Memphis, words about the slick-haired fiddler and the trombone that moaned like a sinner on revival day. Never having heard of a saxophone in a dance orchestra, Norton's lyric had us using a "big bassoon . . . second to the trombone's croon." That was left uncorrected, but I liked the words. Whenever I hear them now, "smoke gets in my eyes." An inner voice begins to scold: "Why did you leave the town where everybody grinned at Handy and every kid knew him? Why didn't you keep that band together, regardless of time and people and money?" Then mist comes in my eyes again and tells me that hairs are white and heads are "blossoming for the grave," and that while some of my best players have gone to the Celestial Band, their sons and grandsons have

taken what I got from Juba and translated it into Jive for their Jitterbugs. Ah, well . . .

Z—— wrote me 20 years later that "a brown-skin gal," who had sung at Persica's in Memphis, finally put the new song over by her renditions at a 105th Street, New York, cabaret. He did not name her, but she must have been either Osceola Blanks or her sister Berliana, both of whom thereafter sang the piece all over the country. From then on it was easy and big money for Z——, till finally he became involved in some manner, lost control of his catalogue and at last died in reduced circumstances.

We met and corresponded from time to time from the Memphis days to his death. In 1933, inspired by a magazine article about me, he wrote me that he had composed a story for the same publication about "the daring man who bought 'Memphis Blues' from you for $100," and he sent me a copy of his script, which was not accepted for publication. In this story, after referring to my bad luck with the New York publishers and crediting himself with the suggestion of publishing 1,000 copies in Memphis to get the public's reaction, he made a statement which would have surprised me greatly at the time, save that I supposed I knew the facts, and passed it over as a bit of romancing. I quote his statement, and the italics are mine:

> *The thousand copies lasted three days.* Handy, *still* affected by his fruitless efforts, was glad to sell for $100 cash as a sure thing.

As I have said, my arrangement with Z——'s associate had been that he should order only 1,000 copies. I had paid him for the engraving and printing, supposedly of 1,000 copies only, and I had parted with my copyright on the statement that the piece did not sell, and had then received back nearly 1,000 unsold copies.

It was only in the winter of 1939–40 that an investigation through the original printer's successors disclosed that the first "Memphis Blues" printing, ordered by X—— and for which I had ignorantly paid, had consisted of not 1,000 but 2,000 copies, of which half were shipped by express, the rest separately by freight. The shipment took place September 25, 1912, and it was on October 7, only nine days after first publication, that Z—— ordered the second edition of 10,000 copies, with a change of imprint.

I do not know just how many copies of my piece had actually been sold when I parted with it. I understand that a fire long since destroyed the records of Bry's, which firm, of course, was in no way responsible for what may have happened to me. But I now know that Z—— and X—— were in a position to sell over 1,000 copies of the "Memphis Blues" to the public and still have nearly 1,000 left, the sight of which would mean to me that there had been "practically no sales" at all and that my creation was a failure. And I received none of the proceeds of the missing 1,000.

I have felt that this story should now be told, because these men constitute a part of the long list of exploiters of the works of composers and inventors. Such men must necessarily ease their conscience, when withholding financial returns, by telling the creator of a work what a great name they have made for him. This was probably the case with Stephen Foster's "Old Folks at Home" ("Swanee River"), dear to the hearts of all Americans, though for years it was the minstrel E. P. Christy's name that went on the copies as composer, and it is related that Christy apparently paid just $5 for this amazing privilege. Although Foster received small remuneration for his works, it is my belief that "Old Kentucky Home" and "Old Black Joe" touched the heart of Lincoln, and thus helped to make this book possible.

The framers of our copyright law, knowing that such practices had long existed, divided the 56 years of copyright protection into two terms of 28 years each, and gave the second term to the author or his heirs, regardless of his previous mistakes. The wisdom of this law I can attest to, since everybody connected with the "Memphis Blues" has made more money from it than I, yet the second 28 years will help to afford me protection in my old age, when I may need it most.

However, things are better for a composer nowadays. Since, with all the protection of copyright, it is still a matter of impossibility for a composer to trace infringements wherever they may occur, powerful and reputable organizations have been formed to assist in the protection of musical creations. Such is the Song Writers' Protective Association, which protects the composer's interests against unscrupulous publishers if there be such. The Music Publishers' Protective Association looks after the interests of both composer and publisher in mechanical reproductions such as phonograph records, electrical transcriptions and synchronized motion picture music, even licensing the last for use throughout the world. Last but not least, the American Society of Composers, Authors and Publishers acts as an agent for authors, composers and publishers when copyrighted music is used by radio, theatres, cabarets and dance halls, and this great agency cares for the composer whose work has shown worth, regardless of whether or not he was disposed of his copyrights.

In the year or two that followed my meeting with Z—— in Bry's music department, I saw the song that I had sold for $50 become a tremendous hit and a gold mine for the new owner.

The Victor Company released a recording by the Jim Europe band. That sent that ball rolling. Meanwhile, as others pocketed the royalties, I reaped some of the glory. Arrangements were made for me to appear before the white women's music clubs of

Memphis. The O. K. Houck Piano Company, which had refused to display the song, not only displayed it now but also displayed me in a life-size picture standing beside a Victor talking machine with ear bent to hear the new Jim Europe recording of my song. And when a big traveling band was announced at the East End Gardens by a great banner, the Alaskan Roof, at which my band was already playing, flung a tremendous streamer high across Madison and Main with these words: *Handy's Band*—ALASKAN ROOF GARDEN—*The Best Band in the South*. It dwarfed the East End Gardens banner.

But the musicians' union did not approve of these proceedings. First, they sent a committee to demand the removal from Houck's window of the Victor talking machine and Mr. Handy's attentive expression. The demand was complied with. They had just attended to this business when the Alaskan Roof unfurled its bold, exasperating streamer. The committee visited the Alaskan Roof and demanded the removal of the banner, which the management refused. Finally, however, they succeeded in securing its removal through the fire and police commissioners.

It was now possible to heave a sigh of relief. All concerned seemed completely satisfied with the accomplishment. That same year, however, this same group of objectors became the greatest boosters of the "Memphis Blues," regarding it with a certain hometown pride. So while I was deprived of the banner over Madison Avenue, nightly I was able to hear E. K. White's Municipal Band playing the "Memphis Blues" in Court Square.

How the "Memphis Blues" had been received in other parts of the country I did not learn till I persuaded Mr. Tuohey, secretary of the Memphis Chamber of Commerce, to engage my men to play for a national convention of the Real Estate Men's Association. The secretary had other ideas about entertainment for the occasion. He had planned an old-time Southern banquet with possum and 'taters, shortnin' or cracklin' bread and persimmon beer, and he had asked me to round up a batch of country banjo players that could sing backwoods songs. It took fast talking to change his mind. I argued that our character artist, Sidney Easton, could handle that sort of darky business even more effectively than could the country boys. Eventually the secretary saw the point and gave us the job.

A great crowd filled the banquet hall on the big night. The secretary requested an opening song, and Sidney gave it to them, his pleasing dark face bright with a pearly smile. An encore was demanded, and then another. Finally Mr. Tuohey suggested that we play a piece with the band. We opened with the "Memphis Blues," since we did not have to have music for that. The real estate men cut loose with one of those rare, spontaneous outbursts that all but shatters your eardrums. I was not only delighted but genuinely amazed. This was the first direct inkling I had gained of the success of my song in other parts of the country. Presently, however, I was to learn more.

After a number of preliminary speeches, Judge Greer, speaker of the evening, stunned us with this astonishing remark: "Gentlemen, I came here with a prepared speech on the old South, but after hearing that boy sing and that band play, I am going to throw away my speech and talk about the Negro, the most wonderful race on the face of God's green earth." That not only baffled us but left me, for one, apprehensive. When a man begins that way, you are inclined to wonder. But Judge Greer went on to say that Easton resembled a playmate of his boyhood days. Then he told the men how he used to slip away from the white church to go to the colored church with his playmate because, as he said, the Negroes seemed to have more religion, and he demonstrated by singing a strain of "Swing Low, Sweet Chariot."

A moment later, when the speaker returned to a portion of his prepared speech to relate his experiences as a drummer boy of 14, following the fortunes of the Confederacy, I began to think that he had said his say and was through with us. But I guessed wrong. He only wanted the real estate men from all over the country to know that when the cause was lost, he had pinned the Stars and Stripes on the lapel of his coat above the Southern Cross. His views, he wished to show, were not based on sectional feeling. He had only commenced to say what was on his mind concerning Negroes.

About that time, he turned to C. P. J. Mooney, editor of the *Commercial Appeal,* and said, "We have made a serious mistake in inviting men from all parts of America to make investments in a city where one-third of its population is painted as vicious. No race that can sing and play as these men have done can be vicious. Why, the 'Memphis Blues,' " he shouted, "has done more to advertise Memphis than all the publicity emanating from the Businessmen's Association." The businessmen gathered there seemed to approve. They applauded heartily. I wanted to join them, but I refrained from using my hands. Only my heart applauded. Curiously, however, it was less because of what he said about my song than because of his kindly generalizations about Negroes as a whole that I felt enraptured.

Judge Greer was followed by editor Mooney. His theme was the same, but he added statistics to show the Negro's contribution to the wealth of that section of the Mississippi Valley. Nothing like this had ever been spoken in my presence before. A Kentuckian, speaking next, felt impressed to make a related point. Once, he explained, the best horses came from Arabia. In his home state they educated their Negroes, and now it could be said that the world's greatest horses were raised in Kentucky.

Another man, while adding his amen to the judge's observations, suggested that the "Memphis Blues" was all the more remarkable when one remembered that Tennessee had probably never spent a dollar on the musical education of a Negro.

My own reactions were confused. I took occasion to thank my stars that I had settled upon music as a career, despite opposition. Nothing made me glow so much as seeing the softening effect of music on racial antagonisms. On the other hand, there was a seed of bitterness in my heart. While I was getting the praise, another man owned the copyright to "Memphis Blues" and was getting the money. As a result of this evening's encouragement, however, I determined to swallow that resentment like a true philosopher, set my head to new things, and see if I couldn't do better next time. In fact, a bee was already buzzing in my bonnet.

Up and down Beale Street, in Pee Wee's saloon, at home—everywhere I went I heard it. A new tune was taking shape, a new hit that I hoped would compensate for the royalties that I was not getting from my first successful song. The inspiration for the new composition was a humorous Negro custom that could be traced to the Gullahs and from them all the way back to Africa. I had first noticed it among the troupers of a minstrel company. Whenever these fellows wanted to say something to one another—something not intended for outside ears—they used words invented by themselves for this purpose. Sometimes they simply attached new meanings to familiar words. For example, a white person was always "ofay," a Negro "jigwawk." The terms, as pliable as silk, were also extended to cover fine distinctions. Thus, if the girl you were sparking at the moment was light colored, you might describe her as "ofay jigwawk." If she was the stove-pipe variety, you might have to hear her called a "jigwawk-jigwawk." I recall that back in the Nineties

Ben Harney wrote a ragtime song entitled "The Cakewalk in the Sky." But when the jigs sang it, the audience heard something like this: "The kigingy kikake wygingwawk higin the skigy."

Of course, in the theatrical profession one meets alert ears and sharp wits, and the public early became familiar with words like "ousy-lay" and "umbay." To meet this cleverness, we used throw-offs to confuse them. "Siging Sigwatney" was such a throw-off—it meant nothing whatever. "Jogo" did have meaning, however. It meant colored and was a synonym for jigwawk. I decided to call my new composition the "Jogo Blues."

Well, the "Jogo Blues" got a play. Michael Markels of New York was one Broadway bandleader who featured it successfully. A St. Louis millionaire, Russell Gardner, "The Banner Buggy Man," liked it so well he sent me a $20 note every time we played it—which was every night when he was present. But "Jogo Blues" never became a hit and never fulfilled the hope I had entertained for a success to compensate for the earlier song.

The trouble may have been partly because "Jogo" was an instrumental number. Then another disadvantage was that only Negro musicians understood the title and the music. On the other hand, while my men liked it a great deal, many bands couldn't play it well because it was considered over the head of the ordinary pianist and too difficult for the average orchestra. I had made an orchestral arrangement too difficult for the average player, and profits in musical compositions come from widely repeated sales, not from an occasional yellow-back from a single rich enthusiast. In short, I was still looking for that second hit.

It occurred to me that I could perhaps make more headway in this direction without the questionable help of my four lively and robust youngsters at home, all bent on using my legs for teeterboards. The noisy rumpus

warmed the heart, but it put a crimp in my work. I could feel the blues coming on, and I didn't want to be distracted, so I packed my grip and made my getaway.

I rented a room in the Beale Street section and went to work. Outside, the lights flickered. Chitterling joints were as crowded as the more fashionable resorts like the Iroquois. Piano thumpers tickled the ivories in the saloons to attract customers, furnishing a theme for the prayers at Beale Street Baptist Church and Avery Chapel (Methodist). Scores of powerfully built roustabouts from river boats sauntered along the pavement, elbowing fashionable browns in beautiful gowns. Pimps in boxback coats and undented Stetsons came out to get a breath of early evening air and to welcome the young night. The poolhall crowd grew livelier than they had been during the day. All that contributed to the color and spell of Beale Street mingled outside, but I neither saw nor heard it that night. I had a song to write.

My first decision was that my new song would be another blues, true to the soil and in the tradition of "Memphis Blues." Ragtime, I had decided, was passing out. But this number would go beyond its predecessor and break new ground. I would begin with a down-home ditty fit to go with twanging banjos and yellow shoes. Songs of this sort could become tremendous hits sometimes. On the levee at St. Louis I had heard "Looking for the Bully" sung by the roustabouts, which later was adopted and nationally popularized by May Irwin. I had watched the joy-spreaders rarin' to go when it was played by the bands on the *Gray Eagle* or the *Spread Eagle*. I wanted such a success, but I was determined that my song would have an important difference. The emotions that it expressed were going to be real. Moreover, it was going to be cut to the native blues pattern.

A flood of memories filled my mind. First, there was the picture I had of myself, broke, unshaven, wanting even a decent meal, and standing before the lighted saloon in St. Louis without a shirt under my frayed coat. There was also from that same period a curious and dramatic little fragment that till now had seemed to have little or no importance. While occupied with my own miseries during that sojourn, I had seen a woman whose pain seemed even greater. She had tried to take the edge off her grief by heavy drinking, but it hadn't worked. Stumbling along the poorly lighted street, she muttered as she walked, "Ma man's got a heart like a rock cast in de sea."

The expression interested me, and I stopped another woman to inquire what she meant. She replied, "Lawd, man, it's hard and gone so far from her she can't reach it." Her language was the same down-home medium that conveyed the laughable woe of lampblacked lovers in hundreds of frothy songs, but her plight was much too real to provoke much laughter. My song was taking shape. I had now settled upon the mood.

Another recollection pressed in upon me. It was the memory of that odd gent who called figures for the Kentucky breakdown—the one who everlastingly pitched his tones in the key of G and moaned the calls like a presiding elder preaching at a revival meeting. Ah, there was my key—I'd do the song in G.

Well, that was the beginning. I was definitely on my way. But when I got started, I found that many other considerations also went into the composition. Ragtime had usually sacrificed melody for an exhilarating syncopation. My aim would be to combine ragtime syncopation with a real melody in the spiritual tradition. There was something from the tango that I wanted, too. The dancers at Dixie Park had convinced me that there was something racial in their response to this rhythm, and I had used it in a disguised form in the "Memphis Blues." Indeed, the very word "tango," as I now know, was derived

from the African *tangana,* and signified this same tom-tom beat. This would figure in my introduction, as well as in the middle strain.

In the lyric, I decided to use Negro phraseology and dialect. I felt then, as I feel now, that this often implies more than well-chosen English can briefly express. My plot centered around the wail of a lovesick woman for her lost man, but in the telling of it I resorted to the humorous spirit of the bygone "coon songs." I used the folk blues' three-line stanza that created the 12-measure strain.

The primitive Southern Negro as he sang was sure to bear down on the third and seventh tones of the scale, slurring between major and minor. Whether in the cotton fields of the delta or on the levee up St. Louis way, it was always the same. Till then, however, I had never heard this slur used by a more sophisticated Negro, or by any white man. I had tried to convey this effect in "Memphis Blues" by introducing flat thirds and sevenths (now called "blue notes") into my song, although its prevailing key was the major; and I carried this device into my new melody as well. I also struck upon the idea of using the dominant seventh as the opening chord of the verse. This was a distinct departure, but, as it turned out, it touched the spot.

In the folk blues the singer fills up occasional gaps with words like "Oh, lawdy," or "Oh, baby," and the like. This meant that in writing a melody to be sung in the blues manner one would have to provide gaps or waits. In my composition I decided to embellish the piano and orchestra score at these points. This kind of business is called a "break"; entire books of different "breaks" for a single song can be found on the music counters today, and the breaks become a fertile source of the orchestral improvisation which became the essence of jazz. In the chorus I used plagal chords to give spiritual effects in the harmony. In effect, I aimed to use all that is characteristic of the Negro from Africa to Alabama. By the time I had done all this heavy thinking and remembering, I figured it was time to get something down on paper, so I wrote, "I hate to see de evenin' sun go down." And if you ever had to sleep on the cobbles down by the river in St. Louis, you'll understand that complaint.

St. Louis had come into the composition in more ways than one before the sun peeped through my window. So when the song was completed, I dedicated the new piece to Mr. Russell Gardner, the St. Louis man who had liked "Jogo Blues," and I proudly christened it the "St. Louis Blues." The same day on Pee Wee's cigar stand I orchestrated the number and jotted down scores for my band.

The song was off my chest, and secretly I was pleased with it, but I could scarcely wait for the public verdict. Blurry-eyed from loss of sleep, I went with the band to the evening's engagement on the Alaskan Roof.

—1941

W. C. Handy plays the "St. Louis Blues" at a benefit for charity in New York City.

# SECTION VI

MUSIC

## Gospel

Clara Ward (in front), with the Ward Singers (left), has taken her gospel into night clubs. She believes that the "message of the Lord" should go wherever there are souls to be reached.

Mahalia Jackson

Brother John Sellers

Sister Rosetta Tharpe

# Rock, Church, Rock!

**by Arna Bontemps**

BACK IN 1925, audiences at the old Monogram Theatre, 35th and State in Chicago, found themselves centering more and more attention on a lanky, foot-patting piano player called Georgia Tom. There was a boy to watch!

Georgia Tom had blues in his mind as well as in his feet and his hands. He had composed Ma Rainey's popular theme music:

> Rain on the ocean,
> Rain on the deep blue sea,

not to mention scores of other blues. The kid was a natural. If the blues idiom meant anything to you, he was your boy. The only trouble was that the more you watched Georgia Tom, the less you saw him. It was downright quaint the way he bobbed in and out of things. Presently the hard-working boogie-woogie player dropped out of sight completely, and the name of Georgia Tom was forgotten.

Five or six years later, observers of such phenomena noticed that Negro churches, particularly the storefront congregations, the Sanctified groups and the shouting Baptists, were swaying and jumping as never before. Mighty rhythms rocked the churches. A wave of fresh rapture came over the people. Nobody knew just why. True, the Depression had knocked most of the folks off their feet and sent them hurrying back to church, but did that explain this tremendous impulse to get out of their seats and praise God in the aisles? It was also true that many new songs were being introduced from time to time—songs which were different—but what did that have to do with this new ecstasy? A few of the more inquiring members discovered that the best and most lively of the new songs were credited to Thomas A. Dorsey, composer, but there were few people anywhere who connected Dorsey with the Georgia Tom of former years. The transformation had been complete. Well—almost complete.

Dorsey—not to be confused with the white orchestra leader of the same name—was born near Atlanta, the son of a country preacher. Gawky and shy, sensitive about his looks, snubbed by the more high-toned colored boys and girls of the city, young Tom early set his mind on learning to play the piano. This involved walking four miles a day, four days a week (since there was no piano in his home), but it was worth the effort.

Within two years, the funny-looking country kid was able to turn a Saturday night stomp upside down with his playing. City youngsters started calling him Barrel House Tom. Such stomp pianists as Lark Lee, Soap Stick, Long Boy, Nome Burkes and Charlie Spann had to move over and make room for the sad-faced newcomer, Barrel House Tom. People who gave the stomps recognized a difference, too. They were glad to pay a player like Tom a dollar and a half a night for dance music. The second-string boys counted themselves lucky to get 50 cents.

Even in those marvelous days, however, young Dorsey had more on his mind than just punishing a piano. For one thing, there was a girl—a girl with curly black hair hanging over her shoulders like the glory of a thousand queens. When she looked at Tom, he felt like a boy dazzled by the sun. Then, quite suddenly, her family picked up and moved to Birmingham, carrying the daughter with them. If they had only known what they were doing to the poor boy's heart! In this mood, as so often happens, ambition was born. Tom determined to be somebody in his chosen field.

First he tried, with such local help as he could get, to teach himself harmony, composition, instrumentation and arranging. But being 20 and broken-hearted, he listened to talk about the steel mills of Gary, Indiana. There was good money in those mills—money that would make the wages of a Georgia stomp musician look sick. Moreover, there were golden opportunities up North, opportunities for study, musical opportunities. Perhaps, too, there were other proud dark queens with shiny black glory hanging down over their shoulders. The lure was too great; Tom couldn't resist.

What he failed to consider was the limitation of a thin, willowy body that weighed only 128 pounds. The steel mill all but did him in, but he kept at it till he got his bearings. Which is to say, he kept at it till he could put a little five-piece orchestra together. This orchestra marked the beginning of Georgia Tom—the barrel house and Saturday night stomp phase having been left in Atlanta. It gave him piano practice, and it enabled him to earn money by playing for parties in the steel mill communities of Gary and South Chicago. It provided exercises in the making of band arrangements and piano scores, and it left enough time for study at the Chicago College of Composition and Arranging. More important still, it started him to reflecting.

One of the first results of this tranquil thought was a little song entitled "Count the Days I'm Gone." The wastebasket got that one, but the effort was not wasted. Song followed song; and when Dorsey joined the Pilgrim Baptist Church the following year, he took to writing church songs as some people take to drinking gin. Why Dorsey's songs should have been different from other church music can be left to the imagination.

As it turned out, 1921 was a good year in which to join Pilgrim Baptist Church, for that was the year the National Baptist Convention met in Chicago. More important still, that was the convention which was lifted out of its chairs by a song called "I Do, Don't You?" A. W. Nix did the singing, and the response by the audience was terrific. More important was the fact that a small wheel started turning in the heart of an inconspicuous young convert. The song lifted the boy like angels' wings. Nothing he had pounded out at parties or stomps had ever moved him so completely. Here was his calling. He would make such music.

The effects of that decision are still unmeasured. Dorsey considers "I Do, Don't You?" the first of the so-called "gospel songs." He credits C. A. Tindley, its composer, with originating this style of music. All of which may be fair enough, but it should be quickly added that the songs of this genre have come a long way since Georgia Tom's conversion.

Tindley's productive period fell between 1901 and 1906. Most of his compositions were gospel songs in the conventional sense: tabernacle and revival songs. His, however, leaned heavily on Negro spirituals. At least one widely-used song book classifies Tindley's "Stand by Me" as a spiritual. "Nothing Between" could go in the same group with equal reason.

Thomas A. Dorsey joined Pilgrim and commenced to write "gospel songs" at a time when Tindley's were catching on—after

15 years of delayed action. It is, therefore, not surprising that Dorsey's first successful songs were distinctly in the mood of his tutor's. The earliest of these, "If I Don't Get There," published in the popular *Gospel Pearl Song Book,* reveals its debt in the very wording of its title. The second followed the same line: "We Will Meet Him in the Sweet By and By." The special edition of the *National Baptist Hymnal* included this one. Both have the Dorsey touch, both have swing and bounce, both are definitely "live"; but there is little in either of the special quality that marks the more mature Dorsey as an "influence." They are standard tabernacle songs. Perhaps there was a reason.

Like most young fellows who join the church in their early twenties, Dorsey had his temptations. Right off the bat, the devil showed him a red apple—a $40-a-week offer to play the blues. Georgia Tom was entranced. He fought against the allurement briefly, then gave up the struggle. The blues are not thrown off by casual resistance. Trifle with them, and they'll get you. They got Georgia Tom. He left the church, rocking and swaying to savage rhythms.

The band he joined was called the Whispering Syncopators. It was directed by Will Walker, and among its members were Les Hite, Lionel Hampton and half a dozen other boys who have since become jazzmen of note. Georgia Tom played with the outfit around Chicago and then accompanied them on an extended tour. When they started a second turn through the country, he was left behind. Instead, he organized a band for Ma Rainey, the "goldneck mama" (thanks to a necklace of $20 gold pieces) of the early blues era. This was a step up, and he went on tour with her at an increased salary. The tricks were running his way.

One day, jittery with excitement, he found himself standing before the dog license cage in the city hall. It was an embarrassing mo-ment, for what he really wanted was a marriage license. When he got himself straightened out, it was just five minutes before the bureau closed. An hour later, all hitched up and everything, he was off with the band for engagements in the South. While his new wife was not the girl who provoked his sighs in Atlanta, she had her own glory, and Dorsey knew that things were breaking his way. Yet his mind wasn't right. Something told him he was straying. God had to put a stop to it.

That was the time he got sick. For 18 months he was unable to work. The doctors couldn't do him any good. His money melted away, and his wife had to take a job in a laundry. Still he grew worse and worse. His weight went down to 117 pounds. It was then that his God-fearing sister-in-law decided to take a hand. She took him back to church. It was just what he needed; he commenced to improve immediately. As a matter of fact, it occurred to him that perhaps his sickness was less of the body than of the mind. To prove it, he sat down that very week and wrote a new song, one of his ringing successes, "Someday, Somewhere."

Even a song that has since been so widely approved by church people of all denominations throughout the Christian world as "Someday, Somewhere" put no meal in the barrel immediately. No publisher wanted it, and when Dorsey had 1,000 copies printed at his own expense, nobody would buy them. With money his wife borrowed, he bought envelopes and stamps and circularized people who should have been interested. Nothing happened—not a single sale. There were no choirs interested in singing this kind of number. No musical directors were impressed. The situation called to mind W. C. Handy's experiences with his blues compositions. The only thing left to Dorsey was to get out and sing his song to the people themselves.

The very next week he made a start, arranging with a preacher to introduce the number in a church service. He arrived as arranged, took his seat in the front row and waited for his call. The preacher preached. The people sang and prayed. The collection was raised. Finally church was dismissed. Dorsey was still sitting in the front row, waiting to be called upon for his song. The next Sunday he tried again. Then the next, and the next. On the latter occasions he got to sing his song, but the rewards were meager. He counted himself lucky when he sold a dollar-and-a-half's worth of song sheets. Still the humiliating business went on. He wouldn't give up. Eventually the Brunswick Recording Company rescued him by giving him a job arranging music for their recording artists.

Thereafter, things went better. He took his wife out of the laundry. In six months he had $1,000 in the bank. But he hadn't learned his lesson yet. Temptation came strolling around again. This time it strummed a guitar, and its name was Tampa Red.

The young singer came to Dorsey's house one evening with some words for a song. He wanted them set to music and a musical arrangement made. Dorsey hemmed and hawed. He had had his fill of blues and stomp music and all the likes of that. Besides, this particular lyric was entitled "It's Tight Like That," and was way out of line. The guitarist pleaded; Dorsey hedged. For two hours the battle raged. In the end Georgia Tom won out over Thomas A. Dorsey. He went to the piano and knocked out the music.

The next day they took it to the Vocalian Recording Company. The record people jumped with glee. They promptly waxed the number and gave it to the world. Result: the first royalty statement brought $2,400.19. Tight? Well, I reckon! Dorsey rewarded his loyal wife with all the fine clothes she had dreamed about while she was working in the laundry and he was ill. The rest of the money he put in the bank. But God didn't like "It's Tight Like That," and he didn't like the money that came from it. The bank failed, and it has never yet paid off. Thomas A. Dorsey took that for a lesson.

He has behaved himself ever since. God is pleased, and the church folks are so happy you can hear them half a mile away. They are clapping their hands, patting their feet, and singing for all they are worth. Why shouldn't they? They have as good a reason as the composer for singing:

> How many times did Jesus lift me?
> How many times did my burdens bear?
> How many times has He forgiven my sins?
> And when I reach the pearly gates, He'll let me in.

Since his return to his true love, definitely and finally, Dorsey has written some songs in the tempered, conventional style of gospel music everywhere. His "Take My Hand, Precious Lord" is a good example. It seems to be almost universally approved and is sung in many churches where there is still a definite resistance to the main body of the Dorsey music. The resistance is understandable. Georgia Tom is still lurking about. The composer of "Stormy Sea Blues" and "It's Tight Like That" is entitled to come out and take a bow when a congregation sings:

> Just hide me in Thy bosom till the storm of life is o'er;
> Rock me in the cradle of Thy love.
> Just feed me (feed me, feed me, feed me, Jesus) till I want no more;
> Then take me to that blessed home above.

It is not surprising that the swing bands fell for the stuff, nor that a church singer like Sister Tharpe could join Cab Calloway without changing her songs. Neither is it surprising that the church folks resented this use of their music and complained bitterly. They have their case, and it's a good one.

Meanwhile, the vogue of the ineptly described "gospel songs" continues. Dorsey's campaigns in the churches resulted in the organization of hundreds of choirs that would not blush at the strong rhythms of the new songs. Where the senior choirs wouldn't handle them, the younger elements in the churches have insisted on the organization of junior choirs to sing them. In Negro communities, school children sing them on the streets. Here is church music that can hold its own with anything on the hit parade.

A flock of other composers have come along since Dorsey showed the way. One is Roberta Martin. Dorsey says he discovered her when she was playing and singing in a storefront church on South State Street. Her "Didn't It Rain?" is miles ahead of the old spiritual which also bears that name. Something has been added.

What these composers have evolved is perhaps a compound of elements found in the old tabernacle songs, the Negro spirituals and the blues. Georgia Tom can probably be thanked for the last. In any case, the seasoning is there now; and, like it or not, it may be hard to get out. Indeed, some churchgoers are now bold enough to ask, "Why shouldn't church songs be lively?"

To this Dorsey would undoubtedly answer, "Amen," but he has also stated his case in verse:

> Make my journey brighter,
> Make my burdens lighter,
> Help me to do good wherever I can.
> Let Thy presence thrill me,
> The Holy Spirit fill me,
> Keep me in the hollow of Thy han'."

Clap hands, church!

—1958

The Grandison Singers

Louis Armstrong (about 1930)

*Jazz*

Kid Ory

King Oliver's Creole Jazz Band (about 1922)

# New Orleans Music

by William Russell
and Stephen W. Smith

EARLY IN the nineteenth century, soon after the Louisiana Purchase, slaves were allowed for the first time to assemble for social and recreational diversion. The most popular meeting place was a large open field at Orleans and Rampart, known as Congo Square. In earlier times the space had been a ceremonial ground of the Oumas Indians. Today, landscaped with palm trees, it forms a part of the municipal grounds called Beauregard Square. The Negroes, however, still speak of the place as Congo Square, in memory of the days when it was an open, dusty field, its grass worn bare by the stomping and shuffling of hundreds of restless bare feet. A century ago, slaves met there every Saturday and Sunday night to perform the tribal and sexual dances which they had brought with them from the Congo.

Before the Civil War, the Congo dances were one of the unusual sights of New Orleans to which tourists were always taken. At times almost as many white spectators as dancers gathered for the festive occasions. That the Negroes had not forgotten their dances, even after years of repression and exile from their native Africa, is attested by descriptive accounts of the times. Dressed in their finest, many of the men with anklets of jingles, the Negroes rallied at the first roll of the *bamboulas,* large tom-toms constructed from casks covered with cowhide and beaten with two long beef bones. Galvanized by the steady, hypnotic rumble of drums, the frenzied crowd was transported to Guinea, their traditional homeland. The men, prancing, stomping and shouting, *"Dansez bamboula! Badoum! Badoum!"* weaved around the women, who, swaying as their bare feet massaged the earth, intoned age-old chants. The shrieks of children around the edge of the square, as they mimicked the dancers, mingled with the cries of vendors of ginger-cakes, sweetmeats and brilliant-hued liquors.

Though discontinued during the War, the Congo dances were again performed after the emancipation and were not entirely abandoned even two decades later, when a correspondent of the New York *World* reported:

> A dry-goods box and an old pork barrel formed the orchestra. These were beaten with sticks or bones, used like drumsticks so as to keep up a continuous rattle, while some old men and women chanted a song that appeared to me to be purely African in its many vowelled syllabification. . . . In the dance, the women did not move their feet from the ground. They only writhed their bodies and swayed in undulatory motions from ankles to waist. . . . The men leaped and performed feats of gymnastic dancing. . . . Small bells were attached to their ankles. . . . Owing to the noise, I could not even attempt to catch the words of the song. I asked several old women to recite them to me, but they only laughed and shook their heads. In their patois they told me—"No use, you could never understand it. *C'est le Congo!*"

The *bamboula*

Voodoo incantations, brought over on slave ships, were the foundation for religious chants and songs of consolation of those who felt the weight of the "Black Man's Burden" and the sting of their master's lash. By nature the Negroes were no less happy than other people. But mirth and laughter find little expression in the song of a people long depressed with thoughts of exile, slavery and oppression. Music born under such conditions can only express a spirit of resignation touched with yearnings. Thus, the primitive African chants, some consisting apparently only of incessant moans, became the basis of the blues.

Before emancipation, the musical instruments of the slaves had to be mainly homemade affairs. Drums were at first hollowed out of logs. After one end was covered with skin, the drums were beaten with bare hands. The term *"bamboula* dance" came from the name of the smallest drum, which was originally fashioned from a tube of bamboo. Other instruments were rattles, such as a pair of bones used as castanets, and the

jaw bones of asses. When the latter were left out in the sun to dry, the teeth loosened and rattled when struck. Other instruments of African origin were a crudely formed banjo and a type of marimba similar to that now used in Cuba.

In New Orleans, after the Civil War, Negroes began more and more to use the usual wind and string instruments of the whites. Such instruments were already widely used by the Creole Negroes, most of whom, though skilled in written music, were not so close to the blues background. (The blues were improvisational in character.) Soon Negro groups, having learned to play by ear, were engaged to play for dances and, by 1880, were found on some of the packets on the Mississippi River. Here they worked as porters, barbers and waiters during the day and entertained the passengers with music at night.

Historians point out that few of these early musicians could read music; that they were "fake" players. This is a highly significant fact when one considers how the music of the jazz band evolved and reached maturity during the last years of the nineteenth century. Although naturally influenced by the music of their former masters, the Negroes retained much of the African material in their playing. The leader of the first great orchestra, Buddy Bolden, was already in his teens before the Congo dances were discontinued. The Negroes were accustomed to endless repetition of short motifs and were not bothered by the brevity of form in the white man's popular song. Nor did they worry about the trite character of the melodies, for, being unaccustomed to read music, they quickly altered the tune, anyway.

With the New Orleans Negro, improvisation was an essential part of musical skill, as is the case with every extra-European musician. In all cultures except that of Europe, where for a century improvisation has been a lost art, creative performance is a requisite.

Thus, where there was no premium on exact repetition and hide-bound imitation, only those with the urge to express themselves and an innate power of invention took up music. When a musician could play only what he *felt,* those without feeling never even got started, and mediocre talents soon fell by the wayside. It is important to note that the greatest talent went into dance orchestras, the *only* field open to those with professional musical ambitions.

The fact that these men were not primarily note readers also explains, when collective improvisation was attempted, the origin of the characteristic New Orleans polyphony, which in its more complex manifestations became a dissonant counterpoint that antedated Schönberg.

The young New Orleans aspirant, having no teacher to show him the supposed limita-

Fred Keppard (fourth from left) with the Doc Cook orchestra (about 1924).

tions of his instrument, went ahead by himself, and frequently hit upon new paths and opened up undreamed-of possibilities. In classical music, the wind instruments had always lagged behind in their development. The brasses, especially, were subordinated to the strings. But the freedom of the New Orleans musician from any restraining tradition and supervision enabled him to develop on most of the instruments not only new technical resources but an appropriate and unique jazz style.

So when Buddy Bolden, the barber of Franklin Street, gathered his orchestra together in the back room of his shop to try over a few new tunes for a special dance at Tin Type Hall, it was no ordinary group of musicians. Nor was Buddy an ordinary cornetist. In his day, he was entirely without competition, both in his ability as a musician and his hold upon the public. The power of his sonorous tone has never been equaled. When Buddy Bolden played in the pecan grove over in Gretna, he could be heard across the river throughout uptown New Orleans. Nor was Bolden just a musician. He was an "all-around" man. In addition to running his barber shop, he edited and published *The Cricket,* a scandal sheet as full of gossip as New Orleans had always been of corruption and vice. Buddy was able to scoop the field with the stories brought in by his friend, a "spider," also employed by the New Orleans police.

Before the Spanish-American War, Bolden had already played himself into the hearts of the uptown Negroes. By the turn of the century, his following was so large that his band could not fill all their engagements. Soon "Kid" Bolden became "King" Bolden.

When he wasn't playing out at picnics during the day, Buddy could probably be found blowing his horn at Miss Cole's Lawn Parties. Miss Cole's was an open-air dance pavilion up on Josephine Street. At night, he might work at any of a dozen places—at private parties, although his music was too "barrel house" for the most refined tastes. The nature of this music may be inferred from Herbert Asbury's description of these taverns in his book *The French Quarter:*

> As its name implies, the barrel house was strictly a drinking-place, and no lower guzzle-shop was ever operated in the United States. It usually occupied a long, narrow room, with a row of racked barrels on one side, and on the other a table on which were a large number of heavy glass tumblers, or a sort of bin filled with earthenware mugs. For five cents, a customer was permitted to fill a mug or tumbler at the spigot of any of the barrels, but if he failed to refill almost immediately he was promptly ejected. If he drank until his capacity was reached, he was dragged into the alley, or, in some places, into a back room. In either event, he was robbed, and if he was unlucky enough to land in the alley, sneak thieves usually stripped him of his clothing as well as of the few coins which he might have in his pockets. Most of these dives served only brandy, Irish whisky and wine, and the liquors which masqueraded under these names were as false as the hearts of the proprietors.

From barrel houses and honky-tonks came many of the descriptive words which were applied to the music played in them, such as "gully-low," meaning, as its name implies, low as a ditch or "gully," hence "low-down," and "gut-bucket," referring originally to the bucket which caught drippings, or "gutterings" from the barrels, later to the unrestrained brand of music that was played by small bands in the dives.

More often, Bolden played at one of the dance halls in the Negro district, such as Perseverance Hall, downtown on Villère Street, or Tin Type Hall, uptown on Liberty. George, the janitor of Perseverance, rented the hall on condition that the clubs who used it would hire the Bolden band. Some of the clubs they played for were the Buzzards, Mysterious Babies, and the Fourth District Carnival Club. In the daytime, Tin Type Hall was used as a sort of morgue, for here the hustlers and roustabouts were always laid out when they were killed. The hustlers, gamblers and race track followers were often hard-working musicians in their off seasons, or when luck turned and they needed a little ready cash. At night, however, the Tin Type trembled with life and activity, especially when Bolden was "socking it out." The "high class" or "dicty" people didn't go to such low-down affairs as the Tin Type dances. At about twelve o'clock, when the ball was getting right, the more respectable Negroes who did attend went home. Then Bolden played a number called "Don't Go 'Way, Nobody," and the dancing got rough. When the orchestra settled down to the slow blues, the music was mean and dirty, as Tin Type roared full blast.

Bolden's band was of the rough-and-ready school, without the polish of the note readers, such as the veteran Claiborne Williams' band, or the sweetness of Robichaux's orchestra. It was usually a small bunch, of from five to seven men. Buddy used William Warner or Frank Lewis, or sometimes both, on clarinet. Warner had a C clarinet, while Lewis played the usual B flat instrument. Willy Cornish, the only member of the original band living today, played a piston (valve) trombone. For a mute, Cornish used an empty bottle. Bolden, who almost always played with an open horn, sometimes used a rubber plunger, water glass, half a coconut shell, derby hat, piece of cloth, or his hand, for muted effects. Bolden, as a rule, played everything in the key of B flat. The rhythm section, as usual in early New Orleans, had no piano, and consisted of Mumford, guitar, James Johnson, bass, and drummer Cornelius Tillman, or McMurray, with his old single-head drum and its bright red snares.

Bolden's band played for a while at Nancy Hanks' Saloon on Customhouse Street, down in the red-light district. They used to sell fireworks out in front, which, on one occasion, set the place on fire. At times, this joint got too rough for even the Buddy Bolden band.

Carnival time always saw New Orleans in its most festive mood. It was also the busiest time for musicians. Everyone was needed in the street parades which celebrated Mardi Gras. There was at least one parade a day for the week before Mardi Gras, and, on the final Tuesday, there were usually five or six. There were six gay weeks of masked balls. During the final week, balconies were decorated and maskers danced in the specially lighted streets. The parades, during the final week of pageantry, always started at Calliope Street and St. Charles Avenue, and after going up Canal, Royal and Orleans, ended at the site of the old Congo Square where, in the case of evening parades, the event was climaxed with a masquerade ball. King Bolden got his share of jobs in the carnival balls, as well as the parades.

In later years, there were several changes in King Bolden's band. Around the corner from the Odd Fellows' Hall, at Perdido and Rampart, there was a regular "gin barbershop" where musicians were accustomed to hang out while waiting to get calls for jobs. Here Bolden picked up Bob Lyons, the bass player, and Frankie Dusen, his trombonist. Others were Sam Dutrey, clarinet, Jimmie Palao, violin, and Henry Baltimore or "Zino," drums. His guitar player was Brock Mumford, around whom Buddy wrote a little song, "The Old Cow Died and Old Brock Cried." On this number the whole band sang the vocal chorus.

Buddy used to hang around a saloon on Gravier and Rampart run by "a guy named Mustache." He called it "my office." But he was never very businesslike. When it came to paying the men, he always had a check but he never got it cashed. When the men cornered him, he'd tell them to go to his office and stay there until he came.

"If you want anything to drink, tell Mustache I said to give you a good hot Tom and Jerry. I'll be there in about ten minutes."

He never got there. So one night the fellows "framed him up." They put him out of the band. That night they were playing at the Masonic Hall, one of the rougher spots on the tough side of town. They replaced Bolden with a fellow called Edward Clem, who had been a member of a rival band, that of Charlie Galloway. When Bolden got in, the band was playing, and he looked up and saw Clem and said to Frankie Dusen, the assistant leader:

"What's the matter, Dusen, we gonna use two cornets tonight?"

Dusen said: "No."

"What're you gonna do with the King, Dusen?"

Dusen replied: "You can go back home."

"You mean to tell me you're gonna put me out of my own band? I got you from Algiers when nobody would have you, Dusen."

"That makes no difference, I'm the King now."

So Bolden said: "Well, I'll shove on back to Mustache's and take it easy."

But a dance was never anything around New Orleans without King Bolden. Whenever he opened up the window at the Masonic or Globe Hall and stuck his old cornet out and blew, people came from far and wide to hear him.

Finally the day came when Buddy Bolden marched in his last procession. For years he had been mentally and physically overtaxed. Under the stress of excitement, his mind snapped and he went on a rampage during a Labor Day parade. Down in New Orleans, there are those who say that women killed Buddy Bolden, but wiser heads know it was also overwork, that at last Buddy had played himself out. The king of them all was committed to the East Louisiana State Hospital on June 5, 1907, where he was listed as a barber, his reputation as cornetist promptly forgotten; he was known only as one of several Boldens from New Orleans. He died there in 1931.

Freddie Keppard, a much younger musician than Bolden, played violin in a primitive style known as "alley fiddle." But he wanted a more forceful instrument. He took up cornet and soon became the "hottest thing" in New Orleans. Though Keppard never learned to read a note and played in the most robust and rough manner, he was associated early in his career with the more finished Creole musicians in the downtown section. He played in the Olympia Band, which had been a rival of Buddy Bolden's band. The earliest clarinetist of the Olympia was Alphonse Picou. Picou composed many of the New Orleans classics, including "Muskrat Ramble," "Snake Rag," "Alligator Hop" and "Olympia Rag." Later, the clarinet in the Olympia Band was played by "Big Eye" Louis Nelson, whose C clarinet inspired many of the younger players, including Jimmy Noone, Sidney Bechet and Johnny Dodds. A little on the French side in appearance, genial in a quiet way, Louis became a changed person when he put a clarinet to his lips. He had a big tone, and while he played in the fluid style characteristic of New Orleans, he brought to it a broad inventiveness.

The drummer of the Olympia was "Ratty" John Vean, who shook all over, each part of his body geared to a different rhythm. Vean was the first to introduce the four-beat bass drum part, the bass drum being played by his right foot, the other leg being free to vibrate with the speed of a trip-hammer. Meanwhile, both hands performed incredible feats of virtuosity on the head of the snare drum, the rim, and various traps. His head, motivated by a two-beat rhythm, protruded and withdrew like a turtle's from its shell, while his stomach whirled spasmodically with a rapidity which would make a dervish dizzy. Later, Louis Cotrelle took over the rhythm. He was also called "Old Man" Cotrelle, and because of his sound, legitimate methods and knowledge of rudiments, was known as the father of New Orleans drumming. He was the inspiration and instructor of many of the younger drummers.

Joseph Petit not only played valve trombone, he was the manager of the Olympia. In later days the slide trombone was played by Zue Robinson for a while. Zue, one of the most picturesque characters of New Orleans music, was a real rambler who could never stay put very long. He played with unbelievable ease sensational stuff which would be impossible for many present-day trombonists. Years ahead of his time, Zue was unquestionably one of the first great modern trombonists. He had a far-reaching influence.

Keppard and others from the Olympia formed the nucleus of the Original Creole Band, the first important group to leave New Orleans. Organized by Bill Johnson, they started on a series of vaudeville tours as early as 1911. Bill Johnson was one of the earliest string bass players. One time, when playing up in Shreveport, his bow broke; so he had to pluck the strings the rest of the night. The effect was so novel and added so much more swing and flexibility to his playing, that he took to slapping his bass entirely thereafter. Johnson's brother, Dink, who fooled around with piano sometimes, was the drummer of the band. The guitar of Norwood Williams filled out the rhythm section. The early bands usually had a violin, and the Original Creoles used Jimmie Palao, who had played with the Olympians and Buddy Bolden. Eddie Venson was the trombonist, and George Baquet, another member of the Olympia Band, the clarinetist. Baquet was also an expert legitimate musician, with a finished technique. In the brass bands, he usually played an E flat instrument. In the funeral marches his tone, full of sweetness and sadness, could be heard wailing high above the other parts.

Since he was the only one able to read music in the Creole Band, Baquet usually had to carry the melody in a fairly straight manner, down low. Keppard, meanwhile, embellished the tune with intricate passage work, utilizing his remarkable range. Keppard, without having too nearly perfect an execution, had the greatest range of any cornetist of his time. He had such imagination in invention that other cornetists found his figurations impossible to copy. With his remarkable range, he could do everything, and was playing music 30 years ago which would sound modern today.

Although Keppard was in and out of New Orleans, much of his time from 1913 to 1918 was spent in touring with the Original Creole Band throughout the country, from Maine to California and from the Mason-Dixon line to the Great Lakes. The Creole Band appeared mainly in vaudeville, but had an extended run at the Winter Garden in New York. They opened the road for other bands which later came up from the South. Everywhere they played the old New Orleans stand-by tunes, and also other favorites of theirs, such as "Steamboat Blues," "Roustabout Shuffle" and Scott Joplin's "Pepper Rag." Early in 1916, the Victor Phonograph Company approached the Original Creoles with an offer to record. Keppard thought it over, and said:

"Nothin' doin', boys. We won't put our stuff on records for everybody to steal."

He persuaded the other fellows to turn down the recording offer. A few months later, Victor signed Nick La Rocca's group, which under the name of the Original Dixieland Jazz Band went on to fame and fortune.

In 1917, Baquet remained in New York, so Jimmy Noone came up and joined the band when they reached Detroit. Six months later, in Chicago, the Original Creole Band broke up, storing the scenery from their vaudeville act in a warehouse down on 31st Street.

After Buddy Bolden had been taken away,

Sidney Bechet

Bunk Johnson

Jelly Roll Morton

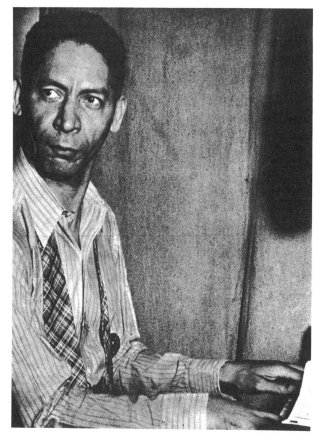

Buster Bailey

Johnny Dodds

Tony Jackson (about 1918)

Louis Armstrong

several members of his band, including Lyons, Brock and Dusen, formed the Eagle Band. They were called "the Boys in Brown" because of their brown military uniforms. At first they had a very good cornetist by the name of Ned, but he soon burnt himself out. Then Bunk Johnson came along, a rather small man who wore his cap far back on his head and was a veritable giant when he picked up a cornet. Of all musicians, Bunk was the ideal successor to the throne of King Bolden.

It may seem paradoxical that Bunk, who hailed from the tough uptown section, had the most refined taste and finished execution of all cornetists. He had an unprecedented sense of swing and feeling for the low-down blues and gut-bucket style, yet a tone unrivaled in its beauty. He was noted for his ability to improvise. He was second to none in his power to swing a band along with him. Bunk never cared to read. When a leader once wrote down some of the music Bunk had played and stuck it up for him to do again, Bunk said:

"Do you think I'm a fool? I can't play that."

Bunk describes his early musical training in the following words:

We will begin; first thing is where I was born. I was born in the city of dear old New Orleans some years ago on December the 27th, 1879. I was born uptown on Laurel Street between Peters Ave. and Octivia St., so now all of you know just where my home is. When I was seven years I started to taking music lessons. After one year I was doing so good that Prof. Wallace he then told me to tell my mother to come over to the school because he would like very much to have a good talk with her. I did just as he told me and my mother went over to the school and seen him. He told her that he could make a real cornetist out of me if she would get me a cornet just good enough to take lessons on and when I became good on the old one then she could get me a real cheap brass cornet. Now me and my old cornet, when my mother got it, night and day I puffed on it and when I did get the slite of it, Oh boy,

I really went. Then my mother saw just what headway I was making with the old cornet. Then she told me, "Son, mama saw a cheap cornet and a new one and as you are doing so good I got to get it for you if you will be a good boy." Now I was that and my dear mother got it for me.

My Prof. was a Mexican; his name was Mr. Wallace Cutchey. He told me that I had a long way to go and a short time to make it in. Boy I got busy and I really made the grade. When I became the age of 15 years old I was good [enough] to go and I really have been going ever since. Now for faking and playing by head I was hard to beat.

The first band I played with was Adam Olivier's and it played by music; that was in the year of 1894. My friend Tony Jackson started playing piano with Olivier's band. I stayed with them about one year until I got a good chance to get with King Bolden. Bolden heard me play with Olivier's band. Then he wanted me to jump Olivier's and come with him because he had the most work and the biggest name in New Orleans. It was town's talk, King Bolden band.

So I told Mr. Olivier that I think I could do better with King Bolden so he told me to suit myself and so I did and went on with King Bolden in the year of 1895. When I started playing with him Bolden was a married man and two children. He must of been between 25 or 30 years old at that time. Now here are the men in the band when I went in to it: Cornelius Tillman, drummer, Willy Cornish, trombone, Bolden, cornet, Bunk, cornet, Willie Warner, clarinet, Mumford, guitar, and Jimmie Johnson, bass. That was the old Bolden band when I went in to it. They were all men; I was the only young one in the band, in short pants.

The picture you have of Bolden's first band was taken just before I started playing with his large band. In those days he only carried a five piece band. In the late years Bolden's five piece band became so great in the city of New Orleans that he had to make his band bigger by putting in drums and cornet which made it a seven piece band.

I stayed with Bolden until 1898 and then I left and started to playing with Bob Russell band. I did not stay very long with it because they could not play very much. I went back to Bolden and when I started playing the second time he had taken Frank Duson [sic] in the band in place of Willy Cornish. I stayed about seven months and then I left and went on the road for two years with P. G. Loral and then

I came in and started playing with first one band and then another. That was the year of 1900. I went to playing with a little band in Tom Anderson dance hall.

In later years, before he finally left New Orleans to settle in the western part of the state, Bunk played occasionally with John Robichaux's orchestra. Robichaux's was for years the class "name band" of New Orleans and was in demand for all the better parties. It played for socials of the whites and had the most desirable spots in the city, the Grunewald (now the Roosevelt) and Antoine's. They played all styles of music, and everything from quadrilles to rags. Monday nights, Robichaux gave balls in uptown New Orleans, at the Masonic Hall.

Bunk, however, reached the zenith of his career between 1911 and 1914, when he played regularly with the Eagle Band. It was Bunk who got Sidney Bechet to join this band:

> Now Sidney Bechet was just starting on clarinet and Leonard Bechet, trombone, and Sidney Desvigne was just starting cornet and Joe Bechet, guitar. I know they had a little band named the "Silver Bell." So there was nothing else for me to do but break into the "Silver Bell." I went to Sidney Bechet mother's house and asked her to let him play clarinet with me in the Eagle Band. She told me yes but here is what I would have to do. "You'll have to bring Sidney home after he is through playing each and every job, that would be the only way I can let him go in your care if you promise me that you will do that."

Every Saturday night at the Masonic Hall was Eagle Band night. The Saturday night mob on South Rampart wasn't an especially high class bunch, and they liked their music hot. And that was the only way the Eagle Band knew how to "serve it up," so they were easily the most popular uptown band.

In the daytime Bunk put on his brown uniform and his Eagle hat and led the band in all their parades. New Orleans could always find an excuse for a parade, not only during Carnival, but for every national holi-

day, Jackson Day, Emancipation Day and election campaigns. The most unusual of all were the funeral processions, under the auspices of the lodges, clubs and societies. Everyone in New Orleans belonged to a secret order or society. When the member died, he had to have a band. "He was nothin' if he didn't have a band!" The societies used one side of their aprons for parades and the other for funerals. When the church bells tolled out mournfully, a couple of the brethren down on Rampart Street paused to remark:

"What's that I hear, twelve o'clock in the daytime—church bells ringin'?"

"Man, you don' hear no church bells ringin' twelve o'clock in the day!"

"Yes, indeed, somebody must be dead."

"Ain' nobody dead. Somebody must be dead drunk."

"No, I think there's a funeral."

"Why, looky here, I see there *is* a funeral."

"I b'lieve I hear that trambone moan."

With a slow, pausing tread, the procession marched to the graveyard. With the exception of a few older downtown cemeteries that had their whitewashed tombs above ground, graveyards were usually a couple of miles "up or back o' town." Most of the cemeteries, such as Cypress Grove, St. Joseph's and Lafayette, had plots for the burial of Negroes. On the way out to the graveyard, the band played in dead-march time, with muffled drums, soft and sombre dirges, including "Free as a Bird," "When the Saints Go Marching In," "Nearer, My God, to Thee" and real funeral marches. But Zutty Singleton says that, once the body was interred, "The mourning got over quick. Right out of the graveyard, the drummer would throw on the snares, roll the drums, get the cats together and light out. The cornet would give a few notes, and then about three blocks from the graveyard they would cut loose."

They came back playing "High Society"

and "King Porter Stomp," but first of all they swung out on "Oh, Didn't He Ramble? . . ."

The funerals and parades always had a "second line" which consisted of the kids who danced along behind. The bands had a way of strutting, of swinging their bodies, and of turning corners in spectacular fashion, and the boys who marched along on the sidewalk with them mimicked every action. When the big band "went crazy" after the funeral, the kids cut up with their primitive version of the "Susie Q" and danced the "shudders." With their leader, the boys joined in the general tumult as they shimmied along and sang, yelled and clapped. Many had tin flageolets or home-made whistles cut from stalks of reed on which they played the tune. Only the tough kids joined the second line. Their mothers did not approve; if they ever caught the kids, they jerked them out of the parade. A few of these future jazzmen were actually helpful. These were the water boys, who carried buckets of water to refresh the tired marchers whose lips were parched after a hot march under the boiling sun.

The Eagle Band and others were often a feature of the picnics held during the summer months. The oldest resort established was Milenburg, out on Lake Pontchartrain, near the old lighthouse and Spanish fort. The many good times at the picnics there in the old days were immortalized in the "Milenburg Joys," a classic stomp played by all New Orleans bands. A casino near the fort and various amusement concessions were added about 1900. For years these offered lucrative employment to musicians. The lake front has since been filled in, and today none of these buildings remain.

In later years, West End became the most popular summer resort. On the lake, by the New Basin Canal, West End has a charming park for picnics. It also has several night clubs. Just across the canal, in the western section of West End, is a small settlement known as "Bucktown," which was at one time a wide-open spot.

On Sunday afternoons, Washington Park, uptown on Carrollton Avenue, was a popular meeting place for bands. Here at the ball games and balloon ascensions, bands fought it out until one emerged the victor. But the real battles occurred when two bands, out advertising in their wagons, locked wheels on some important corner.

Frequently, when there were two dances the same night and the bands ran into one another, there was an honest-to-goodness cutting contest. They hitched on or locked wheels, so that neither band could escape, and went to it, blasting at each other until one band, exhausted, called for mercy. Meanwhile everyone, young and old, gathered from blocks around to shout encouragement and approval for his favorite. The band which received the loudest cheers was the winner and drew the crowd to its dance that night. Any downtown band which ventured across Canal Street was looking for trouble.

Downtown, some of the Creole bands, the "Frenchmen," as they were called, had their following. The Imperial and Armand Piron's were among the most popular downtown bands. The leader of the Imperial was Emanuel Perez, one of the best cornetists in New Orleans. He was an excellent reader and teacher, and could hold his own with any legitimate or symphony man. Perez's first job, at the age of 17, had been with Robichaux's orchestra, when they were playing at Antoine's famous restaurant in 1895. Three years later, he became a member of the Imperial Band with Picou, Peter Bocage and Buddie Johnson, trombonist. When Emanuel finished a night's work, he didn't stay around for a single drink. He always said, "Good night, boys, see you tomorrow night," and took every cent of his two dollars home. He saved his money and was later able to retire to a grocery business.

\* \* \* \* \* \*

Some of the most popular dance tunes of early New Orleans were the Scott Joplin numbers, such as "Maple Leaf Rag" and "Climax Rag." "Tiger Rag" was also known as "Number Two Rag," which came from an old French quadrille, "La Marseillaise." "Cannon Ball Rag" and "Rubber Plant" were other favorites. The prevalence of "rags" among the selections is no indication that the old-timers didn't really swing their music. Then there were always the blues, some, such as the "shags," of the meanest sort. The folk and work songs of the Negroes added their influence; for example, "Good-bye, Bag, I Know You've Gone" came from the song sung by the mill workers as they emptied the rice bags, "Lift 'Em Up, Joe" was taken by Joe Oliver from a song of the railroad hands as they raised the rails.

The absence of pianos in New Orleans orchestras could be explained, in part, by the difficulty of fitting them into the wagons so often used for street advertising.

The pianists did, however, find their place in Storyville, the world-renowned red-light district of New Orleans. Named after the alderman who drew up the ordinance creating it in 1897, Storyville consisted of a dozen square blocks back of the French Quarter. Its principal thoroughfares were Iberville, Bienville, Liberty, Franklin and, most celebrated of all, Basin Street. For 200 years, half of the time under French and Spanish rule, New Orleans had been known for its gaiety and tolerance of human failings, its political corruption, crime and vice. With the founding of the restricted district, Storyville soon became the most glamorous, as well as the most notorious, center of legalized vice in history. It was for 20 years the showplace and scandal of New Orleans. Storyville was bossed by Tom Anderson,

whose "city hall" was his main saloon, the Arlington Annex. Anderson published and sold, for 25 cents a copy, the *Blue Book,* a directory and guide to the sporting district, which listed the names and addresses of all prostitutes and entertainers. There were ads with extravagant claims, and illustrations of all the main houses of pleasure. Some of these, such as Josie Arlington's $5.00 house on Basin Street, were gaily tinseled palaces, full of gaudy tapestries, heavy plush-covered sofas, laces, leopard-skin rugs, gilt statuary, mirrors and cut-glass chandeliers. In every parlor was a piano, and often there was music by a string trio, since the brothels did not favor loud bands. In addition to the musicians, there were dancers and singers.

Ann Cook, one of the very first blues singers, worked for Countess Willie Piazza, under whose roof a Central American revolution had been plotted. Piazza's *maison joie,* which specialized in octoroons, also had the distinction of being the first bordello to hire a pianist to entertain the customers. He was a riot and was known as John the Baptist. At a later date, Tony Jackson was the featured pianist-entertainer and made a big hit with his song, "I've Got Elgin Movements in My Hips with Twenty Years' Guarantee." Tony left New Orleans about 1908 and traveled throughout the tenderloin circuit, later winning national fame as a singer and pianist in New York.

Down in the same block on Basin Street was Mahogany Hall, run by Lulu White. She was called the "Diamond Queen," and her mirror-room and beautiful octoroons were known across the continent. At Lulu's, the pianists at various times were Al Carrel, Richard M. Jones and Clarence Williams, who celebrated Lulu White's establishment in the tune "Mahogany Hall Stomp."

Tom Anderson's Annex usually employed a string trio, with piano, guitar and violin. Among the first to play there was Jelly Roll

Morton. Jelly Roll, who has been called the "Dizzy Dean of music," blew in from Gulfport. Inspired by King Porter, a pianist from Mobile, he wrote the "King Porter Stomp" and a number of other tunes such as "Milenburg Joys," originally called the "Peep Hole Blues," which became part of the standard New Orleans repertory. He left New Orleans a little later than Tony Jackson, traveled up the river and spent several years in Chicago and California before going East.

In 1910, there were almost 200 houses of pleasure in Storyville, including the 50-cent cribs, bare one-room holes, which lined the streets. Also in the district were nine cabarets, many "dance schools" and innumerable honky-tonks and gambling joints.

One of the first cabarets established was the 101 Ranch, on Franklin Street, originally a low dive and hangout for river roustabouts, gamblers and cutthroats. But about 1910, Billy Phillips decided to put some class into his joint. He hired an orchestra and entertainers, raised the prices, and fixed the odds in the gambling games a little more in favor of the house. For the next seven years, some of New Orleans' hottest musicians played here, including Joe Oliver, Perez, Baquet, Bechet, Roy Palmer and "Pop" Foster. Here could be seen future members of the New Orleans Rhythm Kings, the Original Dixieland Jazz Band and the Halfway House Gang, whose first impressions of hot were received while listening to the older Negro musicians.

Peter Lala's cabaret on Iberville Street was one of the most popular and famous. Known also as the 25 Club, it was a favorite meeting place of musicians. Possibly the best "all-star" orchestra to play in New Orleans during that period was at Pete Lala's, consisting of such men as Joe Oliver, Lorenzo Tio, Zue Robinson and Henry Zino. Later, trombonist Kid Ory had charge of Pete's band, and when Oliver left for Chicago, Louis Armstrong came in.

The fanciest decorated resort was the Tuxedo Dance Hall, across from the 101 Ranch. After the killing of Billy Phillips in the Tuxedo, the police clamped down on Storyville. A few places closed up and some cut the size of their orchestras, as the district quieted down for a few weeks. At the Tuxedo, Keppard, when he had to reduce the number of men to cut expenses, fired the guitar, bass, and violin, and hired Buddy Christian to play piano. At other times, Celestin and Bob Frank had bands at the Tuxedo, and, later on, a new clarinetist, Johnny Dodds, worked there.

A colorful part of Storyville life was found in the honky-tonks and barrel houses. The old 28 Club, run by Kyser, was a typical "tonk," jammed every night with river rowdies, card sharks, roughnecks, pimps and all varieties of male parasites. Drunks whose money had been spent or stolen were thrown out into the alley. All the good old crooked gambling games were played: faro, three-card monte, shell, craps and banco. Drinks were cheap, but if a customer wanted to keep a place at the bar, his glass had to be filled often. And if anyone sat down at the piano in the 28 Club, he knew he'd better not play anything else but the blues. In these dives they dragged out the blues with a slow beat and fierce intensity. Apparently there were hundreds of Negroes who could sit down and play and sing the low-down blues. They made up the words to fit their mood and the occasion, but invariably pianists knew only one tune. If someone yelled, "Play somethin' else!" he played the same blues a little faster, and the entire tonk, satisfied, shook in a quicker tempo.

A stimulus to trade was the featured "pig-ankle" night, when handouts of ankles and pigs' feet were given to the patrons. Bessie Smith must have been thinking of New Orleans when, many years later, she shouted the words of her song "Gimme a Pigfoot":

> Check all your razors and your guns,
> We're gonna be wrastlin' when the
>     wagon comes.
> Gimme a pigfoot and a bottle o' beer,
> Send me, Gate, I don't care.
> Gimme a reefer and a gang o' gin,
> Slay me 'cause I'm in my sin.

Storyville was kind to hot music. With a dozen bands, many trios and other musicians employed every night, it is little wonder that jazz first sprang up and flourished in New Orleans. But it was a tough life for the musicians. Hours were "eight until," and the pay ranged from $1.00 to $2.50 a night. Many spots gave them a chance to make a little more by permitting one of the musicians to come down off the balcony to pass the hat. With America's entrance into the World War, the handwriting was seen on the wall, for the Secretary of the Navy ordered the suppression of all open prostitution. A city ordinance was passed, and with a rapid exodus of harlots, Storyville came to an official end in November, 1917. The brothels were closed, and furniture, mirrors and fittings were sold. Countess Willie Piazza's famed white piano, badly out of tune, brought at auction $1.25.

Then the musicians really had the "Basin Street Blues" and began to look for new fields of employment. New Orleans jazz spread fanlike up the Mississippi Valley, from coast to coast and throughout the world. The Original Creole Band had already left years before. Dink Johnson, their drummer, had settled in California and organized his Louisiana Six. He was soon joined by Kid Ory's Brown Skinned Jazz Band, with cornetist Mutt Carey. As early as 1913, Bunk, Clarence Williams, Zino and Sidney Bechet had carried New Orleans jazz to Texas. A little later such stars as Perez, Tig Chambers, Tio, Atkins, Cotrelle and Dominique journeyed to Chicago. In 1914, "Sugar" Johnny, an erratic but sensational cornetist, took north another Creole Band, with Lawrence Dewey, Roy Palmer, Herbert Lindsay and Louis Keppard. In Chicago, he added "Tubby" Hall, Sidney Bechet and Wellman Braud.

The Mississippi riverboats carried jazz not only up the river to Memphis, St. Louis and Davenport, but to cities on the tributaries, such as Kansas City and Omaha on the Missouri, and the Ohio River towns as far as Pittsburgh. Fate Marable, leader of many great bands on the riverboats, settled in St. Louis, where Charlie Creath soon organized another fine band, with the late Tommy Ladnier, "Pop" Foster and Zutty Singleton.

Changing industrial conditions brought an inevitable shift of Negro population to the manufacturing centers of the North. This aided in the dissemination of hot jazz, but the principal reason for the scattering of the New Orleans jazzmen is found in the fall of Storyville. As Lizzie Green, in "Good Time Flat Blues," bemoaned:

> I can't keep open, I'm gonna close up shack.
> The chief of police done tore my playhouse
>     down;
> No use in grievin', I'm gonna leave this town.

—1939

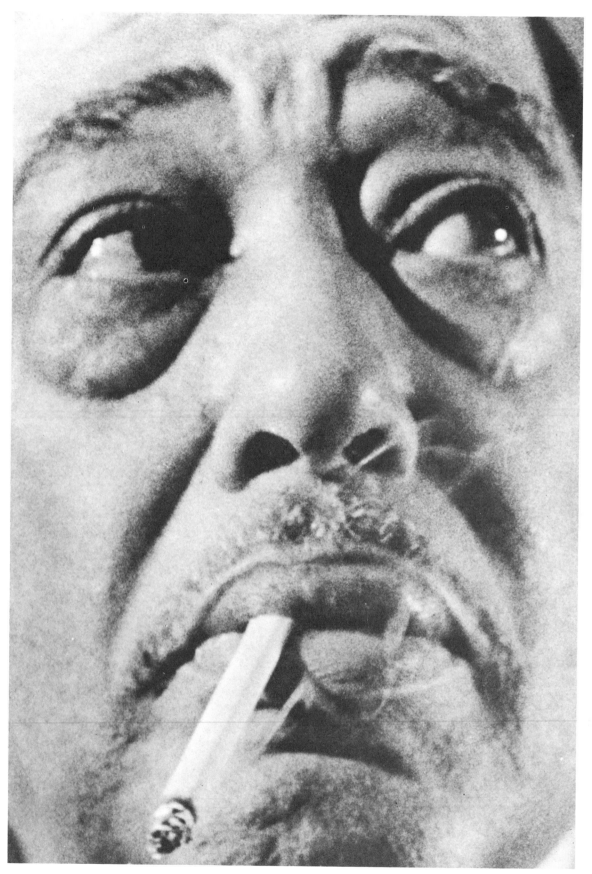
Duke Ellington

# New York Turns On the Heat

by **Wilder Hobson**

THERE WAS probably as much fine jazz playing in New York during the Twenties as in Chicago. Matching the names already identified with the Windy City, the musicians more frequently in New York included Joe Smith, Tommy Ladnier, Albert "Cootie" Williams, Charlie "Big" Green, Jimmy Harrison, Milfred "Miff" Mole, Jay C. Higginbotham, Joe "Tricky Sam" Nanton, Coleman Hawkins, Benny Carter, Buster Bailey, Johnny Hodges, Harry Carney, Barney Bigard and Thomas "Fats" Waller—and it was in New York that Fletcher Henderson, Duke Ellington and Luis Russell developed their excellent big bands, including most of the players mentioned above.

New York's genuine jazz was, of course, like that of Chicago, very obscure as compared with the popular commercial dance music. When the Original Dixieland Jazz Band quit the city in 1919, it left very few *musical* imitators. Most of the "jazz" bands which sought a popularity like that of the Dixieland copied merely the latter's gags and novelty effects, made a syncopated din which had little or nothing to do with the jazz language as the Dixieland had learned it in New Orleans; these Northern combinations were for the most part old-style ragtime "nut" bands with added comedy features, an extra set of pots and pans for the drummer, and the habit of playing their instruments on one knee or in other acrobatic positions. They

were exactly as raucous as a good many ministers of the Gospel insisted they were.

The jazz center of Gotham through the Twenties was, naturally enough, the Negro section—Harlem—which was to New York what the South Side was to Chicago. To this vast, drably architectured district the Coolidge–Hoover boom brought more money than it had ever seen before or has ever seen since, although, by downtown standards, it would have been necessary to call it very small money. A good fraction of it was paid out by sightseers, led off by the downtown esthetes who "discovered" Negro art, music, dancing and vice in the early Twenties. And of that fraction a sizable sub-fraction was siphoned off by entertainment bosses who were not Negroes. Colored Harlem has long been exploited in its own precinct by opportunists not of the race. The well-known Savoy Ballroom, where practically every fine Negro band has played in its time, was not and is not owned by Negroes, and the old uptown Cotton Club of Prohibition days, where Duke Ellington made his name, was operated by a white beer-running syndicate. During the boom, however, enough steady money seeped into Harlem's musical circles to encourage the organization of some of the best bands in the jazz annals. And Harlem gave them the kind of attention which stimulates good playing—from visitors who expected genuine jazz and, more especially, from strenuous, inventive Negro dancers who, as André Gide says of the African natives, were "learned" rhythmically.

The first fine Negro band in New York, however, spent a good part of its time downtown. While Paul Whiteman was filling the expensive Palais Royal, Fletcher Henderson was leading his colored combination at the public dance hall, Roseland, a few blocks up Broadway. Henderson has always had various distractions from his music and has never been much of a self-promoter. He has perhaps joined in more fine jazz performances than any man alive, both with his bands and as accompanist to Bessie Smith and other blues singers, but he has never sustained the discipline and routine, either personal or orchestral, which seem necessary for the really big money and which are apt, at the same time, to cut the spirit of the music. He is recognized today chiefly as the writer of some of Benny Goodman's most effective orchestrations. Fletcher and his younger brother Horace have turned out many fine, unpretentious scores, thoroughly in the spirit of good improvised jazz. Among them are "King Porter Stomp," "Sugar Foot Stomp," "Wrappin' It Up," "Down South Camp Meetin'," "Big John Special," "Hot and Anxious" and "When Buddha Smiles."

But there is a good deal more to be said about Fletcher. His father was a schoolteacher in Cuthbert, Georgia. Fletcher studied chemistry for a while and then played the piano in a road show. Around 1919, he formed his first band for Roseland, where he appeared off and on for the next 15 years. He was the first hot musician to build a big hot band with full brass, reed and rhythm sections and to orchestrate for sections in the manner now familiar, as may be gathered from his record of "What-Cha-Call-'Em Blues" and "Sugar Foot Stomp," which was made in 1924. The personnel of his band changed frequently, but the ensembles were

usually excellent, with several top-rank soloists. First and last, he has had certainly a good 50 per cent of the finest Negro talent in the country. Back in 1924–25, the band included Louis Armstrong, on from Chicago, Coleman Hawkins, who has been to the tenor saxophone what Armstrong has to the jazz trumpet, and Charlie "Big" Green, whose comic trombone "comment" is familiar behind the recorded voice of Bessie Smith and who, with Miff Mole, was one of the earliest expressive trombone soloists. In 1927–28, Henderson still had Hawkins, Buster Bailey on the clarinet, Benny Carter and Don Redman on the alto saxophone, Jimmy Harrison on the trombone and the superb trumpet team of Joe Smith and Tommy Ladnier.

I first heard the band at this period, at a college party. The dozen pieces were spread in front of a set of Gothic windows and flanked, for a while, by three large, well-corseted hostesses sitting on a divan and determinedly giving the impression that they felt quite at home with "Clarinet Marmalade" being delivered ten feet away with five parts brass. Hawkins sweated out chorus after chorus in his more agitated manner, and Kaiser Marshall sometimes exuberantly threw away the drumsticks, not catching them again, like the trick drummers, but lobbing them out over the heads of the crowd. I think this was the evening when the tuba player was high and kept injecting great haarrrumphing notes where they weren't wanted. When this finally annoyed Fletcher, the tuba player said: "Ah usually only play two–three notes; ah'm goin' have some fun this evenin'."

There were alternate trumpet choruses from Smith and Ladnier, Smith's jetting out of the middle range of his horn, with those light, slippery rhythms across the pulse of the band which may be heard in the records of "Stockholm Stomp" and "Rocky Mountain Blues." There were no screams or blasts, and no ornate scrambling, however expert, but the most jubilant, singing trumpet passages imaginable, with lovely inflections in the slow numbers (the closest suggestion of Smith I've heard in recent months was from Muggsy Spanier with his small Ragtime Band). And Henderson usually worked up to seething last choruses of full band faking, like the end of the "Fidgety Feet" record.

It is hard work to develop large, 12- to 16-piece, jazz combinations, to get ensemble finish, precise intonation, unified attack, the sections phrasing and blending well among themselves and with each other. Many currently popular bands are very musicianly in this sense. They have a polish which Henderson seldom, if ever, had, and for which I imagine he never tried. But his best combinations had a quality beside which a high polish seems a rather routine, if difficult, achievement. It might be called ensemble ease and spontaneity—listen to the records of "Fidgety Feet" or "New King Porter Stomp." There was a sense of relaxation, lack of strain, reserve strength. This was perhaps largely a matter of individual talent. With a brass team such as Russell and Joe Smith, Ladnier, Green and Harrison, it would have been too bad to insist on precision. They might have delivered it, but the music would have lost the spirit of these men attacking with their natural enthusiasm. Henderson's best large bands played with the buoyancy of a fine, small, improvising combination. Obviously, few other bands have had such musicians, but, even so, there has recently seemed to be a fetish with regard to precision, and it would seem that, in obtaining it, a lot of the players' gusto is often lost. In the playing of Henderson's "Big John" the premium is on the warm spontaneity, careless in the best sense of the word, which was one of the reasons why, for years, virtually every jazz musician in New York sometimes sat in one of the chairs across the floor from the Roseland bandstand and listened to Fletcher Henderson.

Edward Kennedy "Duke" Ellington, son of a Negro worker in the Washington, D.C., Navy Yard, opened with his band at the Cotton Club in Harlem in 1927, when Henderson's band had long since become a byword with other jazz players. Apart from musicians, however, Henderson's music was known mostly to a limited dance-hall audience. It had had no effective promotion. Ellington, on the other hand, had Irving Mills' plugging management, a bandstand in the purple glow lamps of the Cotton Club, which was a center of the Harlem entertainment vogue, and widespread radio facilities. Also, in addition to being the leader of a remarkable combination, Ellington was a composer of decided interest. In a short time, his radio hookups brought him a large, national audience—his was the first large hot band to attract any such attention.

He has since had all kinds of salutes. Recently it has often been said that Ellington's music has lost the genuineness which characterized it in the late Twenties, that it has become overly suave, elaborate, and virtuoso. In a recent appearance at the downtown Cotton Club on Broadway, Ellington's boys wore white jackets, boiled shirts and dress ties, crimson trousers and shoes. Duke himself opened the evening in a light gray coat and black trousers, moved on to full dress, and finished in a henna jacket and the blacks. The trumpets appeared to be made of platinum, heavily embossed, perhaps suitably inscribed and possibly taken out of Tiffany's each day and put back after the night's work. Even the instrument cases were handsomely lettered in metal. The only feature which marred the general splendor was a battered platter which Rex Stewart produced from some hiding-place and waved over the bell of his trumpet during the last chorus *tutti* of "The Sheik of Araby."

These trappings may have little to do with music, but I think they are fitting and proper

Duke Ellington's Kentucky Club orchestra (about 1925).

The Fletcher Henderson orchestra in 1924 (Louis Armstrong, third from left).

in this case. If any musicians ever earned the right to a dress uniform, Ellington's boys have earned their crimson pants and fancy instrument cases. They have been and are an epitome of a sort. The jazz language, coming out of folk-musical sources, by its own nature bred a lot of remarkable improvising talent. As the players grew more and more interested in the combination of instruments in sections, jazz inevitably acquired considerable orchestral sophistication. Jazz musicians are bound to be more and more experimental *orchestrally*. And it is probably natural that some one organization should most vividly represent *all* the elements of this process in which a folk music is gradually moving into general musical currents. It seems to me that the band which does this is Ellington's. In it you hear improvising in many spirits—the "low-down" rhythmic playing of trumpeter Cootie Williams and trombonist Joe Nanton, the spirited, melodic inventions of the saxophonists Johnny Hodges and Harry Carney, and the floridity of trumpeter Rex Stewart, trombonist Lawrence Brown and clarinetist Barney Bigard. Also, this is certainly the most striking *ensemble* in jazz, with a brilliance, finish *and* ease resulting from long collaboration. Finally, I don't know of any jazz orchestrator as musically fertile as Ellington. His ideas may seldom get sustained development, may often be loosely strung together and over-rich for the thematic material which is carrying them, but in an Ellington performance it is a rare three minutes in which

something of *orchestral* fascination doesn't occur. Of how many other bands can the same be said?

The third big band of fine quality developed in New York in the Twenties was Luis Russell's, which played at the Saratoga Club in Harlem in 1929. Born in Panama, Russell moved up to New Orleans and on up the Mississippi to Chicago in the middle Twenties, and then traveled eastward to Harlem, where he assembled a short-lived group whose chief players have recently been heard, with Russell, behind Louis Armstrong. Toward the end of the Twenties, under Russell's and Henry Allen's names, this band made some of the finest jazz records, with simple arrangements, a good, rhythmic ensemble and a trio of superb soloists. These disks were the first to show to advantage the alto saxophone inventions of Charles Holmes, the playing of Jay C. Higginbotham from Georgia, a trombonist who ran the gamut between the muted delicacy of "Biffly Blues" and the explosive strength of "Swing Out," and the clamorous, lyric trumpeting of Henry Allen, a particularly fine blues player, from Algiers, across from New Orleans.

In the jazz circles of New York, the Twenties ended with the arrival of many of the best Chicago players. But with such bands as Henderson's, Ellington's and Russell's already on location, and their members often playing impromptu late hour sessions in the Harlem basements, the city could scarcely be said to lack for syncopation.

—1939

Lester Young

# Modern Jazz Is a Folk Music That Started with the Blues

by Frank M. Davis

It WAS good to see that an Episcopal minister, the Reverend Alvin Kershaw of Oxford, Ohio, not only chose jazz for his category on that TV quiz show, "The $64,000 Question," but realizes the place of this music in our society.

Only a few decades ago, "respectable" white people just didn't listen to real jazz. They might bend an ear to the musical meanderings of Paul Whiteman, who never could play jazz, or to George Gershwin's *Rhapsody in Blue,* which was 95 per cent foreign to both jazz and the blues, but that was as close as they ever got.

Jazz was born of the musical experience of the Negro people in America. Into it went the highly complex rhythmic patterns and musical conceptions native to those sections of Africa from which the black man came, the spirituals, blues and secular music developed in America following contact with European music patterns in the New World, and the social and psychological experiences of a minority group struggling for equality.

The background was not common to whites, and hidebound critics and musicians, steeped in the traditions and adhering to the standards of Western European music, had little or no patience with African-rooted sounds and techniques which rebelled against everything they had been taught.

As a matter of fact, white America is still not ready to give colored America its due.

Negroes had been playing jazz in and around New Orleans since the 1890's, but this revolutionary new music was not accepted until the Original Dixieland Jazz Band, a white outfit, came out of the South. At the time, there were at least a dozen colored bands immeasurably superior to this white group.

Negro bands such as those of Duke Ellington, Fletcher Henderson, Bennie Moten, Louis Armstrong, Jimmy Lunceford, Don Redman and a number of others had been swinging mightily for years, but it was not until Benny Goodman based a big white band on Negro style that swing became popular with white America.

Although the piano style called boogie-woogie had been known since the early 1900's, and, perhaps its greatest exponent, Pinetop Smith, had died, the general public accepted it only after the Bob Crosby band included "Yancey Special" and "Honky Tonk Train Blues" in its repertoire.

But despite all its enemies could do, jazz grew, and became not only the music of the U.S. but of all sections of the world influenced by U.S. culture. And now we have a white minister who not only is a student of jazz but who has brought it into his church.

The blues are the mother of jazz. To understand jazz, you need to understand the blues.

Nobody knows when the blues began, but they are a folk music which developed in the rural South and became identifiable as a specific type of U.S. Negro secular music after the Civil War and before the 1890's.

Basically, they are personal songs of protest and rebellion, growing out of individual needs. They may have any subject matter, ranging through love, politics, current events, race relations and what not. They may poke fun or they may be deadly serious. A true blues is always realistic; it is never maudlin or escapist.

At first the blues were sung without accompaniment, as a spontaneous expression of the way the singer felt about any topic which moved him deeply. Most of the early blues singers couldn't afford instruments, anyway. Then, gradually, they began using whatever was available as accompaniment—banjo, guitar or what not.

The blues have a distinctive tonal scale, in which the third and seventh tones tend to be flattened. The degree varies. These "blue" notes cannot be reproduced accurately on any instrument with regular tones, such as the piano. On this instrument, the closest approximation is the striking of two keys near the desired tone.

In addition to introducing new tones, the blues also provided new structures and techniques.

Most genuine blues consist of 12 bars of music in common time, divided into three equal groups of four bars. The first group of fours is on the common chord on the keynote, the second four-bar grouping is on the chord of the subdominant and the third on the chord of the dominant seventh.

Each group of four bars has a line of verse. This line of verse rarely fills the entire four bars, often ending on the first beat of the third bar. Usually this same verse is repeated for the second group of four bars, for example:

> I'd rather drink muddy water,
>     sleep in a hollow log;
> Said I'd rather drink muddy
>     water, sleep in a hollow log,
> Before I'd stay in Mississippi,
>     treated like a dirty dog.

Since each line of words did not take up the full group of four bars, the accompanying instruments had to fill in the remainder of the four bars as they saw fit. In other words, they were forced to improvise.

Meanwhile, Negroes were flocking to New Orleans by the end of the last century. Life was faster and there were more jobs and better times than in the rural areas. By now there were many blues which had taken form and were common property.

And since life in New Orleans moved at a far faster tempo than it did on the plantations and in small towns, the music also increased in tempo from slow blues; the improvisation now extended over the entire bar. Thus is was that a new music, to be known as jazz, came into being in the 1890's.

—1955

Randy Weston

Cecil Taylor

## Cool Jazz

WHAT IS jazz? Langston Hughes says, "Jazz is a heartbeat," and that is about as genuine a non-musical definition as anyone could wish for. Jazz has an intricate history, which in human terms means both a terrible and a glorious one. One cannot easily forget the plight of a Charlie Parker and the genius of his music. Along with Lester Young and Miles Davis, he was one of the jazz musicians who, in the late 1940's, began inexplicably to play what was named "modern" or "cool" jazz. Bebop, which preceded it, had provoked violent controversy among musicians, who debated its merits as music, but modern jazz delighted musicians with its complexities of harmony, rhythm and improvisation.

Oscar Peterson

Chico Hamilton

John Coltrane

Horace Silver

Dizzy Gillespie

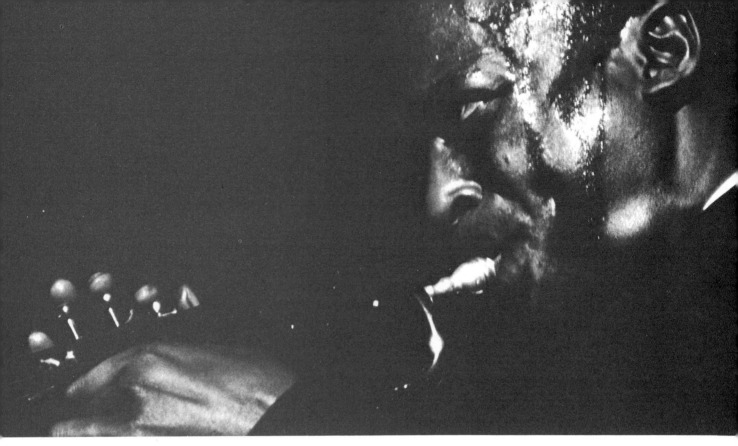

Miles Davis

Charles Davis

Art Blakey

Jackie Wilson

Sam Cooke

Frankie Lymon

LaVern Baker

*Rock and Roll*

The Supremes

The Ronettes

The Marvelettes

The Chiffons

# Rhythm and Blues (Rock and Roll) Makes the Grade

**by Ralph J. Gleason**

EVER SINCE the days when the first jazz bands made themselves heard outside New Orleans, the blues has been a part of America's great popular music, diluted, straight and disguised, but always present.

Recently, however, "rhythm and blues," taken to mean the rocking, rolling beat and the hoarse, sometimes out of tune, sometimes syrupy, sentimental vocal, has emerged into a type of music that has scored on all the hit parades, is belted out by the radio and juke boxes—and is the current number one favorite of the teen-age group.

In New York, several times in the past year [1957], giant shows featuring half a dozen "rhythm and blues" or "rock and roll" groups have filled arenas and brought hordes of teen-agers to the theatres. Road shows with the same sort of talent have toured the East Coast, playing to record crowds.

Last week a group of rhythm and blues artists, headed by singers Al Hibbler, LaVern Baker and Gloria Mann, did a week's stand at the Paramount Theatre. From the opening show on, it was obvious this was no ordinary stage presentation. Bobby-soxers, teen-agers, leather-jacketed motorcycle riders and platoons of high school students stormed the box office to attend. Once inside, equipped with enough hot dogs and hamburgers to last eight hours, they settled in their seats and saw the show over and over again.

They recognized every tune, knew the words and sometimes chanted them. At other times they swayed back and forth, clapping their hands in time to the music, and occasionally, in a burst of uncontrollable energy, they leaped to their feet to dance in the aisles.

Whatever rhythm and blues is, it has certainly captured the teen-age audience.

And just exactly what it is will probably always be a moot point. Like jazz, western music and even the popular song, it defies exact definition.

There's no question about its rhythm. Every act, except for ballad singer Hibbler, performed with a basic rhythm that was as compelling as the simple rhythm of a tom-tom. Slow or fast, the afterbeat was always heavily accented. The appeal was universal to the audience.

As to the blues, it's another story. If you take the standard definition of the blues song as a simple 12-bar pattern with three chord changes, not all the R & B (as the trade refers to it) songs follow it that closely. But all of them have a close general relationship to the blues of Bessie Smith, Billie Holiday and the other great blues singers.

The songs are simple tunes, short phrases, easily understood stories or semi-nonsense songs sung with the beat and the rhythm that teen-agers love.

Right now, the best-selling charts of the record companies in the popular record field (i.e., Frank Sinatra, Rosemary Clooney) list 13 tunes that stem from rhythm and blues or are outright R & B numbers in the top 30. Last year, the top 30 best-selling records included a number of R & B songs, such as "Rock around the Clock," "Ko Ko Mo," "Ain't That a Shame?" and "Tweedle Dee."

Is rhythm and blues something new? Not at all. It has been around a long time, not always in its present form, but with us since the beginning of the phonograph record and possibly before.

In the Twenties and Thirties, rhythm and blues was called "race music" and was a standard part of the catalogues of the major record companies, designed for the Negro audiences in the South and the great metropolitan areas. Bessie Smith's records, which sold by the millions for Columbia and were the salvation of that company in the early Thirties, were rhythm and blues records. Then they were called "race" and, although they had some sale to a white public, it was mostly Negroes who bought them.

On down through the Thirties, a succession of "race record" artists such as Big Bill, Leroy Carr, Blind Lemon Jefferson, Tampa Red, the Harlem Hamfats, Kokomo Arnold, Peetie Wheatstraw and dozens of others recorded for Bluebird, Victor, Decca, Vocalion, Okeh and Columbia and sold as heavily, proportionately, as does many a popular singer today.

Then, during the wartime shellac shortage, the major companies dropped these records to concentrate on the juke box hits, and, in the vacuum thus created, a whole group of new, independent record companies gradually grew up.

Throughout the Forties and the early Fifties, dozens of small companies in Chicago, New York and elsewhere began making records for the Negro consumer. Some of them, such as Cecil Gant's "I Wonder," Jack McVea's "Open the Door, Richard," the

Cats and a Fiddle's "I Miss You So" and Joe Liggins' "The Honeydipper," reached an audience beyond racial lines and became best sellers in the general market.

By the end of the Forties, the business was booming and it became a regular part of the reportage of the trade papers such as *Billboard*. In August, 1949, *Billboard* and *Cash Box* succumbed to pressure and dropped the title "race records" and began referring to them as "jazz and blues." This was not specific enough, so in 1952 they began to call them "rhythm and blues" and the name has stuck. The music is the same, basically, but the nomenclature has changed.

Early last year, considerable attention was drawn to R & B by a series of editorials in *Variety,* the show business magazine, calling attention to what they termed suggestive lyrics; this was followed by a national campaign to get the companies to clean up the lyric content. Disk jockeys and record executives kept predicting that R & B would die, but it has only grown stronger than ever.

What was happening, as Ruth Cage and other writers on publications such as *Down Beat* pointed out, was that rhythm and blues was becoming big business and hence was drawing attention to itself. When the so-called "race records" were not considered a big enough part of the business, nobody paid any attention to them except the fans. But with the advent of the disk jockey as an important element in the entertainment field, records began to reach a greater segment of the public. In areas where there were heavy Negro populations, radio programs playing R & B disks began to appear. In New York there were no R & B records played on the air at all in the Thirties. It wasn't until the Forties that Symphony Sid, a former trumpet player turned disk jockey, began to play a nightly hour of jazz and rhythm and blues and an occasional spiritual. Then, in New Orleans, Oakland, Chicago and other cities, disk jockeys such as Daddy-O Dailey, John Sharpe Williams and Poppa Stoppa began to prove to the stations that such programs could get a solid listening audience and therefore become a practical advertising medium. Now there are hundreds of such shows, with KSAN and KWBR in the Bay Area playing a heavy proportion of R & B.

Once the records were on the air, everybody could hear them, and the disk jockey is the main element in the rise of R & B, according to Dave Rosenbaum of the Rhythm and Melrose Music stores in the Fillmore district.

And it is certainly true that the current rage for R & B followed the exposure of the music on the radio.

Three years ago, R & B began to be noticeably popular with a white audience as well. Jerry Wexler and Ahmet Ertegun, whose Atlantic Records is one of the largest R & B labels in the business, point out that their surveys show the first area in which R & B stepped out past its original audience was the South. In 1952 and 1953, the Atlantic salesmen began to report white high school and college students were "picking up on rhythm and blues—primarily to dance to. A few alert disk jockeys observed this and switched to R & B on their programs. They were deluged with greater audiences, both white and Negro, and more and more sponsors. Conservative, old-line stores found themselves compelled to stock, display and push R & B recordings."

Wexler and Ertegun define the music as "up-to-date blues with a beat, with infectious catch phrases and highly danceable rhythm." And what made it popular? "The need for a music to dance to," they say.

Every parent remembers the hysteria attendant on the swing era and the Benny Goodman band, whose fans danced in the aisles of the New York Paramount much as today's fans dance to R & B. And the prophets of doom regarded that with as much dismay as do today's critics of R & B. But the dance band almost disappeared during and after the War. The kids who learned the fox-trot steps from their brothers and sisters went away to war and weren't around to teach the new generation what to do with their feet. One of the results of this was a generation that couldn't dance.

Since dancing has been a basic human activity since long before the blues, this situation couldn't last. The youngsters searched for something to dance to and they found it in R & B. As a New York disk jockey succinctly put it: "Ever try dancing to a ballad singer?"

Today in the R & B field, according to Rosenbaum, the purchaser comes in and asks for the tune and not the artist. Many times they don't know who made the record, only its name. And a survey made by Key Records in Southern California last year disclosed that 61.7 per cent of the youngsters polled admitted that rhythm was the most important influence to them in purchasing a record.

Another factor, according to Rosenbaum, is that R & B gives the youngsters something they can participate in. Back in the Thirties, Tommy Dorsey's disk of "Marie," with the chorus repeating off-beat phrases behind the vocal, was a big hit. Thousands of high school students, and others, too, learned these phrases and entered into the performance by singing them with the band. Today's teenagers do the same thing, Rosenbaum points out, with another set of performers. "The teen-agers have taken over and everybody is singing," he says.

An indication of the kinship of rhythm and blues of today to the "race records" and blues singers of yesterday is the fact that a number of artists from the Thirties are still active hit-makers today. Joe Turner, one of the great blues singers of all time, is one of the most consistent R & B artists, with such best sellers as "Shake, Rattle and Roll" and "Flip, Flop and Fly." "The only change is really technical," Rosenbaum says. "Now they hit you with the beat and the drums up front. It's like chopping wood."

The teen-agers are very definite about what they want, Rosenbaum says. Count Basie's recent disk "Every Day" was a big hit in the R & B as well as the pop field, but Rosenbaum reports that the kids didn't buy it, only the older people. "And the reason," he maintains, "is that the kids couldn't dance to it. I played it in the store for a group of them one afternoon and they said, 'No, it hasn't a beat.' The Basie 4/4 beat doesn't fit their style of dancing. I find this almost incredible, but it's true. They dance more easily to the groups which have a background that shuffles more than it swings. The kids are experts. They have a grapevine which spreads the news, and everybody's got a phonograph. You have to give the youngsters in each generation something new, some fad. Now it's the way they dance and dress. Each generation requires a new dance—the Susie Q, the Lindy, what have you. But before you know it, they're growing up and then their taste changes and they collect music."

This underlines the experience of Maury Wolohan, Bay Area bandleader who plays dozens of high school and junior college proms each year. "When the kids are all dressed up at a formal, we seldom get a request for a rhythm tune," he says. "Mostly they want smooth, romantic-type music."

The current branching out of R & B into the field of popular music and its acceptance by teen-agers of all classes has brought forth several other developments. A number of singers, usually thought of as popular ballad singers, have made versions of R & B tunes, almost, and sometimes completely, copies of the R & B original. Georgia Gibbs' "Dance with Me, Henry" was first recorded by Etta James, and her disk of "Mama, He Treats Your Daughter Mean" was originally done by Ruth Brown, both R & B artists. The list is long, and LaVern Baker, whose original performance of "Tweedle Dee" was a pop hit when done by Georgia Gibbs, is trying to have Congress amend the Copyright Act to protect the original artist in such cases.

Although R & B copies have been hits in many instances, they have not sold to the teen-age audience or to the Negro audience. "They can tell it in a minute, and they only want the original," Rosenbaum says. "In fact, the only R & B record by a white artist to sell in the normal R & B areas has been Bill Haley's 'Rock around the Clock,' first popularized by its use in *Blackboard Jungle*." (This has now changed, so that R & B disks sell in normal pop territory, pop vocalists sell in R & B territory and so, sometimes, do such country and western singers as Elvis Presley and Guy Mitchell.)

The reactions to R & B have been quite diverse within the music business. Last March, bandleader Les Elgart predicted the R & B boom wouldn't last, but credited it with "getting the kids started dancing." Bandleader Woody Herman also noted the increase in youngsters dancing and attributed it to R & B.

Duke Ellington came right out and called it "folk music. They say anything worth enjoying is worth singing about . . . if it's bad, sing the blues, if the going is good, clap hands."

Yet despite the popularity of R & B today, there are many who criticize it as strongly as their forefathers criticized jazz. And there are many radio stations that refuse to play R & B. One of the reasons given for this is the allegation that R & B songs have double entendre or frankly obscene lyrics. This was the point made so strongly in *Variety* last year when it began its campaign to clean up "song-leerics." This campaign was joined by

The Contours

The Temptations

The Four Tops

The Drifters

a number of pressure groups, including a religious news service which editorialized from coast to coast against obscene lyrics, with the main emphasis on R & B.

However, in a rebuttal that is hard to answer, songwriter Al Stillman, author of "A Room with a View," "Say Si, Si," "The Breeze and I" and other hits, stated in a letter to *Variety:*

> As far as I can remember, practically all lyrics, except "Barney Google," have been dirty, with the carriage trade practitioners, Porter, Hart, etc., contributing their share. What, unless you are innocent-minded, could be dirtier than "You Took Advantage of Me," "Heat Wave," "All of You," "The Night Is Young and You're so Beautiful" (as open a proposition as I ever heard), "Small Hotel" . . . even as ethereal an ode as Oscar Hammerstein's "All the Things You Are" ("that moment divine, when all the things you are are mine") is a refined "All of You" ("the north and south of you").
>
> Actually, the object of all leericists, outside of Gilbert, has always been to get as close to the Main Subject as possible without stating it and/or "cleaning it up" by marrying 'em in the last line. The current crop of rock and rollers are not beating around the bush, but without condoning 'em, it's at least a less hypocritical approach.

And right in the same vein, singer Connie Boswell, one of the great ballad singers, pointed out in a *Chronicle* interview that she began her career listening to Ethel Waters and Bessie Smith records of what could only be termed questionable material. But, she says, "I wasn't listening to the words, I just liked the way they sang."

And that seems to sum it up. No matter what we may think of rhythm and blues, like jazz and soap operas and television, it's here to stay. It's a real music, as earthy and sentimental and solid as anything else. And whether or not anyone will be harmed by it depends more on the individual than anything else. After all, there are not a few bank presidents and high school principals and doctors and lawyers and ministers who were hysterical over Benny Goodman 20 years ago. And in recognition of that fact, and operating on the good old political principal of "if you can't beat 'em, join 'em," *Billboard* reported this winter that the National Council of Churches of Christ had conducted a survey which revealed that teen-agers wanted R & B, and the producer of the Council's TV program "Look Up and Live" is currently trying to work out a way to give it to them.

—1958

*Popular Composers*

Eubie Blake (left) and Noble Sissle (right)

Shelton Brooks

Langston Hughes

Phil Moore

# Popular Negro Composers

ONE DOOR to fame and fortune which the American Negro has opened by himself, without help from freedom marchers, the FBI or National Guardsmen, is the portal leading into the wonderful world of music. Neither racist nor bigot has been able to resist the "charms to soothe the savage breast" exuding from the Negro's spirituals, blues and jazz, which have made music—not only of America but of all the world—what it is today.

Nowhere is there more substantial evidence of the warm welcome accorded the Negro writers of popular songs, and also of concertos and symphonies, than in the membership of the American Society of Composers, Authors and Publishers. All but a very few American Negro composers and lyricists are enrolled in ASCAP, and the society boasts as proudly and loudly of William C. Handy, Louis Armstrong, James Weldon Johnson, William Grant Still, Shelton Brooks and Fats Waller as it does of Victor Herbert, George Gershwin, Irving Berlin, Cole Porter, Rudolf Friml, Hammerstein and Rodgers, Jerome Kern and Lerner and Loewe.

When ASCAP was founded 50 years ago, its charter members included Dr. James Weldon Johnson and Dr. Harry T. Burleigh, two Negroes who had already achieved doctorates of music and won high recognition in the field of symphonic and concert music. Dr. Johnson had attained such prominence as a musicologist, journalist, poet and educator that President Theodore Roosevelt appointed him to the diplomatic corps as a consul. Dr. Burleigh toured the concert halls of the United States and Europe, and was twice honored with summonses to command performances for King Edward VII. He is best remembered as the composer of "Deep River," perhaps the greatest spiritual of all time.

When emancipation came, the Negro, starved for education and culture, was not content with becoming a banjo-plunker or piano-pounder, but reached out for perfection in the highest types of music. Within two decades after the guns of the Civil War were silenced, Negroes were enrolled in conservatories, studying the great masters and displaying a talent for composing and arranging symphonies and concertos. At the same time, these same talented men were composing songs in the popular idiom, some of which became tremendous hits. The eminent Dr. James Weldon Johnson joined his younger brother, J. Rosamond Johnson, in writing "Under the Bamboo Tree," a popular hit 60 years ago and often heard on radio and TV today. James P. Johnson, composer of *Symphonie Harlem* and *African Drums*, laid aside his sonatas, operettas and ballets to write the sensational "Charleston," which set off the dancing craze in the Roaring Twenties. His "Old-Fashioned Love" was almost as big a hit at the same time.

Other Negro composers, such as William

Grant Still, confined their efforts to the classical arena. Dr. Still, winner of several fellowships and holder of many honorary degrees, dipped into the realm of popular music to arrange and conduct for radio and television, but remained steadfast to his loftier ambitions. He was the first Negro in the United States to conduct a major symphony orchestra when he held the baton in a concert given in the Hollywood Bowl by the Los Angeles Philharmonic. Among the works of this prolific composer are four symphonies, three ballets, several symphonic poems and a wealth of chamber music and concert songs.

\* \* \* \* \* \*

But the Negro's most forceful impact has been on the music of the masses. . . . It was the slave, singing his sorrows in the cotton fields, who eventually flavored American music with new, refreshing ingredients. Stephen Foster captured the essence of the music born on the plantations and gave it to the North's minstrels, and the white man's children learned to sing "Old Folks at Home," "Massa's in de Cold, Cold Ground" and "My Old Kentucky Home" from song books in their schoolrooms.

It is interesting to speculate how one of the early slaves may have cajoled his master into letting him have a broken-down old banjo on which he learned to strum chords and improvise melodies; or how he managed to obtain a pair of shoes in which he imitated the white man's clog dance and evolved from it the graceful soft-shoe shuffle and tap dance which culminated in the artistry of Bill Robinson. And one can picture the first colored porter mopping the floor in an empty saloon in the early dawn, surreptitiously fingering the keys of a battered piano, excitedly discovering the chords and eventually learning to play with a new syncopated beat called ragtime— with which Irving Berlin started on the road to success.

Certain it is that the Negro had to get his musical education the hard way, as did the immortal Bill Handy. Handy was born in 1873 in a shacktown called Florence, Alabama. His father was a clergyman, and so was his grandfather, in slave days. He got his early schooling at home and became a schoolteacher. To eke out a livelihood, he worked in the iron mines. Music was his love, and a beat-up cornet became his instrument. Not content with playing it by ear, he somehow managed to learn to read music. He played with a small group of colored musicians at the Chicago World's Fair in 1893, and his cornet solo brought him a job and featured billing with Mahara's Minstrels. Handy became an expert orchestral arranger, and he was always glad to share what he learned with the growing number of colored musicians hungering for musical education. He worked arduously for their welfare and progress in the formation of the National Association of Negro Musicians and of the National Association of American Composers and Conductors.

But to compose was Bill Handy's greatest ambition, and he began early in his career to write instrumentals and songs with an individuality that quickly won him the admiration of fellow-musicians and the plaudits of the public. "Beale Street Blues," "Memphis Blues," "Harlem Blues" and, above all, "St. Louis Blues," brought him the well-merited title of Father of the Blues. He gave the laments of his persecuted brethren a format and interpretation which lifted them to the heights of musical composition. The sound of "St. Louis Blues" has been heard in symphony concerts in Carnegie Hall and in other classical centers all over the world.

Blind in the last years of his life, Bill devoted himself to the W. C. Handy Fund for the colored blind. At his death there was mourning all over the nation, particularly in cities where he had lived at one time or another. In Memphis, a school honors him and a public square was dedicated to his memory.

With the spread of the music hall and the advent of the vaudeville theatre in the Spanish-American War era, the Negro achieved a new status as an entertainer. White minstrels in blackface had been portraying him, sometimes not too flatteringly, on the stage. The Negro undertook to give the public the real article instead of an imitation. Outstanding was the unforgettable Bert Williams, of the team of Williams and Walker, who became a highly popular attraction in vaudeville and then starred in their own all-Negro musical revues which triumphantly toured the United States and Great Britain. In London, one of these revues, *In Dahomey,* was chosen to give a command performance for King Edward VII.

When the dapper Walker was incapacitated, Bert Williams went on as a single act and became one of the highest-salaried performers in vaudeville. He later starred in the famed *Ziegfeld Follies* for many years. Williams wrote many of the comedy songs he sang with unrivaled success. Substantially wealthy at his death, this dignified musician-singer left a fine library of literature, history and philosophy in his home in Harlem.

Other Negroes, following in the footsteps of Williams and Walker in vaudeville, needed songs, and they got them from writers of their own racial origin. One of the earliest of these was Will Marion Cook, a contemporary of Bill Handy. Cook, educated in Oberlin College, began as a student of serious music and became a master of the violin. He studied in Europe under Joachim and, later, in this country under Anton Dvořák. His first composing was for an all-Negro show titled *Clorindy,* which had a successful run in the New York Casino in 1898. He then wrote the scores for Williams and Walker, including the music for *In Dahomey.* Two of his many songs were the big popular hits of that era,

"Bon Bon Buddy" and "Lovey Joe." His son, W. Mercer Cook, holder of several university degrees and winner of a number of fellowships, became professor of Romance languages in Howard University. He has written many books on the history of the Negro and was decorated by the Haitian government. Reflecting the musical gifts he inherited from his father—and from his mother, Abbie Mitchell, the concert singer—he has written many popular songs, notably "Stop the Sun, Stop the Moon" and "Is I in Love? I Is." Like his father, he became a member of ASCAP.

Another prominent figure who took many a bow when the spotlight was turned on the Negro composer and entertainer in the early 1900's was the versatile J. Rosamond Johnson, who forsook his early career in classical music for vaudeville and the popular musical stage. He wrote songs for, and acted in, successful Negro revues which produced some of the most memorable hits of that era. In the later years of his remarkable career, which brought him equal popularity in England, he played in *Porgy and Bess, Mamba's Daughters* and *Cabin in the Sky.* Old-timers recall nostalgically his performance in the Cole and Johnson revue in which he introduced his "Under the Bamboo Tree," "My Castle on the Nile" and "Congo Love Song."

But it was in the Roaring Twenties—the Jazz Age, with its speakeasies, bathtub gin and Scott Fitzgerald—that the Negro songwriter and musician took over and really rocked the popular music world. "St. Louis Blues" and "Charleston" became twin national anthems. Jazz, born in St. Louis, zoomed to Gargantuan stature, and with giant steps, via Chicago, stormed into Harlem and nearby Broadway. White songwriters, musicians and singers rushed uptown to listen and learn. In the Cotton Club, Connie's Inn, the Savoy and other hot spots they heard Cab Calloway singing his "Minnie the Moocher" and "Zaz Zuh

Zaz," and Duke Ellington playing "Solitude," "Mood Indigo," "Sophisticated Lady" and other melodiously rich songs which stamped him as one of America's top-notch popular composers, while Count Basie drove the dancers into a frenzy with his "One O'Clock Jump." In the band of Fletcher Henderson, another composer, the boys from Broadway got their first earful of Louis "Satchmo" Armstrong's cornet. And they heard Mamie Smith, Trixie Smith, Bessie Smith, Billie Holiday and Ethel Waters singing with a new rhythm in a new style far different from what they were accustomed to.

The white writers listened intently and went back to Tin Pan Alley to imitate, which some did quite successfully. The publishers hurried to sign contracts and give advances to colored composers. One of these was Maceo Pinkard, who prospered on the royalties from "Sweet Georgia Brown," "Them Thar Eyes," "Gimme a Little Kiss, Will Ya—Huh?" and numerous other hits. Another was Thomas "Fats" Waller, who started as a boy organist in the church of which his father was pastor. He played the piano in small night clubs, the organ in small and palatial motion-picture houses, made records and piano rolls, played vaudeville in England, Scotland, Norway, Sweden and Denmark, and appeared in Hollywood movies. He finally teamed up with Andy Razaf, and together they wrote Satchmo Armstrong's "Honeysuckle Rose," "Ain't Misbehavin'" and "Keeping Out of Mischief."

Andy Razaf's real name is Andreamenentania Paul Razafinkeriefo. He was born a grand duke; Queen Ranavalone III of Madagascar was his aunt. He started out to be a poet and author, but turned to songwriting with great success. He wrote the lyrics for *Blackbirds of 1930,* which had a long run on Broadway, and several other colored musical shows. His list of hits, one of the most impressive in the ASCAP catalogue, includes "Sposin'," "Stompin' at the Savoy," "Make Believe Ballroom," "My Fate Is in Your Hands," "Knock Me a Kiss" and "12th Street Rag."

In Chicago, where 12th Street was as fertile musically as Lenox Avenue, music publisher Will Rossiter had already made a fortune on two songs he acquired from a colored youth named Shelton Brooks, who wrote both words and music. The first was "Some of These Days," the other, "Darktown Strutters' Ball." Another publisher garnered his "Walkin' the Dog."

Among the young white composers who frequented the hot spots of Harlem were the already famous George Gershwin and a novice named Harold Arlen, and there can be no doubt that their visits had considerable influence on their subsequent compositions. It was soon thereafter that Gershwin wrote his classic *Rhapsody in Blue.* Arlen grabbed an opportunity to write the music for a Cotton Club revue, and out of it came "Stormy Weather," "I Love a Parade" and "I've Got the World on a String." Most of his music has been characterized as a blending of the Negro's music with Arlen's Hebrew musical heritage. It may well be so. Israel is not far from Africa.

Jimmy McHugh, another of ASCAP's top composers, does not hesitate to acknowledge his debt to Harlem for the rhythmic inspiration of "I Can't Give You Anything but Love, Baby," "Diga Diga Doo," "On the Sunny Side of the Street," "I'm in the Mood for Love" and others of his numerous standard hits.

Only a voluminous book could record the Negro's accomplishments in music in the century since his emancipation, but no treatise on the subject could be complete without mention of Langston Hughes. Hughes, a distinguished poet, author and playwright, whose poems "Freedom Road" and "Songs to the Dark Virgin" have been set to concert music,

Duke Ellington

Thomas "Fats" Waller

Cab Calloway

wrote the lyrics for the musical version of *Street Scene* and the libretti of the operas *Troubled Island* and *The Barrier*.

And more than passing mention must be made of Eubie Blake and Noble Sissle, who, if they had written nothing else, would rate a large laurel for "I'm Just Wild about Harry." They wrote many more songs, particularly for the musical revues titled *Shuffle Along* and *Blackbirds*.

One of the most popular younger writers is Jamaica-born Walter Bishop, who is a director of the American Guild of Authors and Composers (AGAC) and active in its administration. He got his first musical training in a Federal music project, then entered New York University. After serving in the Army in World War II, he began his career as a songwriter and clicked with "The Devil Sat Down and Cried." Others that followed are "It's a Military Secret," "Swing, Brother, Swing" and "Bop Goes My Heart."

Never, since the advent of ragtime, jazz and the blues, has the impact of the Negro composer's melody and rhythm on the current popular musical scene been as obvious and as potent as it is today. The beat of Elvis Presley's rock and roll was born, as he was, down South. Out of it came the rhythmic tidal wave of the Beatles and their imitators, which has swept into every corner of the globe.

Anyone who remembers the Harlem of the Roaring Twenties will recognize in the frug and its kindred dances so popular with today's teen-agers—and the socially elite Jet Set—the head-shaking and hip-swinging of the fiery chorus girls who introduced them in the Cotton Club revues. Likewise, the singing style of the present-day recording stars, white as well as colored, bears an unmistakable resemblance to the spiritual vocal nuances which Ethel Waters, Ella Fitzgerald, Sarah Vaughan, Nat Cole and Harry Belafonte injected into their renditions of popular ballads.

It takes no musicologist to appreciate the debt owed the Negro composers by their colleagues, not only in the United States but all over the world.

—1967

# SECTION X

MUSIC

## *Famous Singers*

Paul Robeson

Bessie Smith. Below she is seen in the movie
*St. Louis Blues* (1929).

# Bessie Smith

**by George Hoefer**

BIG BILL Broonzy began one of his blues: "Oh, I feel like hollering but the town is too small."

Bessie Smith often felt the same way, but she hollered anyway. For Bessie, not only were the towns too small for the deep and free living she knew could be; but even her big body was too small for all the living and enjoying and drinking and hating and eating and loving that she wanted, needed to jam into one small lifetime.

Bessie sang the blues to make a living; but she also sang the blues to communicate who she was, who she wanted to be, and why. And basically, she told the blues as a Negro who grew up in the South with Jim Crow, who moved through the North but couldn't shake Jim Crow and who, as some stories have it, may have died because Jim Crow ran a hospital that didn't take in colored, even when they were bleeding to death.

Her blues could be funny and boisterous and gentle and angry and bleak, but underneath all of them ran the raw bitterness of being a human being who had to think twice about which toilet she could use. You can't hear Bessie without hearing why Martin Luther King doesn't want to wait any more.

Bessie was born in blunt poverty in Chattanooga, Tennessee, around 1900. She grew up with no money and not much more hope. She bumped into an unlikely fairy godmother, however, when Ma Rainey's Rabbit Foot Minstrels came through town. Ma, perhaps the first of the classic blues singers (although she may never have heard *that* said about herself), liked the way Bessie hollered and took the girl on the road with her.

Bessie sang her hungry blues through years of tent shows and carnivals that barnstormed all through the Southern states, as well as in the honky-tonks, gin mills, and small theatres of the larger ghettos, like those in Atlanta, Savannah, Birmingham and Memphis.

Frank Walker, recording director for Columbia Records, heard Bessie, and he sent New Orleans pianist-composer Clarence Williams to find her. Walker had a feeling that Bessie could reach a lot of record buyers with the truth of their own lives. He was right.

Bessie Smith made her first session on February 17, 1923. Her stomping record sales made her a "star," and she began to work regularly with her own show in New York, Chicago, Boston and Philadelphia, as well as in the large Southern cities. It must be remembered that during her period of wide acceptance, between 1923 and 1930, she played almost always to Negroes. What she had to say was as naked and yet untranslatable as a Jewish cantor piercing his congregation with "Kol Nidrei."

Bessie's legacy consists of 160 recorded sides and a two-reel motion-picture short. Some of the records, especially those made after 1928, are quite rare, although they do exist in isolated hot-jazz record collections. This rarity is accounted for by the fact that her later recordings did not sell well. Around 1926–27, she had begun to change her repertoire and, in a way, she tried to sing her songs differently, sensing that tastes were changing. But it was hard for Bessie to change with them.

But before going into the twilight of Bessie's blues, there is much to be said about what happened before. She had three sisters—Viola, Tinnie and Lulu—and a brother, Clarence. After Bessie began to earn money, they all moved North and made their home in Philadelphia. Bessie had beaten being poor for a time, but she had picked up other demons that kept riding with her.

The years of barnstorming made Bessie tough, ribald and able to fight for herself. From all indications, she seems, in her early years, to have been an extrovert, tending to accept things as they were. This was to change radically during her years of success. According to George Avakian, she became two diametrically opposed personalities. Her drinking, an emotional release, became progressively more compulsive through the years. She was basically an embittered woman, who not only didn't know all the answers but found many of the questions unfamiliar. At the same time, Bessie was gentle, sentimental, and full of sympathy for the downtrodden among her people. When she had money, she was inclined to squander it, or let her favorite man throw it away. She is said once to have bought a rooming house in New York so that a group of her friends could live together under one roof.

Bessie was married to a policeman named Jack Gee on April 5, 1922, in Philadelphia. He left the force and became her manager. His managerial abilities were such that the two of them are said to have gone through $16,000 in six months' time. Some of Bessie's early blues compositions were registered in her husband's name. The couple separated in 1930, but continued friendly and close relations until the time of her death.

A poignant insight into the kind of woman Bessie wanted to be is revealed by an episode that occurred at the height of her success in 1926. Bessie, who thought her days of cleaning up after whites were long past, volunteered to be a maid. During a busy and professionally triumphant period, she cancelled her bookings. Frank Walker's child had suddenly become ill, and Bessie came to this man to whom she was grateful and offered to care for his child. Despite protests, she insisted on helping with even the most menial tasks and did not return to her tour until the child was well.

At other times, Bessie could be brutal and violent. Her addiction to gin took hold during her teens, and, as she grew older, it kept pace with her added responsibilities, troubles and frustrations. Bessie, who as a child had been dominated by people and situations, acquired an insatiable desire to dominate people and situations. When thwarted, she was inclined to start drinking and was soon ready to take on the world. There were times when her recording dates and public appearances had to be cancelled because she was on a rampage. It was also during these bad periods that she made an exhibition of spending money.

Bessie Smith was always a very attractive woman. Pictures taken when she first came North reveal her as fairly slender and rather tall. In one famous early photograph, her sad eyes are open to love, and there is sensitivity in the way her hands rest. In another early picture, she is doing the Charleston and wearing her hair in bangs.

By the time Bessie became a headliner and the star of her own show, she had attained considerable stage presence. She always came on in the headline spot next to the closing act, a well-groomed, formidable personality. Her black hair was combed close to the top of her head, and her large earrings sparkled in the spotlight. If she played a week in a theatre, she would usually save a particular white evening dress for the last show. According to drummer Zutty Singleton, who played in the pit orchestra for her whenever she appeared at the Lyric Theatre in New Orleans, the audience was always awed when the colored spotlights shone on this white dress and the regal headdress that she wore with it. When Carl Van Vechten heard Bessie for the first time in Newark, on Thanksgiving night, 1925, she was wearing a crimson satin robe embroidered with multicolored sequins. He recalls her round, beautiful face, a deep, bronze-like shade of brown which matched her bare brown arms.

In her performance, Bessie would walk slowly to the footlights, accompanied by the pounding of the drum, augmented sometimes by muted brasses. It is interesting to note that Bessie had a strong antipathy to percussion and on her records used drums only once or twice. On stage, she would sometimes remain in the spotlight singing a repertoire of her most popular tunes as she had recorded them, swaying slightly to the beat. Art Hodes, the jazz pianist, says that when he heard her in Chicago, she walked slowly around the stage, with her head somewhat bowed. Either way, her blues numbers were greeted with "amens" from the audience, whose attention she commanded completely, and after her final encore the applause and shouting were deafening. Her people called her the Queen of the Blues. It was the Columbia Record Company that labeled her the Empress of the Blues when she signed an exclusive contract with them in 1923, to distinguish her from other "comediennes" on their roster.

Bessie had a rich, full-toned contralto voice. It was as powerful as any voice that has ever been heard in jazz. When the microphone made its appearance on the stages of the country, Bessie pushed it away in dis-

dain. The late Oran "Hot Lips" Page, who accompanied her on the trumpet once, was greatly impressed by her powerful delivery. "Man," he said, "she could sing over and drown out the loudest swing band going."

Pictures of Bessie during her good days, 1923 through 1926, show her with a laughing face. She had a strong, earthy sense of humor. Milton Mezzrow has described his first meeting with Bessie at the old Paradise Gardens in Chicago. She came to his table and he asked her to sing "Cemetery Blues." Bessie ruffled Mezz's curly hair and said, "Son, what you studying cemeteries for? You ought to be out in the park with some cute little chick."

Shots of Bessie taken during the late Twenties and early Thirties show the ravages of hard living and an insatiable thirst for tall glasses of gin. She was still beautiful, but had aged considerably, and much of the luster in her eyes and expression was gone. She had become increasingly moody in those years, and it was plainly to be seen in her face.

Sometime in 1929, Porter Grainger, one of her piano accompanists, took her to Carl Van Vechten's studio in midtown Manhattan. It was then towards the end of the so-called Negro Renaissance, a time when Negro performers were welcomed to intellectual parties and fawned over by Park Avenue.

Other guests on this occasion were the late composer George Gershwin, actress Constance Collier and opera singer Marguerite d'Alvarez. Bessie entered the room and immediately demanded a drink—not a cocktail, but a full tumbler of straight gin—which she downed in one lusty gulp. She then got down to business. With a lighted cigarette drooping from a corner of her mouth, she gave them the blues with Porter at the piano. Van Vechten has stated, "This was no actress, no imitator of woman's woes; there was no pretense. It was the real thing: a woman cutting her heart open with a knife until it was exposed for all to see. . . ."

It would be interesting to know what Bessie thought of the reaction to her performance. Would it have been a "my best friends are my enemies" sort of feeling? After all, Bessie had a need to *belong* as well as to be the main attraction. But if she couldn't belong, she could at least try to boss as many as she could of those who did. As far back as 1920, Bessie had attained enough stature as a leading blues singer to be able to dictate theatre policy to managers. She insisted that no other act or acts on the bill with her were to perform blues songs. This didn't always work.

Once Ethel Waters was on the same bill with Bessie at the 91 Theatre on Decatur Street, in Atlanta. Ethel was advised to stay away from singing the blues. Before she had finished her first number, the audience was clamoring for her blues. The manager went to Bessie and said he would have to go back on his agreement and permit Ethel to give the crowd what they wanted. Miss Waters recalls overhearing a stormy battle in Bessie's dressing room, with Bessie yelling things about "these Northern bitches," who came down into her territory.

Some years later, after Bessie had won acclaim through the phenomenal sales of records to her own people, she was on a road tour with her show called the *Harlem Frolics*. For one week in the summer of 1927, they were playing in the Grand Theatre, a leading Negro house on the South Side of Chicago. That same week Ethel Waters was appearing before a white audience at the Palace Theatre in Chicago's Loop and taking the town by storm. This sort of double-edged irony was to occur many times and undoubtedly made Bessie's inner life darker.

It is probably true that Bessie was shunned by the more urbane and sophisticated Negroes. There is evidence that even Negro show people were reluctant to welcome her into their homes. For instance, Mrs. James P. Johnson, wife of the late pianist, who was one of Bessie's favorite musicians, has been quoted as saying, "Bessie would come over to the house but, mind you, she wasn't my friend. She was very rough."

In accounts of activities and gatherings of Negro show people during the Twenties and early Thirties, Bessie Smith's name is conspicuous by its absence. For example, Ethel Waters is listed as an honorary pallbearer at Florence Mills's funeral, and everyone else with a name in show business seemed to be there to pay tribute to the beloved entertainer. But not Bessie.

No artist is without detractors, and the great blues singer has had many. When Bessie's blues touched a listener, he usually became a convert. On the other hand, there were, and are, many who do not appreciate her work. She was an artist whose work was either loved or hated with a vengeance.

Jazz is a highly individual art for both the performer and the listener. Bessie sang her life story, just as others have written autobiography. A good many listeners, even jazz fans, are prone to allow an allegedly archaic style, or non-hi-fi archives, to cause them to close their ears to a message so throbbingly alive that it should become dated only when automation has replaced us all.

There is available today a fairly complete collection of Bessie Smith recordings. These sides embrace her career from the 1924 "Weeping Willow Blues" to the four sides she made on her last date, in 1933.

Bessie signed an exclusive contract with the old Columbia company, for Walker, in 1923. Her recording activity with Columbia came to an end in November, 1931, when the record market became almost nonexistent. John Hammond produced a Bessie Smith record in November, 1933, expressly for England. These sides were issued in this country on the Okeh label. Before joining Columbia, she had been asked to make sides for the old Black Swan Record Company, owned by Harry Pace. The story goes that she was fired in the middle of her first side because she said, "Hold on a minute while I spit." Ironically, Bessie went on, a few months later, to pull the Columbia company out of receivership, while Black Swan went bankrupt.

\*   \*   \*   \*   \*   \*

At first, Bessie sang the songs assigned to her. Clarence Williams handled the selection of tunes and musicians for Walker. This situation did not last long, however, and Walker chose Fletcher Henderson as her recording supervisor. After this, most of her accompanying musicians were men from Fletcher's band. Once she was furious with Fletcher for sending her a young cornetist from Chicago in place of another Henderson hornman, Joe Smith. In spite of Bessie's skepticism, the Louis Armstrong accompaniments resulted in several of her greatest records.

As she grew older and more experienced, Bessie began to assume complete control of her recording activities. She also began to write her own tunes and lyrics, and these became some of her more memorable recordings.

Sometimes, on her road tours, her stage setup resembled an old-fashioned recording studio, with an old-time horn featured. She would explain to her audience how she made her records and then sing the tunes she had recorded. Whatever she sang turned into blues. She could take the popular tunes of the day and transform them. For example, hear her "Aggravatin' Papa" and "Baby, Won't You Please Come Home?"

The blues can be broken down into categories. Among them are: happy blues songs and satirical blues; blues based on catastrophes of nature; poverty and work songs; blues for a city, street, or some other locale, like the jailhouse or cemetery; drinking blues; and sex blues built around a complete man-woman relationship. There are Bessie Smith records illustrative of each of these types.

Bessie's happy blues renditions include such numbers as "Jazzbo Brown from Memphis Town," "At the Christmas Ball," "Cakewalking Babies," "There'll Be a Hot Time in the Old Town Tonight" and "Alexander's Ragtime Band."

With the exception of "Jazzbo," all of these tunes were recorded by Bessie in an attempt to attract a wider audience. She may have been making a play for some of the popularity that Ethel Waters was enjoying. Both "Cakewalking Babies" and "At the Christmas Ball" were rejected by Columbia when they were made in 1927 as being too far from the style of the commercial Smith records, and it was not until the middle Forties that they were finally released. Bessie's excuse for making them was that her people were tired of the "depressed" type of blues.

In 1930, there was another radical departure. With James P. Johnson on the piano, and a male quartet called the Bessemer Singers, she assailed the field of the spirituals. Bessie's lusty shouting wasn't enough to make successful records of "On Revival Day" and "Moan, You Mourners." The quartet drowned out James P.'s piano, and the sides were unsuccessful both musically and commercially.

One of Bessie's finest records is "Backwater Blues," on which she was accompanied by James P. Johnson's fine solo piano. Bessie once witnessed the Mississippi flooding the Louisiana backlands, and in this song her original words are movingly poetic. It is a simple twelve-bar blues with overtones of social protest. She sings a complaint addressed to God against the five days and nights of rain that forced the people from their homes. James P.'s accompaniment is beautiful in its spare and lyrically poignant power.

Poverty has always been a familiar subject in the literature of the blues. Again, one of Bessie's classics can be cited as an example

—her May, 1929, waxing of "Nobody Knows You When You're Down and Out." It is significant that this record was made when Bessie was already on the decline. Her road tours no longer brought her $2,000 a week, and her records were not selling. The Depression was yet to come, but Bessie had little left of her fabulous earnings. And Bessie's mood was sadly prophetic when she put all the pathos, bitterness and protest she could muster into her performance of that song.

Of the many blues songs about places, some are just praise for a locale, others have to do with traveling back somewhere to see a woman, and some are songs of identification. Many people consider Bessie Smith's version of "St. Louis Blues," with Louis Armstrong's cornet and Fred Longshaw's harmonium, the finest rendition of the classic song in existence.

Bessie recorded two sides on which she discusses her favorite beverage. They are autobiographical in content and are entitled "Gin House Blues" and "Me and My Gin."

A considerable part of Bessie Smith's output had to do with men and women in love, and the universal interest in the subject accounts for her great success with such recordings. She was the master storyteller of love tales for her own people. They understood all the symbolism, the frustration and the seesaw of joy and sorrow. When Bessie sang of love, there was no expurgation. She was able, in some non-mailable cases, to convey meanings through voice inflections, without using the exact words.

Bessie preferred to sing her blues in slow tempo; she left the fast-stepping dance tunes to others.

At the peak of her career, in 1926, she made several sides that can be classified as formal city blues and that are jazz landmarks. Included are "Young Woman's Blues," "One and Two Blues," "Baby Doll" and "Lost Your Head Blues." On all of these sides,

there are beautifully organized accompaniments by Joe Smith's mellow cornet. Smith's unique use of the mute was pure artistry. He plays intense, precisely conceived notes in answer to Bessie's phrases on "Lost Your Head," while on "Baby Doll" he is in another mood, projecting light, floating tones with an open horn. Very rarely in jazz have there been two artists whose work blended as beautifully as did Joe's and Bessie's. Bessie also had perfect rapport with trombonist Charlie Green.

These three artists—Bessie, Joe and "Big" Green—all died at about the same time. Bessie ended in an automobile accident under horrifying circumstances, Charlie Green was found frozen to death on a Harlem doorstep, and "Little" Joe succumbed to tuberculosis in a mental institution.

One surviving record of Bessie is the film drama *St. Louis Blues*. It was made in 1929, but was immediately banned because it was considered too uninhibited. Ten years ago it was found in Mexico and is now shown from time to time at the Museum of Modern Art in New York. It is still not available for public exhibition because of frankness and realism. The two-reel short was made from a scenario by W. C. Handy, in collaboration with Kenneth W. Adams, and was directed by Dudley Murphy.

Bessie plays the role of a cast-off woman, and the most impressive aspect of the film is the beauty of her movements and the sensitivity of her facial expressions. She apparently had considerable talent as a dramatic actress.

Musically, the film is limited because of the inadequacies of early sound techniques. A primitive crystal microphone was used, and the sound track is muddy. Even so, the great blues singer's magnificent and powerful voice is very much there.

After 1929, Bessie's star plunged straight down. Even without the impact of the Depression, the record industry was temporarily

doomed by radio. Where Bessie had been accustomed to receiving a $1,000 advance against a five per cent royalty for her recordings, she had to settle for $50 a side in 1933. Bessie had to give rent parties in Harlem in order to pay for her keep. She tells about these gatherings very effectively in "Gimme a Pigfoot," made on her last record date, in 1933.

Unfortunately, it was sometimes necessary for her to resort to pornographic songs, and even a "mammy" get-up, in order to get jobs. In 1930, she lasted only two nights in a Negro musical at the Belmont Theatre in New York. She was unable to compromise her art for Broadway audiences, and engagements at Manhattan's Kit Kat Club and Connie's Inn were also "flops." She finally went back on the road with a show similar to the ones with which she had started barnstorming the South 25 years before.

Yet, strangely, some jazz researchers found a newspaper interview with Bessie Smith in 1936, in which she is quoted as being very optimistic about the future and feeling that she was on the brink of new successes. The interview gave her birth date as April 15, 1898, which would have made her only 39 when she died in 1937. Most reports gave her age at death as being between 45 and 50. She may, when she died, have appeared older than she was, or she may have wanted the story to make her as young as possible.

She may have been utilizing press agentry when she stated that she had won the Tennessee roller-skating championship with a pair of skates bought with her first week's salary on her first job at the age of eight, on the stage of the Ivory Theatre in Chattanooga. While professing her love for diamonds, fur coats and sporting events on the one hand, she said that her ambition was to retire in 1960 to a farm in the country where she could settle down with her pets.

These years, 1936 and 1937, were the ear-

ly days of the acceptance of jazz by the white public, and this may have given Bessie hope. In February, 1936, she sang her blues at a jazz concert held at the Famous Door on 52nd Street. Eddie Condon has written that her performance was wonderful, and has added that Mildred Bailey was also there but refused to sing after Bessie.

September, 1937, found Bessie traveling with Winsted's *Broadway Rastus* show through her home state. They had been to sites where Bessie could recall former triumphs—like Nashville, where, in August, 1923, the papers reported, "Bessie Smith . . . knocked all the tin off of the theatre roof. People cried for more and refused to leave the theatre." And then there was Beale Avenue in Memphis, where, in February, 1924, she had given a special performance for whites at 11 P.M. on the stage of the Beale Avenue Palace.

Early on Sunday morning, September 26, 1937, Bessie was riding in a car bound for Memphis. Near Coahoma, Mississippi, the car piled into a panel truck parked on the side of the road, and overturned. Bessie sustained an arm injury. It was reported that her arm was almost severed from her body. She also suffered bruises about her face and head, and internal injuries.

There were many conflicting stories of what happened after the accident. Some of these have undoubtedly been exaggerated because of the racial issues involved. Piecing together the various reports, however, the following appears to be reasonable.

The accident took place on the outskirts of Coahoma, a town too small to have a hospital. The closest town of any size was Clarksdale, Mississippi, a few miles away. A prominent Memphis surgeon came upon the accident a few minutes after the crash. An ambulance had already been ordered, but the doctor could see that Bessie was in danger of bleeding to death. He was attempting to put her into the back of his car (she weighed about 200 pounds at the time), when another car rammed into the back of his car, wrecking it completely. Five minutes later, the ambulance arrived and rushed Bessie to the Negro ward of the G. T. Thomas Hospital in Clarksdale, where one of the town's best surgeons amputated her arm. She died fifteen minutes past noon that same day. The doctors reported that her death was probably due more to her internal injuries than to the loss of blood.

Bessie's brother, Clarence Smith, of Philadelphia, had her body sent to Philadelphia for burial in Mount Lawn Cemetery.

Bessie Smith set a pattern for many blues singers among both her contemporaries and those who followed her. She was outstanding in her own time, the day of the direct, driving blues shouters. There were five other blues-singing Smiths—Clara, Trixie, Mamie, Laura and Hazel—and not one was related to the other.

The Bessie Smith influence on the jazz that followed has been deep. Louis Armstrong recorded with her early in his career and has been quoted as saying, "She used to thrill me at all times, the way she could phrase a note with a certain something in her voice no other blues singer could get. She had music in her soul and felt everything she did. Her sincerity with her music was an inspiration."

Bix Beiderbecke used to throw money at her feet at the Paradise Gardens in Chicago every time she hit a note or phrase that pleased him. Eddie Condon has said that the Chicagoans were raised on her records.

Billie Holiday used to run errands for the girls in a Baltimore bagnio just for the privilege of coming into the parlor to listen to Bessie Smith's records.

The outstanding gospel singer of our day, Mahalia Jackson, whose vocal style is very reminiscent of Bessie's, tells how, as a child, she had to sneak away from her religious household to go to a New Orleans theatre to hear Bessie, whenever the great blues singer came to town.

As recently as 1954, an English blues singer named Beryl Bryden showed up in Paris singing the words and using the intonations of Bessie Smith—with a British accent!

When you hear Jack Teagarden or Joe Sullivan improvise, you are very likely to hear a phrase or an idea that originated with Bessie Smith. Her phrases and ideas, and the life-filling sound of her, will be remembered as long as there are reasons for the blues.

—1957

Billie Holiday at the peak of her career. Below, she is seen in the 1935 movie *Symphony in Black*.

# Billie Holiday

## by Charles Edward Smith

THERE WAS nothing about living on the sidewalks that I didn't know," Billie Holiday told a writer for *Tan* [February, 1953]. "I knew how the gin joints looked on the inside; I had been singing in after-hours joints —damp, smoky cellars, in the backs of barrooms.

"It was slow, this attempt to climb clear of the barrel. But as I grew older, I found those trying to keep me in it were not always the corner hoodlum, the streetwalker, the laborer, the numbers runner, the rooming-house ladies and landlords, the people who existed off the $25- and $30-a-week salaries they were paying in those days.

"They, I found, were the ones who wanted to see me 'go,' to get somewhere. It was their applause and help that kept me inspired. These 'little people,' condemned as I have been ever since I can remember, gave me my chance long before the mink-coated lorgnette crowd of Fifth Avenue and Greenwich Village ever heard of me."

Which could be said of most outstanding hot musicians. No one begins at the top; few even reach it. And if Lady was condemned now and again—and she has been, plenty— it was by essentially smaller minds and smaller people than the "little people" she knew in Harlem during the Prohibition era. But her talent has never been without recognition. Indeed, it was in the small spots of Harlem that people like John Hammond, Paul Muni, Mildred Bailey and others heard her, encouraged her and got others to listen to her voice.

She is an altogether remarkable singer and, like her great predecessor, Bessie Smith, deserves the best. In backgrounds, the two have little in common. Bessie, when she was a kid, sang in a choir in Memphis and left home to become a protégé of Gertrude "Ma" Rainey in Negro minstrels, in the South, the only place where the blues were "big" until Bessie, Louis and others rescued them from an unfair charge of country contamination. Billie ran errands for a madam in East Baltimore, so that she could listen to records on the parlor phonograph by Bessie and Louis. But when she began singing in second-string Harlem hot spots, the material most in demand consisted of pop songs and show tunes, especially Negro show tunes, for few Negroes in those days could afford the charges in the swanky night clubs (such as the Cotton Club, where oftentimes there were more whites than colored at the pink-lit tables).

In joints such as those Billie worked in, there were any number of kids doing miserable imitations of Ethel Waters. She was different. Not that her style was perfect, but it was shaping up, and already the direction was clear. For, whatever she sang, she had a voice born of blues. And if she sang in the cellars, as she says, she probably sang more blues there—her rather sophisticated vocal style still shows the influence of lowdown and "dirty" blues intonation—than she ever did in the lesser night clubs of the Harlem circuit. There was a speakeasy around the corner from Jerry's Log Cabin, for example, where, at the very time Billie sang at the Log Cabin, at this basement bistro (which hardly deserved the name; there was a dirt floor and old boxes for chairs) one could hear harshly sung, moaning blues and "primitive" polyphonal and antiphonal spirituals that, years later, were to give root-nourishment to rock and roll. And this, too, was part of the Harlem scene, but one the visiting public seldom got to know—"down home" blues and spirituals close to the field holler and the chant, gone underground in the urban North. But Billie knew it and, mixed up in her singing, as she went to work on the latest romantic ballad, were the beat and burning fire of the blues.

Essentially, hers has been a jazz, an *instrumental* style of singing for as long as critics have known it. She may have got it mostly from Louis, from his records and from hearing him at theatres, but style comes in bits and pieces so infinitesimal that not even a singer can be aware of every last influence. What is significant is that she has been, and is, an artist in reshaping songs and ballads, and in this, of course, Louis was the first great master.

Billie Holiday (Eleanora Fagan) was born in Baltimore, April 7, 1915, of teen-age parents who married three years later. When she says she was a woman at six, she may have been thinking of other things than physical development. Her father, Clarence Holiday, was a musician (McKinney's Cotton Pickers, guitar; he'd formerly played trumpet), almost always on the road. He and Billie's mother had separated when Billie was little more than a baby, so that she was, in effect, a fatherless child (as were so many during slavery days); the little mother called "Mom" was the rock she clung to. And even her mother left her with relatives, to go up North in search of work. It wasn't merely that Billie had traumatic experiences—life slaps all of us around—but it slapped her viciously, when she was very young and didn't know what it was all about.

Albeit she lacked Job's eloquence, her recital of grievances reminds one of him as he inculpated the powers of darkness with a kind of sulky solemnity. Job, in his way, was salty, and so was Billie, and in each case there seems an obvious merit. For instance, Billie was accused by her arch-tormentor, a cousin named Ida, of having indirectly caused the death of her great-grandmother, one of the few people who gave her love and to whom she gave love in return. Her great-grandmother had been a plantation slave (and Billie is descended from the owner), who used to entertain her with stories of the old days. She couldn't read or write but knew the Bible intimately. When her great-grandmother—who was not supposed to lie down (but rest in a chair) because of illness—asked Billie to let her lie down, she only thought to ease the old woman's pain. She spread a blanket on the floor and, being tired, lay down herself. She woke up hours later, with her great-grandmother's arm around her neck, and the arm was growing stiff and cold with death. She was scared and panicky and couldn't free herself and began to scream. After that she was in a hospital for a month, recovering from shock.

At the age of 10 she was attacked by a man who lived in the neighborhood. The man was sent to prison, and Billie was sent to a Catholic home where, as a punishment for infringement of rules, a refractory girl had to wear a raggedy red dress; once, Billie claims, she was locked in a room where a girl (who'd met with an accident) was lying out dead. In between such harrowing experiences, she lived the "normal" life of a slum kid, snitching stuff from the dime store and sneaking into movies. When her father nicknamed her "Bill" because of her tomboy ways, she changed it to Billie, after Billie Dove, her idol of the silent films.

As she describes her early years in her autobiography, she sounds like a tough little kid, running scared, and makes one realize how meaningless terms like "juvenile delinquent" can be when applied to specific persons. She didn't run in gangs. She was a lone wolf and a lonely little girl who, when barely old enough to be out on the streets, learned to spit and scratch and howl. Years later, at the Grand Terrace in Chicago, she threw a lethal threat and an inkwell at the manager, exploding in blind hostility just as she had as a small child when a boy teased her with a dead rat. On that occasion she had whacked the boy over the head with a stick. On another, in a 52nd Street club, she dunked a maid (who'd called her a dirty name) in a toilet bowl, and a jurist, measuring the provocation, refused to press charges. Now that she is famous, such incidents are categorized as temperament. Yet all of these acts, and more, were less than adult and other than childish, for the child's act was defensive and, in its context, more than reasonable.

Billie came to New York when she was 13, in 1928, the year Louis recorded one of her favorite numbers, "West End Blues." She decided to get off at Pennsylvania Station and visit Harlem before going on to meet her mother at Long Branch. Instead of which she got lost. A social worker for the Society for the Prevention of Cruelty to Children took her in hand and set her up in a beautiful hotel where she had a room and a bed to herself. This was living it up. Years later she looked up the place, out of curiosity, and to her amazement it turned out to be the YWCA.

In her autobiography, Billie tells of her experiences, in and out of jail, as a teen-age prostitute, and describes, at first hand, the seamy sides of seamy streets during the late 1920's, when corruption and gangsterism were rampant in many parts of the city, but nowhere more so than in Harlem, where white gangsters were in control of the more plush night clubs and street-corner loafers could steer you to after-hours joints, prostitutes or marijuana pads—whatever your wayward heart desired. Billie took to smoking reefers (marijuana) when still in her teens. This was not unusual elsewhere—a "Kinsey report" on the subject would shock and surprise only the very sheltered.

Billie didn't expect to be a call girl even temporarily, but apparently looked upon the world of pimps and prostitutes as a way to make a fast buck. Since she was allowed to visit a house of prostitution and run errands for a madam before she was 13, it is logical to suppose that she thought of the girls in the house as making a living (which, in fact, they did), without moral theorizing. To a slum kid the more affluent prostitutes may have seemed like fashion plates. Billie was sent into transports of happiness when "Mom" got a floppy, big, red velvet hat, such as Billie had seen on good-time glamour girls, decorated with birds of paradise feathers. But *she* only ran errands and, anyway, wasn't paid in money. She was paid in being allowed to listen to records by Bessie and Louis on the parlor phonograph.

So the two roads beckoned in a good-time parlor on the corner, and she knew she would take the one that meant singing, even as she walked the streets in Harlem in a silk dress and spike heels. "I know this for damn sure," she says in her book, "if I'd heard Pops and Bessie wailing through the window of some minister's front parlor, I'd have been running errands for him."

In low-class joints, where she worked for a while when young, she refused to pick up bills from tables without using her hands. She wanted to be a singer without tricks, sexual or otherwise. This was consistent. In the sort of hustling she had experienced there was nothing at all glamorous—one wonders if there ever is, except in books—and the whole pattern of life, from stealing white socks in the dime store to accepting a blue mink coat from her man, *paid for out of her own earnings as a singer,* found her trying to live up to the Lady, perhaps with an eye on the one for whom a day of the year, Lady Day, is listed in the Calendar of Saints.

In an interview with Dave Dexter, Jr., she tells of the Depression period when her mother couldn't find work as a housemaid and when she herself tried scrubbing floors and just couldn't make it. "We lived on 145th Street near Seventh Avenue," she explained. "One day we were so hungry we could barely breathe. I started out the door. It was cold as all hell, and I walked from 145th to 133rd down Seventh Avenue, going in every joint trying to find work. Finally, I got so desperate I stopped in at the Log Cabin, run by Jerry Preston. I told him I wanted a drink. I didn't have a dime. But I ordered gin (it was my first drink—I didn't know gin from wine) and gulped it down.

"I asked Preston for a job . . . told him I was a dancer. He said to dance. I tried it. He said I stunk. I told him I could sing. He said: *sing.* Over in the corner was an old guy playing piano. He struck 'Travelin' All Alone' and I sang. . . . The customers stopped drinking. They turned around and watched. The pianist, Dick Wilson, swung into 'Body and Soul.' Jeez, you should have seen those people—all of them started crying. Preston came over, shook his head and said, 'Kid, you win.' That's how I got my start." [*Down Beat,* November 1, 1937.]

The influx from downtown wasn't long in starting. Tipped off by Hammond, Benny Goodman and other musicians dropped in, and Benny used Billie on a record date for Columbia. This was before he'd organized his regular band. Teagarden, Krupa and Joe Sul-

livan were among those on the date that made "Your Mother's Son-in-Law," in November, 1933, and, the following month, made "Riffin' the Scotch." Wrote Dave Dexter of the first Holiday record: "The disk is an item today, not only because of the fine instrumental work, but because it was Holiday's first side. She was pretty lousy. You tell her so and she grins. 'But I was only 15 then,' she says, 'and scared.' " (I'll buy the "scared" but not the age; she had to be 18 or born in wedlock; she can't have it both ways.)

She continued to sing in Harlem night spots and at theatres, but outside the professional world of music and entertainment she was surprisingly little known.

Like most other hot musicians who have since become famous, Billie got very little for her work. Bernie Hanighen fought for her, to get her more money and wider recognition. "A lot of guys were big tippers uptown," she says in the autobiography, "but when it came to fighting for you downtown, they were nowhere. Not Bernie. He was the cause of me making my first records under my own name —not as anybody's damn vocalist, but as Billie Holiday, period—and then the list of musicians backing me. Bernie Hanighen is a great guy."

When she opened at the Apollo, she sang one of his tunes. She had a bad case of stage fright, but by the second tune the house was with her and she was all right. There was an interesting crowd there, as there often was where she sang. They not only knew current song hits but knew the composers of them, and if they liked the composer, that was it; he was in; he was applauded just as loudly as if he'd been there in person. "There's nothing like an audience at the Apollo," says Billie. "They didn't ask me what my style was, who I was, where I'd come from, who influenced me, or anything. They just broke the house up."

Billie said that she'd always wanted Bessie's

big sound and Pop's feeling. What she got, as her style developed, was altogether her own sound, big, brash, subtle, soft-sensitive, a sour-sweet sound, the shape of which she manipulates so that it comes out flat, round, harsh, *pianissimo*—one of the most beautiful vocal sounds in jazz, once you get to know it—and, out of a raw, emotional maelstrom, come feelings which are disciplined in song.

She met Lester Young at a jam session. "I used to love to have him come around and blow pretty solos behind me." She once said that she was first called "Lady" because she wouldn't take customers' money off tables, an old-established (frankly obscene) gin-mill custom. Then Billie, who can use a rough, tough, nasty vocabulary when she wants to, blew a gasket at the loose and dirty talk of some Basie-ites. Whereupon Lester took the "Day" out of Holiday and that made it—Lady Day. She called him "Prez" for "President"; "Mom" was "Duchess"; to complete the list, her boxer was "Mister."

"If you find a tune and it's got something to do with you," she says [autobiography], "you don't have to evolve anything. You feel it, and when you sing it other people can feel something, too. With me, it's got nothing to do with working or arranging or rehearsing. Give me a song I can feel, and it's never work. There are a few songs I feel so much I can't stand to sing them, but that's something else again."

From this statement, it is clear that the lyric is part of the material she has to work with, yet in treatment of it, melodically and rhythmically, she confutes semantics. "I don't think I'm singing," she says [*Hear Me Talkin' to Ya*], "I feel like I am playing a horn. I try to improvise like Les Young, like Louis Armstrong, or anyone else I admire. What comes out is what I feel. I hate straight singing. I have to change a tune to my own way of doing it. That's all I know."

\*    \*    \*    \*    \*    \*

Billie's chapters on road tours with Basie (1937) and Shaw (1938), playing dates that took them overnight from riff-raff joints to class hotels, are as frank and revealing as those on the seamy side of Harlem, when she was trying to make a fast buck the fast way. There also emerge from these pages her respect and love for musicians (some of them; for others she had no damn love at all, so to speak) and her growing maturity as a musician among musicians (though she didn't read music). For example, she says, "With Basie we had something no expensive arrangements could touch. The cats would come in, somebody would hum a tune. Then someone would play it over on the piano once or twice. Then someone would set up a riff, a ba-deep, a ba-dop. Then Daddy Basie would two-finger it a little."

Already, with groups led by Teddy Wilson and others, Billie had proved herself on blues, ballads and pop songs that, in her interpretation, could be as poignant or portentous as *crimes passionels*. In handling tone and rhythm she was infinitely subtle, as is essential in a capable blues singer; usually she dragged the beat, but she fooled around it (as Louie does) and sometimes gave it a nudge. The timbre of her voice changed to suit the mood of the song, and her beautiful, strong vibrato could also be as delicate as an angel dancing on the head of a pin. Many of her metamorphoses of pops and ballads—some of the best vocals in jazz—are out of print, including the first version of "Summertime," that she did in 1936, with Bunny Berigan and a small band.

By 1939, according to her (Dexter interview), she had loved three men. (There were others, subsequently, but only much later did she seem to radiate any real sense of contentment.) "One was Marion Scott, when I was a kid. He works for the post office now. [Another] was Freddie Green, Basie's guitar man. But Freddie's first wife is dead and he has two children, and somehow it didn't work out. The third was Sonny White, the pianist, but like me, he lives with his mother and our plans for marriage didn't jell. That's all." Even her book lacks what one could call any moving romantic interest, though it is not at all lacking in revelations of tenderness and feeling. (Frank and revealing as it is, it sometimes leaves one with an odd sense of incompleteness, as if it did not always "dig" the real Billie, who is perhaps best felt in the sinuous line of a song. I was reminded, perhaps irrelevantly, of Freud's concept of dreams: that there is a manifest content that *appears to be* the reality of the dream, and a *latent* content that is real, and that *is* the dream.)

\*    \*    \*    \*    \*    \*

The human reality of segregation . . . dogged the Lady east, west, north, south. Unless your skin is the appropriate color, you may not be aware of the humiliation that one out of ten of our citizens experiences, every day, as regular as clockwork, but with more wheels within wheels. At a Detroit theatre she was asked to apply dark grease paint, so that she wouldn't be mistaken for off-white. Then, when she played a Detroit theatre with the Artie Shaw orchestra there was some apprehension about her appearing on stage (with a white band) because of her dark complexion. Billie, in her memoirs, called it "dynamic-assed Detroit."

Once, at a joint where some members of the Artie Shaw orchestra were having a snack, everybody got waited on but Lady. Chuck Peterson (trumpet) called the waitress over and Tony Pastor (saxophone) bawled her out. "This is Lady Day," he said; "now you feed her." At some stops on the road, such as roadside diners, there weren't even outdoor toilets for colored. Said Billie [autobiography], "At first I used to be so ashamed. Then finally I just said to hell with it."

When the band went into the Blue Room of the Lincoln (New York City), the treatment accorded Billie griped the whole band. Yet there seemed no way to cope with it. As Billie explained later, Artie and the men had taken months of hell-on-the-road for this New York engagement and a radio wire. This was the big one. So Lady came in the back door and didn't sit on the bandstand—as girl vocalists almost invariably did in the great days of swoon and swing—but went upstairs to a little room until she was called to sing her number. She was, she said, given fewer and fewer spots on the air time. It got to her, it got to her more than it ever had in the South, where it was all a part of somebody else's gracious way of living, and she blew up a storm and quit.

When Billie opened at Café Society Downtown (New York City) in the late 1930's —her favorite flowers, white gardenias, in her hair—it was seven years and thousands of gut-torn, satin-sheathed songs from the Log Cabin. Café Society was filled to capacity with the sort of cosmopolitan audience for which it became famous—celebrities, artists, society people, and just people. And top-drawer jazz. Said Billie [autobiography]: "Meade Lux Lewis knocked them out; Ammons and Johnson flipped them; Joe Turner killed them; (Frankie) Newton's band sent them; and then I came on. This was an audience."

When she sings from the guts—and that was the only way to sing her big tune there, "Strange Fruit" (Lewis Allen wrote it with her in mind, and she's the only one to sing it) —she reminds one of Bessie on a deeply felt blues. There is no hip-twisting or flirting with the microphone, but there appears to be an almost imperceptible tremor. Like Bessie, she sings with her whole body.

Once, at a Miami night club, a customer asked for "Strange Fruit" and "Gloomy Sunday!" She couldn't figure out why he asked for either but she finally sang "Strange Fruit" as an encore. "When I came to the final phrase of the lyrics," she said, "I was in the angriest and strongest voice I had been in for months. My piano player was in the same kind of form. When I said '. . . for the sun to rot,' and then the piano punctuation, '. . . for the wind to suck,' I pounced on those words like they had never been hit before." [ auto-biography.]

The Commodore record of this song is one of the great vocals of jazz, described with penetrating accuracy by Glenn Coulter as "that uncanny expression of horror which transcends its willful lyric when Billie sings it, and becomes a frozen lament, a paralysis of feeling truer to psychology than any conventional emotionalism could be." [*Cambridge Review*, December, 1956.]

The 1940's, for Billie, began near the top and ended as near the bottom as one could get with any hope of climbing up again. She made trips to the Coast, where moving-picture stars became her friends and where she met Norman Granz ("Jazz at the Philharmonic" concerts and recordings) who, in the 1950's, helped her to get back on her two feet and stand up straight professionally. She sang and acted in the film *New Orleans,* with Louis Armstrong. (She was given the usual, ig-nominious role of a maid, but at least she got to sing.) By the time the film had its première in New York, she was in trouble with the law because of using heroin.

Before the timbers shoring up the roof (that was to fall on her) began to creak, Billie recorded songs that are among her most moving performances. Among these was "God Bless the Child," worked out with Ar-thur Herzog after she had had a quarrel with her mother. She said [ autobiography], "This will gas the Duchess, I thought. And it did." In fact, it gassed a lot of people, sardonic lyrics twisting and squirming under the scal-pel of Billie's membranous reed.

"In a reversal of the usual story," wrote Glenn Coulter, "Billie's popularity in-creased during the same time that her style became more complex. This was also the period when her life seemed tangled and diffi-cult . . . if drama intensifies, it may do so by means of irony. To this weapon Billie now turned, and as she sang a love song, it became a cry of hatred and contempt. . . ." Of her uneven output at this time he remarks, "Most of these bad performances take place in an over-arranged, be-violined setting, and the gait never seems to be an honest jazz tempo, or indeed any tempo that allows music to breathe naturally." Mr. Coulter noted what appeared to be an attempt to convert Billie "into a super-personality cranking out mil-lion-copy best sellers. . . . It is a shock to re-call that Billie saw no incongruity in this at-tempt; we even learn with dismay that the throbbing violins are there at her express wish; it is only the demon that kept her against her will from abandoning her art for the big money."

Lady's demon had many faces. One was the big H, heroin. On Tuesday, May 27, 1947, she appeared in United States District Court, Ninth and Market, Philadelphia, and was arraigned for violation of Section 174, Title 21, U.S.C.A. (violation of Narcotics Act). In the course of his remarks, the district attorney said: "She has given these agents a full and complete statement and came in here last week with the booking agent (Glaser) and expressed a desire to be cured of this addiction. Very unfortunately she has had following her the worst type of para-sites you can think of. We have learned that in the past three years she has earned almost a quarter of a million dollars, but last year it was $56,000 or $57,000, and she doesn't have any of that money."

Billie volunteered to take a government-su-pervised cure—she had previously tried to "kick" it off with a private hospital cure, but it hadn't worked—and was committed to the segregated Federal rehabilitation establishment for women at Alderson, West Virginia, for a year and a day. After a brief but rough "cold turkey" treatment, she was fitted into the routine, starting out as a "Cinderella," washing dishes and peeling potatoes; then for a spell she was assigned to work with the pigs on the farm. Nevertheless, and despite Jim Crow, she found it a better environment than the city prison had been and remarked at one point, "There were any number of heartwarming experiences." [*Ebony,* July, 1949.]

Billie gave a concert at Carnegie Hall 10 days after leaving Alderson. She played to a packed house, and hundreds were turned away. Coming north from West Virginia, she got off at Newark and went direct to Morristown to stay with Bobby Tucker's family. Bobby was her accompanist, and the first song they rehearsed was "Night and Day," which she described as "the toughest song in the world for me to sing. I'll never forget that first note, or the second. Or especially the third one, when I tried to hit 'day' and hold it. I hit it and held it and it sounded better than ever. Bobby almost fell off the stand, he was so happy. . . . We did all our rehearsing there. We never went near New York, or Carnegie Hall. Bobby and his mother made me feel I was home and everything was cool."

The user of narcotics is the eternal fall guy. Pushers, themselves *pushed* by the tycoons of the multi-million-dollar dope racket, harass them with all the slimy persistence of bloodsuckers and blackmailers. Narcotics agents keep tabs on users and, it would seem, on those who have "kicked" the habit, in the hope of getting a line on the higher-ups. In New York, Billie was refused a performer's license for work in cabarets—but this was standard procedure; she was in no sense singled out. "Billie is not self-pitying," Nat Hentoff commented in reviewing her book for *Down Beat* [August 8, 1956], "but she does

make several valid complaints, including a plea that America adopt the British system of treating addicts as 'sick people' under medical care."

In the interests of rehabilitation, at various times, Billie had a talk with a priest, spent loads of money on new clothes, bought a sleek Cadillac the color of chlorophyll-happy green peas, and a plot of land in New Jersey. Later (she doesn't give an exact date), she went to a psychiatrist, and was proud to have fought down an urge to die and gotten back the love of life and the will to live that goes with it.

As often happens with people who've been on dope, some previous friends and acquaintances were wary of associating with her. In the vernacular, she was *hot*. Others, such as Bobby Tucker and John Simmons, acted as though she had merely been away for a while, which was the truth. John took her down to the Strand to hear Lena Horne. Lena had been told that Billie was out front and came down from the stage and up the darkened aisle to take Lady in her arms. As Billie said, people like Lena took the sting out of the others.

The storm that blew her house of cards apart in 1947 had a vicious backlash that caught her while on the West Coast two years later. A news item in *Down Beat*, datelined San Francisco, July, 1949, reads:

> Broke and alone after her manager, John Levy, left her to face the trial here, at which she was acquitted, Billie Holiday decided to go back to work. . . . But despite the fact that the jury said they believed Billie had been framed by Levy, she said, "If he was to walk into the room this minute, I'd melt. He's my man and I love him."

> The trial appeared to confirm that a package of opium had been planted on Billie just before the raid. Billie came to trial with a black eye she said Levy gave her before he left. "You should see my back," she added. "And he even took my silver-blue mink—18 grand worth of coat. He said he was going to give it to his sister to take care of for me. *I got nothing now and I'm scared.*

> "I turned all my life over to John. He took

all my money. I never had any money. We were supposed to get married. On January 22, John came back from Los Angeles. We had been arguing about money. . . ." While Levy was unpacking, the telephone rang. Immediately afterwards, she said, he handed her a package and told her to get rid of it. "I went into my room. John closed the door behind me. . . . Then someone grabbed me. . . . John told me to throw some trash away. I did it. . . . My man makes me wait on him, not him on me. I never did anything without John telling me. . . ."

The story of the San Francisco trial and her acquittal is told by Billie in her book and by Jake Ehrlich, the famous West Coast lawyer who defended her, in a paperback, *Never Plead Guilty*.

In the late Forties, Billie had her own show on Broadway, backed by Bob Sylvester and other true believers; it flopped after three weeks. She has had very successful tours of Europe, the last one in the 1950's when, in a group shepherded by Leonard Feather, she wowed them in Copenhagen. Some time after the San Francisco trial she married Louis McKay. She was also once married to trumpet player Joe Guy, but this time it showed signs of taking.

During the present decade she has steadily recaptured her sureness of style and, along with it, a mellowing and maturity. Happily, however, her intonation has not lost its caustic undertones and her voice can still be as tight as Montgomery Clift's levis. In the spring of 1957, contracts were signed for a film biography of her life.

Sardonic and sophisticated as her singing style is, it has retained and made stronger and deeper an affinity to such honky-tonk styles as that of Alice Moore, whose "I'm black an' evil an' I did not make myself . . ." sears the eardrums. No one since Ma Rainey has sung the "My man"-type blues with such sullen, sultry pathos. No one has given such point and passion to popular song lyrics.

\*    \*    \*    \*    \*    \*

Billie Holiday, born Eleanora Fagan and dubbed Lady Day, was a product of the East Baltimore slums, where a star cracked on her cradle, leaving her star-born and star-crossed. Some years ago the Lady of the White Gardenias, in a Cadillac whose whiteness matched the white steps of Baltimore she'd scrubbed as a kid, drove slowly through the old neighborhood. Even in this she appeared to pay homage with the clumsiness and belligerence of the fear-ridden, the guilt-gotten. But, if so, this was a deeper guilt than the unreasonable but conventional reaction that her past might have instilled in her—of the deep and dark places of the mind, having only a tangential relationship to all manner of hustling, a hurt and a haunt that could be exorcised only by a song.

But we're all of us love hunters, some stalking the prey, some wooing it, some finding it by giving it, others folding before it like night flowers in sunlight, resistless in the coils of an indiscriminate and emotional hunger. Insight is not enough. Not unless it becomes part of one, as in some precious moments when there is no longer the chasm between what one knows, deep within one's self, and what one believes and is, outwardly. Lady comes closest to this fusion of knowing and feeling when she says: "I've been told that nobody sings the word 'hunger' like I do. Or the word 'love.'

"Maybe I remember what those words are all about. Maybe I'm proud enough to *want* to remember Baltimore and Welfare Island, the Catholic Institution and the Jefferson Market Court, the sheriff in front of our place in Harlem and the towns where I got my lumps and scars, Philly and Alderson, Hollywood and San Francisco—every damn bit of it. You've got to have something to eat and a little love in your life before you can hold still for any damn body's sermon."

—1957

Billy Eckstine

Aretha Franklin

The Ink Spots

Gloria Lynne

## Popular Singers

THE HISTORY of popular singing in this country can be partially charted by the appearance of Bessie Smith, Billie Holiday and Ella Fitzgerald. Each has been imitated but never successfully copied. As little as a decade ago black singers were forced to work under unbelievable conditions. One only has to read the autobiographies of Ethel Waters and Billie Holiday to get an idea of the abuse popular black entertainers were subjected to. But now, thanks to television, it is no longer necessary for most singers to perform in backwater towns and suffer the verbal, physical and financial abuse that was constantly being heaped on the performer.

Today, young singers such as Aretha Franklin and Dionne Warwick are able to pick and choose their engagements, often performing in huge civic auditoriums, on university campuses and in the best nightclubs. And whereas once upon a time the black singer was merely a guest on television, he is now also being asked to participate in the overall programming.

However, though his status is much improved, the black singer is still not accorded all of the commercial outlets that white singers take for granted when they have made it big.

Carmen McRae

Nat "King" Cole
Nancy Wilson

Pearl Bailey

Ella Fitzgerald

Ray Charles

Sarah Vaughan

Nina Simone

Marian Anderson with Governor Nelson Rockefeller of New York.

Miss Anderson in 1962, with President Kennedy, before giving a concert at the new State Department auditorium.

# Marian Anderson

by David Ewen

THE SUCCESS of Marian Anderson represents the triumph of genius over the greatest single obstacle an artist can be called upon to hurdle: race prejudice. There have been excellent Negro musicians before Anderson, and comparatively successful ones, too. But none, not even so sensitive an artist as Roland Hayes, has risen so high as she. To call Marian Anderson the greatest living Negro musician, as so many have done, is to qualify her reputation unwarrantably. She is more than that: she is one of the great artists of our generation *regardless* of race, color or nationality. And, in some respects, she stands alone, majestic, incomparable.

Both as artist and as human being, she holds a regal position in music with rare stateliness. In her art, she has ever clung tenaciously to the highest standards alone; one can go through her career with microscopic thoroughness without discovering any hint of concession to expediency. So, in her everyday life, she has always behaved with rare integrity and dignity. I do not refer to her many benefactions to her race, which she prefers to keep unpublicized; I refer rather to the noble spirit and the beautiful pride with which, throughout her life, she has walked, in spite of the prejudice, the hatred, the ignorance surrounding her. This is what was meant when the Spingarn Award given her in 1939 carried the additional citation: "Equally with that achievement which has won her world-wide fame as one of the greatest singers of our time, is her magnificent dignity as a human being."

She has never descended to the level of those who have been hostile because of their color; on the contrary, she has always worn her color as a medal of honor. It is her practice to include at least one group of Negro spirituals in every program, not because it is expected of her, but because it is the music of her race, the eloquent and poignant voice of her people. It is also her practice, when she appears on the stage of any concert hall that segregates Negroes, to bow to her own people first, and only afterwards to the rest of the audience. She does this simply, unostentatiously, almost with humility—telling the world that she cannot forget that she is a Negro, only because the world refuses to let her race forget its color.

The climax of her lifelong struggle against race prejudice came during the first months of 1939. Her manager tried to hire Constitution Hall in Washington, D.C., for a recital in February, 1939. Because the Daughters of the American Revolution looked with undisguised disfavor on the appearance of a Negro in Constitution Hall, the theatre was barred to her. Such barefaced discrimination evoked a chorus of protest throughout the country. Musicians, statesmen, clergymen, writers, vehemently denounced the D.A.R., and Mrs. Franklin D. Roosevelt resigned from that organization. Secretary of the Interior Harold L. Ickes then invited Miss Anderson to give her concert at the Lincoln Memorial. She consented, offering to sing for nothing to whoever cared to come to listen. On April 9, an audience of 75,000 assembled before the Memorial, among them Supreme Court judges, congressmen, Cabinet members; and another audience of several millions heard the concert over the radio. She sang Lieder and Negro spirituals. Before her stretched an enthusiastic throng which was paying homage in no uncertain terms to a great artist. Behind her loomed the massive and benign figure of Abraham Lincoln, seeming almost to serve as spiritual godfather to the proceedings. (This concert, incidentally, is the subject of a mural design decorating the new Department of the Interior building, in Washington, D.C.)

One week later, at a concert at Carnegie Hall, a capacity audience rose to its feet spontaneously when Marian Anderson came onto the stage and gave her one of the most impressive demonstrations ever to be seen in that august hall. Here, surely, the Daughters of the American Revolution had their answer.

It is true that this occurrence put Marian Anderson's name on the front page of every newspaper in the country—threw the limelight of national publicity sharply on her. But it revealed either an abysmal ignorance of the truth, or a blinding prejudice, to say that it was this that transformed an obscure singer into a famous one. Marian Anderson obscure in 1939? Here are the facts.

In August, 1935, she electrified what is perhaps the most discriminating music audience in the world at the Mozarteum in Salzburg—an assemblage of world-famous musicians, esthetes, journalists, critics. "A voice like yours," remarked Toscanini, who was at that concert, "comes once in a century." A half-year later, she gave that concert in Town Hall, New York, at which she was unreservedly

acclaimed one of the greatest concert artists of our generation—"mistress of all she surveyed," as the critic of the *New York Times* put it. Her concert at Carnegie Hall, a month later, was sold out in advance. She was invited to sing at the White House before President and Mrs. Roosevelt. An extensive European tour followed. In the Soviet Union, she expected to stay one month, but such was her success that she had to stay three. In Vienna, she sang under Bruno Walter to triumphant acclaim. In Finland, Sibelius was so stirred by her singing that he dedicated one of his songs to her, "Solitude." Concerts in Spain, Switzerland, Monte Carlo, Scandinavia, Egypt, Palestine, South America (in Buenos Aires she gave 12 consecutive concerts to full houses!), were scenes of personal triumph. Again, between January 2 and May 28, 1938, she traveled 26,000 miles and gave 70 concerts (believed to be the most ambitious tour ever undertaken by any artist). By this time, her concerts in New York were automatically sold out weeks in advance, while an appearance abroad had to be booked two years ahead. On July 2, 1939, she was given the Spingarn Award for the greatest achievement by a Negro "in an honorable field of endeavor."

By 1939, she had arrived at the full richness of her vocal powers. As Toscanini suggested, her voice was truly without equal, gracefully spanning as it did three full octaves without betraying a flaw. In sheer beauty of tonal production, in variety of colors, from the deep purple of her low tones to the bright crimson of her falsetto, her voice was like a Stradivarius in the hands of Heifetz. Destiny had indeed given her an incomparable instrument, and she did justice to it. With voice were combined brains and scholarship, heart and sensitivity, taste and refinement. Simply, she brings a wealth of humanity and culture to every song she sings in her extensive repertoire of more than 200 compositions, whether an aria by Purcell, a Lied by Brahms, or a spiritual. She fashions a lyric line like that of Casals on the cello, each note having its precise role to fill, and assuming its inevitable place in the design of the whole. Drama and heightened tragedy she brings with the most economical use of shade and nuance. I have heard many world-famous Lieder singers interpret the chant of Death in Schubert's *Death and the Maiden,* but no one that I can recall brought such an overwhelming sense of doom as Anderson did merely through the subtle use of tints and hues. She can change her mood magically, as she draws from Scarlatti or Handel or Schubert or Brahms or Hugo Wolf the very essence of their art.

Her rendition of Negro spirituals is, of course, a deeply personal expression. To these songs she brings the full tragedy of a race despised and rejected. "Nobody Knows de Trouble I've Seen"—the expression of sorrow becomes more poignant and heartbreaking because of the restraint with which she speaks her woe. "Were You There When They Crucified My Lord?"—she brings the immense and shattering sorrow of one who knows what it means to be crucified. "Deep River"—with those unequaled low tones of hers, luscious in texture, the melody acquires wings and soars as never before.

Marian Anderson was born in South Philadelphia in 1908. Her father sold coal, and his income was so meager that her mother (an ex-schoolteacher) had to supplement it by taking in washing. But Marian's was not an unhappy childhood. Music brought a glow and warmth into the Anderson household. On many an evening, the family gathered with friends to sing spirituals.

Singing, from the first, was both an artistic compulsion and a financial necessity for Marian. When she was six, she made her first public appearance singing in a duet at the Union Baptist Church. Soon after this, she joined its junior choir, graduating into the senior choir

after seven years. At the same time, she helped support her family by singing at church concerts, earning money that was even more needed after 1920, on the death of her father. She had earned her first singing fee (50 cents) when she was eight years old, but before many years had passed she was paid as much as $25 a performance. In a community where dollars were not plentiful and incomes were small, this eloquently attests to her extraordinary popularity with her neighbors.

At the South Philadelphia High School her voice attracted a Negro actor named Thomas Butler, who recommended her to her first voice teacher, Mary S. Patterson. A few months later, the Philadelphia Choral Society held a benefit concert for her, the profits of which enabled her to become a pupil of Agnes Reifsnyder.

She was just 17 when the principal of South Philadelphia High School urged the well-known vocal teacher Giuseppe Boghetti to accept her as a pupil. Her lessons were paid for by the nickels and dimes gathered among the members of her church. To this day, Boghetti recalls the audition. It was dusk. Behind him lay a hard day of teaching. He was too weary even to put on the lights. Sinking deep into his chair, he motioned to the somewhat self-conscious visitor to sing. She sang "Deep River," and "it was as if the sun had suddenly flooded the rooms."

She worked industriously under Boghetti and made such rapid progress that, in a few months, her teacher made ambitious plans for her. She gave a recital at Witherspoon Hall in Philadelphia, and another at Town Hall in New York. She also entered a contest conducted by the New York Philharmonic at the Lewisohn Stadium. There were 300 contestants. Marian—singing "O Mio Fernando"—won the prize: an appearance with that orchestra. She was engaged for an appearance with the Philadelphia Orchestra. A concert manager signed her to a contract.

But engagements were not easy to get. She was unknown; she was a Negro. Even some of those who themselves were not prejudiced, and who were ready to acknowledge that she sang magnificently, would not sponsor her for fear of unfavorable public reaction. "If only she were not a Negro," they would say sadly. That she was rejected, not because she was artistically inadequate, but because of her race, was a galling dose to take. But Anderson would not yield to bitterness, nor descend to hatred. She brushed aside her disappointment and worked all the harder.

Her manager decided that the climate of Europe might be healthier for a Negro singer. She went to London where many leading musicians, amazed by her singing, worked for her.

The Julius Rosenwald Scholarship, which she won in 1929, enabled her to travel and study for a few years. Finally, an appearance in Berlin in 1933 (for which, incidentally, she had to pay $500!) launched an extensive concert tour that brought her to France, Belgium, Holland, Italy, Scandinavia, the Soviet Union. And in August, 1935, there took place the Salzburg concert, with which her wonderful career as an artist of first importance can be said to have begun.

It was a historic concert, and it has been eloquently described by Vincent Sheean in *Between the Thunder and the Sun* [New York: Random House, 1943]:

> Into the wealth of European classical and romantic music that was heard in Salzburg in 1935, there was introduced a note that was new and strange. A musical hostess, Mrs. Moulton, invited three or four hundred people to an afternoon of songs at the Hôtel de l'Europe. The guests included Toscanini, Lotte Lehmann, Bruno Walter and practically all the other musical powers of Salzburg. The artist was Marian Anderson. I do not think anybody there had heard her before. . . . She sang Bach, Schubert and Schumann, with a final group of Negro spirituals. Her superb voice commanded the closest attention of that audience from its first note. The Archbishop was sitting in the front row, and at his insistence she repeated the Schubert "Ave Maria." In the last group she sang a spiritual, "They Crucified My Lord, and He Never Said a Mumblin' Word." Hardly anybody in the audience understood English well enough to follow what she was saying, and yet the immense sorrow—something more than the sorrow of a single person—that weighted her tones and lay over her dusky, angular face was enough. At the end of the spiritual, there was no applause at all—a silence instinctive, natural, and intense, so that you were afraid to breathe. What Anderson had done was something outside the limits of classical or romantic music: she frightened us with the conception, in musical terms, of course, but outside the normal limits, of a mighty suffering. Without the conventional training of an art-singer she would probably never have been able to do this, and yet she did it most of all by a quality of tone and expression which transcended even her rare gift and related her to millions of others; it was most of all a racial quality. To find it in a great singer was something that had not happened before. It made some of the more self-conscious of our festival manifestations seem pallid and absurd. . . .

In December, 1945, a testimonial dinner was given to Marian Anderson, honoring the tenth anniversary of her historic debut in New York. The great of the music world attended to pay tribute to a fellow artist. In these ten years, she had given more than 700 concerts in 289 cities, at which more than 4,000,000 attended. She had been selected for five consecutive years by national polls as the foremost woman singer over the radio. She had established the Marian Anderson Award—initially with the $10,000 Bok Award she received from the city of Philadelphia in 1941, and subsequently with additional funds from her own pocket—to help the careers of young, struggling singers.

In short, in these 10 years, Marian Anderson has proved herself to be one of the great artists of our time, and one of its great women. As Fannie Hurst put it: "Marian Anderson has not grown simply great, she has grown great simply."

—1949

Marian Anderson as United States Delegate to the
United Nations. She was appointed by
President Eisenhower.

Miss Anderson being congratulated by President
Johnson at the White House in 1963, after receiving
the Presidential Medal of Freedom.

Easter Sunday, 1939

Leontyne Price during a concert.

In *Antony and Cleopatra*, with Justino Diaz.

In *Porgy and Bess* in 1952, with William Warfield.

In Cilea's *Adriana Lecouvreur*.

# Leontyne Price

Leontyne Price in Verdi's *La Forza del Destino.*

LEONTYNE PRICE is considered one of the great dramatic sopranos in opera today. She was born in Laurel, Mississippi, where she began to show musical talent at an early age. From there she went to Central State College in Wilberforce, Ohio, and, later, on a scholarship, to the Juilliard School of Music in New York. It was in 1952, as Mistress Ford in a Juilliard production of *Falstaff,* that she first received wide critical notice, with the result that she was chosen to sing Bess in a revival of Gershwin's *Porgy and Bess.* This production had a triumphant tour of Europe and a long Broadway run. In November, 1954, Miss Price made her Town Hall recital debut; in the three years following, she appeared with the NBC-TV Opera, successively as Tosca, as Pamina in *The Magic Flute,* and in the television première of Poulenc's *Dialogues of the Carmelites.* This last, she sang with the San Francisco Opera in 1957, at the time of her first performance in *Aïda.* Engagements followed at the Vienna Staatsoper, London's Covent Garden and the Arena di Verona. In the fall of 1959, she made her debut with the Chicago Lyric Opera. She appeared in *Il Trovatore,* which opened the new Salzburg Festspielhaus in 1960 and was also the work in which she made her Metropolitan Opera debut in the 1960–61 season. She opened the Metropolitan at its new home in the Lincoln Center for the Performing Arts in 1966, as Cleopatra in *Antony and Cleopatra,* an opera written especially for her.

Marian Anderson at her Metropolitan Opera debut, January 7, 1955, as Ulrica in Verdi's *Masked Ball*.

# The Negro in Opera

**by Phil Petrie**

EVEN DURING slavery the melodic gift of the Negro was appreciated. The most rabid of Negrophobes were wont to point out the "natural" musical abilities of the Negro. In the words of Paul Laurence Dunbar: "He jes' spreads his mouf and hollahs! Come to Jesus."

Both points—the Negro is a natural singer, and the Negro is a natural singer of spirituals —reflected the national attitude toward the Negro extended into music. Being a "natural" singer deprived him of the discipline of his craft. It denied training, cultivation and an artistic use of the voice. In other words, the term was another use and modification of the "noble savage."

Since the spirituals were an Afro-American creation, it was only proper that Afro-Americans should sing them. The tragedy was that Negroes were relegated to singing spirituals only. Few people saw these songs as "art," and even fewer imagined that the voice singing them might also sing grand opera. The step from the plantation to the opera house was such a big one, such an ironic step, it was easy to accept the rationale that Negroes simply had not made the long walk, had not had enough time to be trained. Generally speaking this was true, just as it was true for whites in America. In the 1800's America was not noted for the opera singers it produced. But singers are individuals, and there were several Negro vocalists equipped to sing in grand opera.

Thirty years before the Metropolitan Opera House came into existence, an ex-slave, "colored as dark as Ethiopia," was presented, and accepted, in London as a great singer. The "Black Swan," as Elizabeth Taylor Greenfield was called, was said to equal the great Jenny Lind. Much of her success was due to the rarity, at the time, of a Negro singing classical music. The very existence of Elizabeth Taylor Greenfield should have alerted the disbelievers, the doubters, to the fact that some Negroes could sing opera.

The notion that Negroes were meant to sing spirituals and minstrel songs, however, persisted. A young tenor from Philadelphia told a friend that "what induced me more than anything else to appear in public was to give the lie to 'Negro serenaders' (minstrels), and to show to the world that colored men and women could sing classical music as well as the members of the other race. . . ." This was certainly not the attitude that expressed "art for art's sake." Thomas Bowers, the author of that statement, was pushed onto the concert stage, not by the Muses, but by a passion to affirm the Negro's right to take his stand in music with anyone. This was not just a grand gesture. Bowers was possessed of a "mellow" and "sweet" voice. His talents were so prodigious he was called the "American Mario," after the great Italian tenor Mario. Thomas

Bowers sang for a purpose. He gave the country a great voice, a voice, in spite of its greatness, that could not push open the operatic door for Negroes.

Even the great Sissieretta Jones could not push open that door. Madame Jones, like Bowers, had a great voice and was compared with the leading singer of the times, Adelina Patti. The comparison was so favorable she was called "Black Patti." Madam Jones became prominent in the 1890's and performed in the principal cities of Europe. She established her own company, Black Patti's Troubadours, and remained at its head for 19 years.

America obviously recognized the talent of these people, giving them such sobriquets as "Black Swan," "American Mario," and "Black Patti." Unfortunately, the recognition of talent does not give one the opportunity to enjoy it fully. These singers would have set new standards for American opera. I know of no others of the period who compared so decidedly with European stars.

But opera in America has not been an art form for the majority of the people. I am told that in Europe peasants flock to the opera in droves. But here, at least in its formative years, opera was the child of the wealthy. Those who were spectators belonged to "top society." Those who performed were "artists," worthy of all the honor accorded to genius. Such honor to black artists in a society that lynched, ridiculed and segregated Negroes would have been, to say the least, incongruous.

In spite of the successes of Greenfield, Bowers and Jones, the Negro was still relegated to singing "coon songs" and spirituals. He did pray and sing in church, and it was the church that helped him to carve out a future in opera.

The historic aid for the Negro singer has been the church. Many of the best choirs in the larger churches engage soloists. Most of these are professionally trained and partially, if not fully, prepared to make an entrance into grand opera. Ellabelle Davis, a church soloist, made her operatic debut at New York's Museum of Modern Art, in an opera called *The Chaplet,* without having had formal training. Five years later, in 1946, she stunned Mexico City with a performance of *Aïda.*

The church organization that sponsors concerts is just as important as the church choir in the development of singers. These organizations put the performer before an audience. Young talent needs to hear applause—needs a place in which to make mistakes. But opera, by its nature, is secular and cannot flower within the monastic walls of the church.

The young singer needs the experience of working in an ensemble of his peers. This being the case, Negroes organized their own opera companies. The first of these was the Colored Opera Company, established in 1873. This was a company composed entirely of amateurs. A Philadelphia newspaper, in reviewing a performance of the Colored Opera Company, said that though "the opera, *The Doctor of Alcantara,* has frequently been given previously by various English companies, we venture to say, never so perfectly in its ensemble as by this company."

The Drury, another early company, was established in 1900. It was run by Theodore Drury and was primarily a touring company appearing in New York, Philadelphia, Boston and Providence.

\* \* \* \* \* \*

Other Negro opera companies were the American Negro Opera Company and the Harlem Opera Workshop. These companies built admirably upon the foundation laid by the Negro church. But they were too few, presented too few performances, lacked permanent houses to work in and were constantly in need of funds.

In 1919, thirteen young musicians, feeling

Madame Sissieretta Jones

Caterina Jarboro

Lillian Evanti

Camilla Williams with Geraldine Farrar after the former's debut in *Madama Butterfly*, in 1946.

a need to help themselves and other musicians, organized the National Association of Negro Musicians. They wanted their organization to encourage the development of musical talent through scholarships for needy students; they wanted it to enrich the careers of professional musicians through workshops, seminars and conferences; they wanted it to be a showcase for the cultural contribution of the Negro in music. These aims were not only noble—they were Gargantuan. It is a tribute to those founders that this organization continues to exist. Not only is it still with us but it is a force within the community. It gave Marian Anderson her first scholarship and, in 1953, awarded Grace Bumbry, a brilliant mezzo-soprano, similar aid.

In spite of what the Negro community did to sustain its opera singers, there was much more to be done. The opera singer was still in a land where opera was not king. Young voices, professionally trained, had few places to soar, few places to rise where one might gauge their glory. Home was not the place to hang one's hat, and the opera singer headed for Europe.

Lillian Evanti was one of these. "I had no sponsors on the other side," she said. "And I knew I had a big mountain to climb. I would be alone and I had to make good. In America the Negro was accepted only as a buffoon in big-time music. A World War had been fought for democracy, but it did not extend to democracy in musical opportunities. That alone was enough motive to go elsewhere. I guess I would have gone if I had had to board the boat as a stowaway. . . ."

She was there for six months before she made her operatic debut in *Lakmé*, with the Nice Opera Company. She was the first Negro to appear with an organized European opera company. *Lakmé* was a role "not in conflict with her color," but it was a role. She was not restricted to it or to the Nice Opera Company. When her contract with the company ended she contracted for herself and began a career that sent her to the principal cities of Europe. Her major roles were in *La Traviata, Le Coq d'Or, Romeo and Juliet, Lakmé* and *Lucia di Lammermoor.* Even in Europe color seems to have been a barrier for the Negro singer. Madam Evanti, in spite of her success, did not perform in the major European opera houses.

Evanti did not have the voice for *Aïda,* or surely she would have been asked to perform it. But Europe was not without an Aïda *senza trucco* (without makeup). In 1930, Caterina Jarboro, a young singer from Wilmington, North Carolina, made her debut at the Puccini Opera House in Milan as Aïda. Her success was immediate. The Paris Opera offered her a contract for six performances, and Jarboro became popular in the *Queen of Sheba* and *L'Africaine.* She returned to America in 1933, after having spent over six years in Europe.

The director of the Chicago Opera Company, Alfredo Salmaggi, heard her and was impressed. "I recognized that she had a real soprano voice and that she was a good artist," he later said. He so admired her that he hired her. "Her color made no difference with me." Thus, in July, 1933, Caterina Jarboro performed *Aïda* with the Chicago Opera Company. She was the first Negro to perform with an American opera company.

"Was her performance immortal? Was it all that one could ask? Was there something to be desired?" a Negro reporter inquired. "The untrained ear of a mere newspaper reporter," he continued, "could not tell. But the trained eye of this same reporter could watch the faces of perfect strangers as they passed each other during the intermission and smiled a smile which seemed to say, 'Another milestone, Lord!' "

Jarboro also realized the significance of her performance. "My debut here means so much more than my debut in Italy," she declared. The debut was a success, at least artistically. Jarboro appeared in two more performances of *Aïda* with the company, and the door was once again closed against the Negro. Jarboro returned to Europe. She never performed with an American opera company again.

No Negro appeared with an American company after Jarboro's success until 1945. In that year Todd Duncan, already celebrated for his portrayal of Porgy, in *Porgy and Bess,* was contracted by Laszlo Halasz, director of the New York City Center, to play the part of Tonio in *Pagliacci.*

One year later, a young Negro soprano was sent by her music teacher to audition for Halasz. Camilla Williams, the young soprano, went to Halasz and sang. The conductor was at once awed by her voice. Here was a voice, he thought, that already was capable of performing a lead role. Camilla Williams needed no secondary parts in which to make her debut. The conductor gave the young singer his impressions and said that he thought *Madama Butterfly* should be her vehicle. Williams was pleased. Owing to the closeness of World War II, *Butterfly,* an opera dealing with a Japanese woman and an American sailor, was banned in America. As soon as the opera could be performed, Halasz promised to send the young singer a telegram. Williams was skeptical. After all, sending a telegram is very much like saying, "Don't call us; we'll call you." Negroes had traveled that road before.

One month passed and there was no telegram; month slipped into month, and still no telegram. Another dream, another hope, deferred. Then, eight months after her audition, the telegram came. Camilla Williams was to play the lead in *Madama Butterfly.* In 1946, Williams did portray Cio-Cio San to great acclaim. This was followed up by other roles, and Williams became a fixture at the New York City Center Opera Company. One

can imagine that Negroes cried, "Another milestone, Lord!"

The New York City Center gave opportunities to many Negro singers. In the late Forties, Lawrence Winters and Margaret Tynes appeared there. Both of these singers moved on to become international stars.

The New York City Center had cracked open the operatic door for the Negro—but it was only a crack. Only four Negroes appeared there between 1945, when Todd Duncan made his debut, and 1955, the year Marian Anderson first sang at the Metropolitan.

When, in 1955, Marian Anderson made her debut—and the debut for the Negro—at the Metropolitan Opera Company, it was thought that the barriers were down, that Jericho's walls had tumbled. Shortly after her performance Robert McFerrin, a first-prize winner in the Metropolitan auditions and the first Negro to enter the Metropolitan's opera training course, made his Metropolitan debut as Amonasro, the Ethiopian king. Rudolph Bing, general manager of the Met, announced that he was "looking for voices, not color." He continued: "Eva in *Die Meistersinger* might be difficult with a Negro singer, nor could I easily envisage a Negro Elsa in *Lohengrin.*" The two statements offset each other. It appeared as if the Negro was going to be assigned special, or "typed," roles to play.

Howard Taubman, critic for the *New York Times,* stated in 1959 that the "usual routine is to have Negro singers appear in roles not in conflict with the color of their skin. Roles like Aïda and Amonasro have always been regarded as their right. . . ." It is interesting to note that Marian Anderson made her operatic debut, and the operatic debut of the Negro at the Metropolitan, as Ulrica, a gypsy.

This does not mean that Negroes have sung only "Negro parts." True, Robert Mc-

Grace Bumbry as Eboli in *Don Carlos*.

Martina Arroyo as Aïda.

Felicia Weathers as Lisa in Tchaikowsky's
*Queen of Spades*.

Reri Grist as Rosina in *The Barber of Seville*.

Robert McFerrin with his teacher, Zitomirsky.

Charlotte Holloman

George Shirley as Pinkerton in *Madama Butterfly*.

Todd Duncan

Ferrin made his debut at the Metropolitan as Amonasro, the Ethiopian king. But he also portrayed Tonio in *Pagliacci,* Valentin in *Faust,* Count Di Luna in *Il Trovatore,* and *Rigoletto.* The assigning of typed roles, though prevalent, was not inflexible. It was merely one of many things that the Negro singer had to be aware of. His first problem, however, was to be hired.

When it was announced that Leontyne Price would appear with the Metropolitan Opera Company in 1961, there was great excitement. Why? She was not the first Negro to appear at the Metropolitan. Indeed, she was the fifth. This was not her first appearance in America. She had already appeared with the San Francisco Opera Company and the Lyric Opera of Chicago. Besides, millions had seen her on television with the NBC Opera as Tosca. Why the excitement about Leontyne Price? Why indeed! Leontyne Price came to the Metropolitan with the reputation of having one of the finest voices of the century. Her debut was successful. And when she was given the honor of opening the Metropolitan the following season, one could imagine a voice saying, "Another milestone, Lord!"

But in spite of Leontyne Price's success, Negro singers still found that the doors to American opera companies were not wide open. Like their predecessors, Evanti and Jarboro, they turned their faces toward Europe.

After World War II, Europe had a manpower shortage. There were not enough native singers to fill her opera houses. This on a continent that fostered Mozart, Wagner and Verdi was unthinkable. Outsiders would have to be brought in. The people must have their opera! Young Americans heeded the call and, in the tradition of Evanti and Jarboro, found their way to Europe. Many, such as Vera Little, Gloria Davy, Kathleen Crawford, Leonora Lafayette, Grace Bumbry and Gwendolyn Simms, made their operatic debuts there. Today, there are approximately a dozen young Negro singers working in Europe. Here is a list of singers presently working, or who have recently worked, in European opera companies: Annabelle Bernard; Grace Bumbry; Kathleen Crawford; Mattiwilda Dobbs; Reri Grist; Charles Holland; Charlotte Holloman; Rhea Jackson; Junetta Jones: Ella Lee; Vera Little; William Ray; Gwendolyn Simms; William de Valentine; Felicia Weathers.

This list is certainly not a definitive one, but it is a fair indication of the number of young Negro singers performing in Europe.

The war has been over for 20 years now, and Europe is ready to give its own singers opportunities to perform. Outsiders will be limited even more than they have been. What will happen to the young performers now working in Europe, one cannot say. It is safe to say, if her present and past history is any indication, that America is not yet ready to receive them.

This country does not have an operatic tradition. The prevailing attitude is that opera is for the rich and well-to-do. Thus we have a few opera companies in a few urban centers. As the situation stands today, there would be too few opera houses to accommodate the American singers now in Europe. To speak of using a large number of Negro singers in American opera houses is to speak optimistically.

In its entire history, 11 Negroes have appeared with the Metropolitan Opera Company, 11 with the San Francisco Opera, 15 with the New York City Center, five with the Lyric Opera of Chicago, seven with the Boston Opera Company and one with the Pittsburgh Opera. In 1933, Caterina Jarboro and Jules Bledsoe appeared with the Chicago Opera Company. The total number of different Negro singers to have appeared in all American opera companies is 34. The bulk of these have arrived on the operatic scene since Marian Anderson's debut at the Metropolitan in 1955. When one takes into consideration the fact that some performers appeared only in one role for one season, and that other performers were local singers who did not intend to have careers as opera singers, the number of 34 is not a true indication of the number of professional singers used by American companies. In fact, only nine Negroes appeared in American opera companies during the 1966 season. The number of Negroes performing in American opera companies is not legion.

This is especially true of the Negro male. Since 1933, only 12 have appeared with American companies. Six have had lead roles.

The Metropolitan has used two Negro male singers (Robert McFerrin and George Shirley), while the Lyric Opera of Chicago has used none. The San Francisco has used more than any other company, with five (Lawrence Winters, McHenry Boatwright, André Montal, Eugene Jones and George Shirley). Most of these are baritones. Where are the tenors?

The Negro singer in American opera has moved from a position of complete rejection to one of partial, if not complete, acceptance. He still must strive continually "to be a co-worker in the Kingdom of Culture." Many have made the effort and failed, and their failure has not been related to their talent. Many others have succeeded. Talent, after all, is not embedded in a race but in an individual.

—1967

## *Classical Music*

Dean Dixon

William Warfield

Thomas Greene Bethune (Blind Tom)

# Musical Pioneers

by Maud Cuney Hare

TURNING back the pages of history, we find it remarkable that, in a period as early as from 1847 to 1876, there had arisen a number of Negro musicians and singers whose work was of sufficient merit to bring recognition from the white press and from cultured people of the country. New Orleans, Philadelphia and Boston were the exceptional cities, particularly New Orleans.

Eugene V. Macarty, a Negro musician of a century ago, has been remembered by historians of New Orleans. He was born in that city in 1821, and studied piano under J. Norres. In 1840, having won the interest of the French ambassador to the United States and of Creole friends, he was accepted as a pupil in voice, harmony and composition at the Imperial Conservatory in Paris. In his own city, he became known as a man of versatility. He was a singer who possessed a rich baritone voice, a composer of light music, an actor of ability and a man of public affairs. He was also considered an excellent pianist.

Basile Barés, pianist and composer, was born in New Orleans, January 2, 1846. He was a student of piano under Eugène Prévost, at one time director of the French Opera House orchestra, and of harmony and composition under Professor Pedigram. During 1867, he spent some time in France and played in Paris, after which he returned home. His dance compositions, a number of which the author has in her collection, were very popular. They were published in 1869 and 1870. His salon pieces, in the style of that period, show an effective use of the glissando, an embellishment that was in vogue and was often found in the Mexican and Spanish Creole music of that area. His best-known pieces included "Les Cent Gardes," "Minuit Polka de Salon" and "Basile's Galop." Barés was a man of fine literary tastes, as well as a musician.

Samuel Snaér, a versatile musician, was born in New Orleans about 1834. He played the violin, cello, organ and piano, and was organist at the Church of Ste. Marie, on Chartres Street. He possessed a good tenor voice, but did not sing professionally. Joseph A. Moret, later a violinist, was among his first pupils. While active as a teacher of piano and violin, Snaér devoted time to composition. His first work, "Sous Sa Fenêtre," was published by Louis Gruenwald. Snaér did nothing to further his own career and preferred to live a retired life in New Orleans. A catalogue of his compositions includes "Rapelle-Toi," "Le Vampire," "Le Bohémien" and "Le Chant des Canotiers." In addition to his orchestral pieces, he wrote works in the dance forms of the day—polkas, waltzes, mazurkas and quadrilles.

The vocalists Mrs. Lucy Adger and John Mills, with the violinists F. J. R. Jones and Edward Johnson, and the pianist M. Inez

Cassey, were sponsors of oratorio societies. Sarah Sedgwick Bowers (later Mrs. Bell) was a fine singer. She gave recitals of operatic arias and classical songs in Philadelphia and New York and was active musically with her gifted brothers. She was a member of the well-known Negro families, the Turpins and the Howards, who fostered salon music in their social life. The most noted member of the musical Bowers family was Sarah's younger brother, Thomas.

William Brady, who died in March, 1854, was actively engaged in composing songs and dances, and also anthems and other pieces for church services. His "Anthem for Christmas," published in 1851, is among his best-known compositions.

Another composer of this period was the violinist Edwin Hill, who was the first Negro to be admitted to the Philadelphia Academy of Fine Arts (1871). Among Mr. Hill's compositions, about 30 in number, one finds songs and anthems. His son, Edwin Hill, Jr., is now known in Philadelphia as a teacher of violin and a choral conductor.

Thomas J. Bowers, tenor, known as the "American Mario," was born in Philadelphia in 1836. His father was for many years the warden of St. Thomas' Episcopal Church, which first opened its doors on July 17, 1794, under the guidance of Absalom Jones. An elder son, John C. Bowers, became organist of St. Thomas'. At the age of 18, Thomas, who had been taught by his brother, followed John as organist. He then began the study of voice under Elizabeth Taylor Greenfield and in 1854 appeared in a local concert as her pupil. Shortly afterwards, he was engaged for a concert tour and traveled in the Eastern and Middle Western states. Colonel Wood, a former manager of the Cincinnati Museum, arranged concert appearances for him in New York and Canada. In Hamilton, a difficulty arose concerning the admission of a Negro party of six to first-class seats. The contention

that Negroes were not allowed to occupy first-class seats in Canada was protested by the purchaser, Dr. Brown. He was upheld by the singer, who refused to give the concert should there be any discrimination shown. His argument that he did not leave home to encourage racial prejudice won the point and established a principle for Bowers and his colleagues.

The Sedgwick Company, with Bowers as the tenor soloist, was highly praised by the press. The critics early called Bowers the "American Mario" in comparison with the noted Mario of that day [the Italian tenor, who was the leading singer of his time].

The *Daily Pennsylvanian* of February 9, 1854, commented on a concert given by Bowers in Samson Street Hall in Philadelphia, and concluded that, "He has naturally a superior voice, far better than many of the principal tenors who have been engaged for star opera troupes. He has, besides, much musical taste."

Peter P. O'Fake was a versatile musician who was active in New Jersey at this time. He was a skillful artist and became proficient on the flute and violin mainly through his own efforts. O'Fake was often called upon to take part in the activities of various white musical organizations, and at one time he conducted the orchestra of the Newark Theatre (1848). The musician organized a small orchestra, which was engaged for entertaining purposes by the wealthy citizens of Newark. His dance compositions, mainly those written for the popular quadrilles of the day, had a certain vogue.

Among the singers of the early period was Elizabeth Taylor Greenfield, who was born in Natchez, Mississippi, in 1809, brought to Philadelphia when one year old and reared by a Quaker lady, Mrs. Greenfield. Her musical gifts were early shown and encouraged. Following her patron's death in 1844, she went to Buffalo, New York. In October,

1851, she sang before the Buffalo Musical Association and was received with such acclaim that her voice was likened to those of Jenny Lind and Parodi, and the sobriquet the "Black Swan" was bestowed upon her.

At Albany, New York, in January, 1852, she was heard in the lecture room of the Young Men's Christian Association before a representative audience which included Governor Hunt and his family, members of both houses of the legislature and other state officials. On February 3, 1852, she sang in Boston at the Melodeon.

After Miss Greenfield's tour of the Northern states, she went to Europe (aided by New York music-lovers) with the hope of studying and of singing in public. She arrived in London on April 16, 1853.

Miss Greenfield's success was immediate. The London *Times,* the *Morning Post* and the *Observer* commented on the range of her voice, its power and sweetness. Many concerts were given in London under the patronage of titled ladies, and on May 10, 1854, she was commanded to sing at Buckingham Palace for Her Majesty Queen Victoria. The singer returned to America in July, 1854. Miss Greenfield then located in Philadelphia, where she opened a studio for vocal students. She died in April, 1876.

Some other interesting musicians of that time, the Luca family, consisting of the father and three sons, made their home in Connecticut. Alexander C. Luca, the father, was born in Milford in 1805. He became a shoemaker by trade and studied music in the village singing school. He removed to New Haven, where he married a Miss Lewis, who also possessed musical taste. For some time he held the position of chorister in a Congregational church, and at the same time organized a small concert company with his wife, his sons, Dinah Lewis, his wife's sister, and himself.

The family had their first wide hearing at the May anniversary of the Anti-Slavery Society, held in the Tabernacle in New York City in 1853. Their respective talents were: John W. Luca, the eldest son, bass-baritone and violinist; Alexander C., tenor and violinist; Simeon G., tenor and violinist; and Cleveland, pianist. The group traveled throughout New England and the Middle West until 1859.

Cleveland Luca migrated to Liberia about 1860, and composed the national anthem of that country. He died there March 27, 1872.

An instrumentalist of this period, Henry F. Williams, was born in Boston, August 13, 1813. He possessed natural talents, played many instruments, and was engaged by P. S. Gilmore of the celebrated Gilmore's Band. He wrote many pieces which were published by Oliver Ditson from 1842 to 1866. Among his compositions, most of which were of a sentimental order, was an anthem, the authenticity of which was doubted by the noted pedagogue Lowell Mason. Finally admitting Williams was the composer, and impressed by his ability, Mason advised him to go to Liberia in order to win recognition, as he felt that race prejudice would deter him in America. This advice Williams refused to heed.

A well-remembered name is that of Justin Holland, born in 1819, the son of a farmer, Exum Holland, who made his home in Norfolk County, Virginia. At the age of 14 he came to Boston and located in Chelsea. He had shown marked musical gifts at the age of eight; so, having had no opportunity of furthering his love of music, he was overjoyed at the chance which came his way of taking guitar lessons under Simon Knaebel, a member of Kendall's Brass Band. He later took lessons with William Schubert, guitarist, and Pollock, flutist. In 1841, realizing the limitations of his general education, he went to Oberlin College.

In 1845, he located in Cleveland, Ohio. There he gave guitar lessons and studied French, Italian and Spanish, that he might have access to technical works on guitar playing, many of which were written in foreign languages. When living in Boston, he became entranced by the playing of Mariano Perez, a Spanish guitarist who was heard with a visiting company at the Lion Theatre, and he determined to learn for himself how to explain how certain effects were produced. Holland had not at that time access to many scientific works which treat the subject of acoustics, and so he wrote:

> I . . . thus discovered the true theory of the harmonic tones to be the vibrations of a single string in a number of equal sections, more or less, and all at the same time; and that their production was at the pleasure of the operator as he desired higher or lower tones. Having fully verified my discoveries, I then corrected the erroneous theory on this subject of the great guitarist, F. Sor.

Holland made many arrangements of standard pieces for solo guitar, and wrote more than 35 original works. His most important contribution is *Holland's Comprehensive Method for the Guitar,* which was published in 1874 by J. L. Peters of New York. In 1876, a revised edition, *Holland's Modern Method for the Guitar,* was published by Oliver Ditson, Boston. According to that house, the book offers to this day the favorite method of guitar playing.

From the first, the cause of good music and encouragement to trained Negro musicians came from the Negro church. In the East, the choir afforded an outlet both for trained singers and for organists, even though in most instances it was a labor of love. The pioneer work of the majority of instrumentalists and vocalists who aspired to a concert career was accomplished through church societies, which were always willing to arrange a concert, for a division of the profits. For many years the Negro church

remained the artist's most willing "manager."

Interest in vocal and instrumental ensembles grew. About 1872, the Colored Opera Company was formed in Washington, with John Esputa as musical director. The company appeared in Philadelphia on February 21, 1873, at Horticultural Hall, and was highly praised by the *Philadelphia Inquirer,* which said of their chorus, "Their singing is really unsurpassed by the finest choruses in the best companies." Other papers were equally impressed by the efforts of this little group of ambitious singers.

The Philharmonic Society of New York City, which was organized in 1876, had a junior division in which young people of musical taste could study and might take a test for admission to the senior section, which gave public performances. P. H. Loveridge was the society's conductor.

Musical New Orleans remembers with pride the Philharmonic Society which was in existence about that time. It was composed of a group of trained musicians under the direction of experienced conductors such as Constantin Deberque and Richard Lambert. The latter musician, a teacher of music, was the father of the talented Lambert brothers. The Philharmonic, an all-Negro group of instrumentalists, was organized for the study and presentation of the classics.

While meritorious concert performances were being given by trained Negro virtuosos before 1846, brass bands were also organized simultaneously with the growing musical associations. Many bands were the outgrowth of small orchestras. The most noted of these bands was Frank Johnson's band, which was organized by a man of that name in Philadelphia. As an orchestral and band conductor, he toured the United States with his own group from 1839 to 1841, played before Queen Victoria in 1841, and returned to continued popularity in this country. Johnson was a skillful performer on the bugle, besides playing many other instruments. He died in Philadelphia in 1846, and at his funeral, the silver bugle presented to to him by the English Queen was placed under his casket. The organization was continued under the leadership of Joseph G. Anderson, and the band was heard on tour until his death in 1874.

Certain cities tended to become popular as centers with Negroes prominent in music. Old programs of the year 1874 bear the names of the best-remembered pioneer musicians of Boston. At this time, the pianist Samuel W. Jamison was at the height of his popularity. Jamison was born in Washington, D.C., in 1855, and died in Boston in February, 1930. He began his studies in Boston at the age of 11, as the pupil of James M. Tracy and F. K. Boscovitz, a Hungarian pianist. He later studied under B. J. Lang, and had the distinction of playing with the Boston Symphony Orchestra. In 1876, he graduated from the New England Conservatory, but gave concerts a year earlier, when he received praise for his Chopin and Liszt interpretations. Jamison, who later devoted his time to teaching pianoforte, remained a brilliant pianist until his death.

Benjamin J. Janey, tenor, a private pupil of New England Conservatory professors, a flutist as well as a singer, was often heard in duets from the Italian operas with Nellie Brown and Fannie A. Washington.

James Caseras, pianist and organist, was one of the best organists in the East. His musical training was received abroad, before he came to this country from England, sometime before 1877.

Frederick Elliot Lewis, born in 1846, was a well-known musician of Boston. His father, of New England birth, was a performer on the flute, piano, cello and violin, while his mother was a choir singer. He took his first lessons in piano from his mother. At the age of about 12, he began to study the organ and

harmony, and continued his piano lessons under Rachel Washington. A most gifted and eager student, he afterwards studied other instruments under local teachers. In 1861, he made his debut as a violinist, in New Bedford.

His purpose in studying so many instruments was that he wished to be the better fitted to write orchestral and band music. Lewis was a member of the large orchestra that played at the World's Peace Jubilee held in Boston in 1872. From 1861 until 1878, he was engaged in arranging and composing music for piano, orchestra and band. His "Fantasia for Piano, Opus 3," is in the style of Gottschalk's pianoforte pieces. For some years he maintained a well-equipped studio and enjoyed the association of the prominent musicians of the city. He was a member of white music societies, one of which was the Haydn and Mozart Club of Chelsea, an instrumental group which he sometimes conducted as first violinist. He also enjoyed the esteem of the musicians Julius Eichberg, director of the Boston Conservatory (at that time), and P. S. Gilmore, the band director.

John T. Douglas, violinist, was born in New York City, in 1847. He studied in New York and in Europe, and is remembered as a devoted lover of music. He gave David Mannes (now a celebrated violinist of New York) his first violin lessons when he was a young lad without means. Mr. Mannes has not ignored this favor of his Negro teacher. Douglas was acquainted with several instruments, and was known as a fine guitarist as well as a proficient violinist. He composed many pieces for orchestra and for piano. Those that the author of this volume has examined are in the salon style of the Eighties. For some years, the musician traveled, and taught music in New York, where he died a few years ago. Like many ambitious musicians, he met with frustrations which saddened his later years.

Thomas J. Bowers

Elizabeth Taylor Greenfield

Justin Holland

Flora Batson

Madame Marie Selika

Sidney Woodward

A remarkable musical prodigy of the Eighties was Thomas Greene Bethune, known as Blind Tom. He was born without sight, in Columbus, Georgia, in 1844, and was of unmixed blood. He possessed absolute pitch, an unerring ear and a marvelous memory. He was said to have a repertoire of 5,000 pieces, which he had learned by having them played to him. He traveled extensively and created a stir in America and in Europe.

Of those especially gifted persons whose contribution was of real musical value to the race, we find two sisters, Anna Madah and Emma Louise Hyers, who at the ages of seven and nine years showed a predilection for music to such a degree that they were placed under a German instructor in Sacramento, California, the city of their birth. They were students of voice and piano, and of languages. Later they received instruction from Josephine d'Ormy. Their parents refused to allow them to appear in public until their debut on April 22, 1867, when they were presented before an audience of 800 at the Metropolitan Theatre in Sacramento.

Their father, who seems to have shown considerable wisdom in furthering his talented daughters' careers, insisted upon further study before allowing them to undertake an extended tour. The western press, particularly the daily papers of Missouri, Illinois and Ohio, praised the singers widely in reviews. Anna's singing of E flat above the staff with the greatest ease, and her bird-like trills, caused her to be likened to Jenny Lind, while Emma's voice was said to be one of remarkable quality, and richness "rarely heard."

The father, who traveled with the sisters, engaged Wallace King of Camden, New Jersey, who was the rising tenor of the day, and John Luca, bass-baritone of New Haven, as assistant artists. Concerts were given at the Young Men's Christian Association hall in Brooklyn, New York, and at Steinway Hall in New York City.

The sisters lived in Boston for some time, in order to continue their training, after which they traveled in New England, where they performed to crowded houses.

About 1877 and 1878, the Misses Hyers widened their activities by taking part in a drama, *Out of Bondage,* a play in four acts written expressly for them by a white writer, Joseph B. Bradford of Boston. Samuel Lucas was a member of this company when they toured throughout the West in 1878.

Emma Louise Hyers died some years ago. Anna Madah Hyers became the wife of Dr. Fletcher of Sacramento. Visiting California in December, 1920, the author had an opportunity to call on Mrs. Fletcher. In the autumn of her life, she lived quietly, still actively interested in art music, especially as it pertained to the church. She was most gracious in showing souvenirs of her happy career.

Nellie E. Brown (Mitchell), soprano, who was born in Dover, New Hampshire, early came under the tutelage of Miss Caroline Bracket, a vocal teacher of Dover, who advised her to prepare for a public career. In 1865, she began her lifetime service as a church singer, as a member of the Free Will Baptist Church (white) of Dover. In November, 1872, the young soprano was engaged as soloist of Grace Church, Haverhill, Massachusetts. After four years as salaried singer, she resigned to accept an engagement as director of the choir of the new Methodist Episcopal church in her native city. Since 1874, she had commuted between the two cities in order to sing leading soprano parts in the latter choir. Before this, she had come regularly to Boston to study at the New England Conservatory; her teachers included Madame J. Rametti and Professor O'Neill. In November, 1874, she sang in Steinway Hall, New York City, with much success. She appeared in concerts from Canada to Washington, D.C.

The New York papers spoke of her beauty of voice and "rare charm of manners." During the year of 1876, she was actively engaged in organizing groups of young people for musical presentations.

During her career, Nellie Brown had the distinction of being the leading soprano of four prominent white churches in Boston, among which were the Winthrop Street Church, Roxbury, and the Bromfield Street Church. She married Lieutenant Charles L. Mitchell, of the famous Negro regiment, the Fifty-fifth Massachusetts. After retiring from the concert stage, she devoted her time to teaching, and singing at local affairs. While her recognition was first gained as a singer of French songs and Italian operatic arias, she did the old Scotch and Irish songs particularly well. Her later reputation was sustained by her charming singing of ballads. Until her death, which occurred in Boston in January, 1924, Nellie Brown Mitchell remained willing to encourage younger musicians.

Flora Batson was a younger singer, who was born in Providence, Rhode Island, in 1870. She possessed a remarkable soprano voice of great range as well as sweetness. As a ballad singer, she traveled throughout the United States, in Europe, Australia and New Zealand, and touched African soil. In 1887, she organized a concert company, and on March 21 of that year, she was heard and acclaimed at Music Hall, Boston, after which she became popular on tours. At the height of her career, she married Mr. Bergen, a white business man, who for some time was her manager. She died suddenly in Philadelphia, on December 2, 1906.

\* \* \* \* \* \*

The greatest of the Negro prima donnas of yesteryear was Madame Marie Selika (Mrs. Sampson Williams). About 1879, while visiting in San Francisco, California, Mrs. Fran-

ces Bailey Gaskin heard the young soprano sing, and, recognizing the exceptional quality of her voice, persuaded her to come to Boston. This she did, and while making her home with Mrs. Gaskin's mother, Mrs. Williams continued her studies and became proficient in German, French and Italian.

In 1880, Mrs. Williams gave concerts in various centers, and under the efficient management of Lieutenant Dupree, who aided and encouraged many young struggling Negro artists, she created a furore with her marvelous coloratura voice. For a stage name she took that of Selika, the heroine of Meyerbeer's opera L'Africaine. A fine testimonial concert was arranged for her by John Boyle O'Reilly, a friend of Mrs. Gaskin's father.

Soon afterwards, Madame Selika visited Europe with her husband, who was an aspiring baritone singer known as Viloski. She achieved immediate success. The Paris paper Le Figaro said:

> Madame Selika sang in great style. She has a very strong voice, of depth and compass, rising with perfect ease from C to C, and she trills like a feathered songster. Her range is marvelous and her execution and style of rendition show perfect cultivation. Her "Echo Song" cannot be surpassed. It was beyond any criticism. It was an artistic triumph.

Of her appearance in Berlin, the Tagblatt reviewer wrote:

> The concert by Madame Selika was given before a well filled house, and this distinguished artist gave us a genuine pleasure. Madame Selika, with her singing, roused the audience to the highest pitch of enthusiasm, and after her first aria, she was twice recalled, and could quiet the wild applause only by rendering a selection with orchestral accompaniment. Of this wonderful singer we can only say that she is endowed with a voice of surpassing sweetness and extraordinary compass. With her pure tones, her wonderful trills and roulades, her correct rendering of the most difficult intervals, she not only gains the admiration of amateurs but also that of professional musicians and critics.

After some years of successful concertizing,

Madame Selika and her husband located in Philadelphia. After Mr. Williams' death, which occurred in Philadelphia about 15 years ago, his devoted wife went to New York City, where she has for the past few years been a teacher of voice at the Martin-Smith School of Music in Harlem.

Frederick P. White, a cultivated musician of Boston, was born in Providence, Rhode Island. Among his instructors was the noted teacher, B. J. Lang. White began his career as accompanist for Madame Selika, and has become one of the best accompanists of recent years. On one occasion, when Madame Selika's trunk and box of music had been delayed, on concert tour, White played the entire program of operatic arias and songs, without notes. His talent embraced more than a gift of good memory, as can be seen from later criticisms. For over 25 years, he was organist at the (white) Methodist Episcopal church in Charlestown, Massachusetts. He is now organist and teacher of piano in Boston.

\*   \*   \*   \*   \*   \*

William H. Bush, organist, was born in New London, Connecticut, on February 15, 1861. He was the son of a mechanic, Aaron Bush, and a musical mother who was encouraged to give her son lessons under Charles B. Jennings of New London. When a young man, he was given cast-off parts of old organs by a Negro organ builder, Preston Hamilton, and made a pipe organ for himself. When 18 years of age, he was permitted to use the organ of the (white) First Congregational Church, and until his 23rd year he studied organ, English and German under private instructors. An opportunity to prove his ability as an organist came when Jennings, because of an injured hand, was unable to play, and William Bush was called in to take the place of his teacher as church organist. After six months, he was engaged by the (white) Methodist church at a

salary of $150 a year. Continuing to perfect himself in the study of composition and musical theory, as well as organ, he finally became organist at the Second Congregational Church, the richest in the city.

Bush went weekly to New York for study with Dr. Samuel Warren, and, in 1887, gave his first recital at Grace Church, New York. With the assistance of Dr. Warren, he gave annual concerts for 35 years. Bush was made chorister as well as organist at the Congregational church. In 1904, he was chosen as one of the musicians to represent his state at the St. Louis Exposition, where he played before an audience of 5,000 persons. The organist is a lover of Bach. As a teacher he has been most successful. He is a member of the American Guild of Organists.

M. Hamilton Hodges, baritone, of Boston, possessed fine natural talent. He joined the Stewart Concert Company and traveled extensively through the Middle West. He later joined the McAdoo Jubilee Singers, whose leader had a fine bass voice. After traveling abroad with this company, he settled in Auckland, New Zealand, in 1896, and there he became prominent as a concert singer and teacher of voice.

In 1898, Hodges returned to this country on a visit and gave many recitals in and about Boston. Here he won favorable reviews from the distinguished music critic Philip Hale, of the *Boston Herald*, and other reviewers of note. He was assisted by Frederick P. White, accompanist. The excellence of the two artists may be comprehended in this review by H. T. Parker, musical editor, which appeared in the Boston *Evening Transcript* of January 26, 1910:

> In a group of songs by Schubert, two by Strauss and Von Fielitz, a group of French songs by Masse, Bemberg and Godard, and English songs by Mallinson and Wallace, Mr. Hodges used a baritone voice of great richness, full of subtle inflections, full of adjustments of tone to the mood of the songs, and with reserves of great power and sonority. When he used the

soft tones of his middle register, as he was invited to do by several of the lighter songs, it was without a hint of monotony. He gave his *sotto* voice as varied a color as his full voice. This effect brought to Mallinson's song "Four by the Clock" the vague and eerie quiet of the moments that precede the dawn, and left in due prominence the rhythm of the pianoforte accompaniment, which marches to the regularity of the pendulum's swing or the sifting of sands in the hour glass.

Two others of the group of songs by Mallinson compelled admiration for their music, for the singing and for the work of the accompanist. Mr. Frederick P. White made the accompaniment what it rarely is in a recital of any kind—an integral part of the performance.

The year 1912 found Mr. Hodges in New Zealand. In December of that year, he sang the part of Mephistopheles in a performance of Gounod's *Faust,* given in oratorio form by the noted Wellington Musical Union. His services were in demand as an oratorio singer in many parts of the country. In 1913, he was engaged to sing in the *Messiah,* which was produced by the Finding Choral Society, and in Coleridge-Taylor's *A Tale of Old Japan,* which was given by the Wellington Royal Choral Society.

In February, 1913, he gave exacting programs with such excellence that the New Zealand *Free Lance* said of his recitals:

> Mr. Hodges is helping to raise the standard of musical taste in this community, for he includes nothing tawdry in his program. He has a cultured, artistic judgment, and as he is always on the alert for new music of a high standard, we are indebted to him for a knowledge of many fine songs.

In 1925, Mr. Hodges returned to Boston, where he died in 1928, at the age of 59.

\* \* \* \* \* \*

Sidney Woodward was one of the finest tenors that the race has produced. He was born on a Georgia plantation, October 16, 1860. Early orphaned, he encountered many hardships while working his way through school. In 1889, with the aid of Miss Clark, a student of Frank E. Morse of Bos-

ton, who heard the young man sing in Peoria, Illinois, he went to Boston and became a pupil of Mr. Morse and later of Madame Edna Hill. About 1890, Woodward undertook an extensive Southern concert tour in order to add to his means so that he might prolong his vocal studies. In Galveston, Texas, his talent and ambition won the interest of the author's father, Norris Wright Cuney, Collector of Customs, who, giving him substantial aid and encouragement, enabled the singer to continue his travels in the state after his Galveston concert.

In Boston, Woodward's first public appearances were so successful that he was engaged as first soloist at the People's Baptist Church. Later he accepted a position at another white church, the Second Congregational Church, where he remained for five years at a salary of $500 a year. He continued his vocal studies and gave a recital at Chickering Hall on February 15, 1893. Philip Hale, writing of him in the *Boston Journal,* said, "He sings as a rule with ease, his tones are pure and well sustained, his attack is decisive, and he does not abuse the portamento; he knows the meaning of the word legato, he phrases intelligently and holds himself in control, and his enunciation is admirable."

In 1892, Woodward's beautiful voice won him the friendship of Madame Nordica, who became his close friend and helped him to rise to higher levels. Between 1897 and 1900, after Woodward had joined a musical comedy company, John W. Isham's *Oriental America,* in order to reach England, he was engaged in singing in England, Ireland, Scotland, Wales, Germany, Austria, Holland, Belgium and Russia. In England, he sang a number of times at the garden parties given at Buckingham Palace. After the singer's return to the United States, he served as a teacher of voice at the Florida Baptist Academy in Jacksonville, Clark University in Nashville and the Music School Settlement in New York City. During this last period, he gave a concert in Carnegie Hall, New York, in celebration of his 31st anniversary as a singer. He died February 13, 1924.

Some years ago, attention was called to an exceptional and beautiful lyric soprano voice, heard at Hammerstein's Roof Garden in New York City. It was the voice of Rachel Walker, who went to Europe, where she met with signal success. She won the notice of Madame Marchesi, the teacher of voice, and, while in London, became a pupil of Sir Henry J. Wood. After a concert in Paris, the correspondent of that city for the New York *Journal* wrote:

> Her voice is one to catch the ear and hold it. Pure, clear, sympathetic, it unites the lyric qualities of the soprano with the passion and power of the dramatic soprano. . . . Her tones are rich and melodious, and the difficult aria brought out the beautiful cultivation of the voice. In the scene and prayer from *Iphigenia*, she stood transfixed into the part she acted. Of soulful face and fine physique, she might well be taken for the passion-stirred heroine of Gluck's masterpiece.

While abroad, Miss Walker sang before Her Majesty the Queen of Spain; the Duchess of Albany; Her Royal Highness, the Princess of Saxe-Coburg and Gotha; and the Gaekwar of Baroda. She received compliments from the great modern French composers, Massenet and Saint-Saëns. She returned to America in 1914, at the threatened outbreak of the war. During the seasons of 1914–16, she sang in many Northern cities in concerts and in Negro musical festivals. Since 1924, she has lived quietly in her native city of Cleveland, Ohio.

The foregoing survey is by no means a complete record of the many Negro men and women who were active in the field of music in the pioneer period. We can but recognize that from 1840 to 1880, within 40 years, there arose in this country a considerable number of Negroes who were not only ambitious and earnest, but who possessed talent befitting their desires and were able to attract the attention of the thoughtful and intelligent people of America.

\* \* \* \* \* \*

The Negro musicians of New Orleans deserve here a little more than general treatment. They lived and labored in a different environment from that of any other musical group in this country. Many of them were of French extraction. A goodly number, having parents of wealth, were sent to Paris to complete their education. For these very reasons they have been misunderstood. One marvels at the tendency, now evident, to describe these people as "Negro Creole." To call their music "Negro Creole" is absolutely incorrect and shows a woeful ignorance of the history of that particular section—a distortion of facts which even prejudice does not excuse.

An important name of the early school of musicians of New Orleans, from 1840 to 1879, is that of Lambert. Richard Lambert, a member of a talented family of seven, was a teacher of music in Louisiana. His son, Lucien, who was born about 1828, received his first instruction in New Orleans, where he became known as a pianist, teacher and composer. Unhappy under Southern racial prejudice, he went to Paris, where he continued his studies. He was called to Brazil to be the chief musician to the court of Dom Pedro. When about 50 years of age, he entered the piano manufacturing business in that country. A list of his compositions includes: "La Brésiliana," "L'Américaine," "Paris Vienne," "Le Niagara," "La Juive," "Le Départ du Conscrit."

Sidney, another son of Richard Lambert, was also a brilliant pianist, who wrote for the piano and other instruments. For his method of pianoforte study, he was decorated by the King of Portugal and called to that country to be a musician at court. He later became a teacher in Paris, where he added to his list of compositions, which includes: "Murmures du Soir," "Anna Bolena," "L'Africaine" and "Transports Joyeux."

One of the most widely known musicians of that section was Edmund Dédé, who was born of free parents in New Orleans in 1829. They had migrated from the French West Indies. He, however, seems not to have been of mixed blood. He learned to play the cornet, then studied the violin under a noted Negro violinist, and continued his studies with L. Gabici, director of the orchestra of the old St. Charles Theatre. In 1848, his father sent him to Mexico in order to complete his musical education. In 1857, he went first to England and then to Paris, where he entered the Conservatory. There he became a pupil of Halévy and Alard and won a number of medals.

For many years Dédé was the director of the orchestra of L'Alcazar in Bordeaux. In 1894, he returned to this country to visit relatives. The steamer on which he was sailing was wrecked at sea, and with other passengers he was taken aboard a Texas coal steamer and landed at Galveston. He remained there for two months and was acclaimed by the best musicians of that section, both white and black. The author's parents, ever appreciative of musical talent, entertained him. After giving many concerts, Dédé went to New Orleans, where he received a royal welcome.

After playing in many cities, as far north as Chicago, he went back to France, never to return. Shortly before her death in 1920, Madame Erado, an aunt of Dédé, sent the author the words of a song which he had written as his farewell. The burden of the poem was his return to France:

> My adopted mother, France, who so often has consoled me—Eternal is my destiny to live far from my native country, the land of my birth; but the prejudice that pursues, it is implacable —my country which refuses my love, it is the land of my birth.

Dédé died in Paris in 1903. He had been married for some years to a French lady, and a son, George, is said to have survived him. The violinist-composer's works include *Les Faux Mandarins* and *La Sensitive,* played by many orchestras, "Le Palmier Overture" and a number of songs. His last composition was an opera in four acts, called *Sultan d'Ispahan.* A dramatic aria from this work, "Le Serment de l'Arabe," was revived by the concert singer William Richardson, as an example of art music written by an early Negro composer. It is written in the style of Verdi and the Italian school.

—1936

Betty Allen, mezzo-soprano

## The Current Scene

### by Raoul Abdul

In THE United States today hundreds of composers are writing serious music. There is hardly a symphonic concert which does not include a new work. But one seldom encounters the name of a Negro composer. When such a rare occasion takes place, it is usually an opus by Ulysses Kay. His *Sinfonia in E* has been performed by the Cleveland Orchestra under George Szell; *Of New Horizons,* by the New York Philharmonic under Thor Johnson; and *Serenade for Orchestra,* by the Louisville Orchestra.

Another composer to gain high acclaim is Howard Swanson, whose *Short Symphony* was played by the New York Philharmonic under Dimitri Mitropoulos and won a New York Music Critics' Circle Award. Hale Smith's *Contours* was premiered by the Louisville Orchestra and later performed by the Cleveland Orchestra, the Symphony of the New World (New York) and the Cincinnati Orchestra. His *Music for Harp and Orchestra* was commissioned and played by the Symphony of the New World.

Under the direction of Newell Jenkins, Julia Perry's *Stabat Mater* was performed by Clarion Concerts (New York), with mezzo-soprano Betty Allen. Coleridge-Taylor Perkinson's *Concerto for Viola and Orchestra* was performed at Philharmonic Hall under the auspices of the National Association of Negro Musicians, with Selwart Clarke as soloist. John Carter's *Requiem Seditiosam,* dedicated to the memory of Medgar Evers, was premiered by the Symphony of the New World.

Without question, the leading Negro concert singers today are soprano Adele Addison, mezzo-soprano Shirley Verrett, mezzo-soprano Betty Allen and baritone William Warfield. The spectacular success of pianist André Watts opened heretofore closed doors to Negro instrumentalists. Some years before, Natalie Hinderas became the first Negro pianist to join the roster of a major management—Columbia Artists. Two other highly gifted pianists, Armenta Adams and Eugene Haynes, are now with major concert managements. Other instrumentalists who are building major careers are cellist Kermit Moore, violinist Sanford Allen, flutist Harold Jones and violist Selwart Clarke. In the field of conducting, Dean Dixon has an international reputation, Everett Lee is permanent conductor of an orchestra in Sweden and Henry Lewis was named musical director of the New Jersey Symphony.

—1971

Henry Lewis, conductor

Coleridge-Taylor Perkinson, composer

Natalie Hinderas, pianist

Margaret Bonds as guest soloist with the Women's Symphony
Orchestra in 1934, in a program devoted to women in music.
Her selection was Florence Price's *Concerto in F Minor*.

# A Reminiscence

by Margaret Bonds

ABBIE MITCHELL, whose mother was a Negro and whose father was a Jew, was one of the great singers of her day. During my late teens it became my good fortune to become closely associated with her. Though she sang Schubert's "Erl King," and all of the German Lieder, and the art songs of Debussy and Fauré, in an indescribably beautiful manner, she was equally devoted to the music of the American Negro. Often when I would spend the day with her, she would say to me, "Let us go excursioning." Out of her vast library of vocal literature would come volume after volume of a cross section of the world's great songs. Since Abbie Mitchell was a fine actress as well as a fine singer, she was a great interpreter and extremely word conscious.

From her I learned the importance of the marriage between words and music which is demanded if one is to have a song of any consequence.

During one of these daily "excursions," I was introduced to a song of Harry T. Burleigh (a composer of African descent). The name of the song is "Ethiopia Saluting the Colors." The poem of Walt Whitman tells of a black slave woman watching a United States army passing in review. (I believe it was General Grant's army.) The melody of the song is in the minor mode, and, although Burleigh did not actually use a spiritual melody, the idiom is unmistakably

Negroid—simple, minor and syncopated. The accompaniment is a steady four to the bar, representing the marching feet of the army.

I also learned during this time a song cycle of Burleigh's, the *Saracen Songs,* with poetry by Fred G. Bowles. In one of these songs, "Ahmed's Farewell," Burleigh used the spiritual theme "Somebody's Knocking at Your Door." I doubt that any music historian has ever written about this experiment, and I wouldn't be surprised if, had Negroes themselves realized that Burleigh had used a Negro spiritual melody as a principal theme of a love song, they would have severely attacked him for having desecrated a spiritual.

In my teens and highly impressionable, I began unconsciously to copy Harry T. Burleigh. In a basement of the Evanston Public Library, I found the works of a poet named Langston Hughes. I was intrigued by his first published poem, "The Negro Speaks of Rivers." I myself had never suffered any feelings of inferiority because I am a Negro, and I had always felt a strong identification with Africa, but now here was a poem which said so many different things I had known and was not able to verbally express. Burleigh's "Ethopia Saluting the Colors" became Margaret Bonds's "The Negro Speaks of Rivers."

Thirty years ago a teacher of mine objected to the music. It was "too far out," then, not only because it had a Negro spiritual flavor, but because, in the last part of the song, in which the poet speaks of America, it becomes very "jazzy." My teacher said that maybe it would be all right if I took out those "jazzy augmented chords."

I changed not a note, because God had "gotten at me" for several hours during the song's creation, and I believed that I had recorded what He wanted me to record.

I gave the song to Marian Anderson. She was very polite, but I think the "jazzy augmented chords" frightened her. She never sang the setting I did but later did a more sombre one of Howard Swanson's.

Nadia Boulanger liked "The Negro Speaks of Rivers." She liked all of my music, though in a passage of about 16 bars in a spiritual setting she asked me, "Why did you write that, Margaret? Puccini has written it already." I was perturbed at the time, but later I came to realize that most composers at one time or another reflect their friends.

Incidentally, Boulanger refused to take me as a student. She said that I "had something" but she didn't quite understand what to do with it. She added, however, that whatever it was I was doing "felt right to her," and that I should continue to do it, but I shouldn't study with anyone, and I certainly should never study fugue. Recently I had to experiment further, so I wrote a fugue in the Negro idiom in a choral work.

With Abbie Mitchell, then, I had close analysis of the works of all the composers, and from my mother, a church organist, Estella C. Bonds, I had actual physical contact with all the living composers of African descent. My mother had a collector's nose for anything that was artistic, and, a true woman of God, she lived the Sermon on the Mount. Her loaves and fish fed a multitude of pianists, singers, violinists and composers, and those who were not in need of material food came for spiritual food. Under

her wings many a musician trusted, and she was my link with the Lord. Many a time when I would compete in a contest I'd say, "Oh, God, please let me win. I know I'm not much good, but my mother is so good; please good God, let me win for her." And generally I won.

I was sent to study with the Negro composers William L. Dawson and Florence Price. (You know Miss Price from "My Soul's Been Anchored in the Lord.") At one point Miss Price was in such bad financial shape that my mother moved her into our house with her two children in order to relieve her mind of material considerations. Then we all prayed, and Florence won $500 for a symphony (awarded by the Wanamaker Foundation). Our prayers were powerful, because Florence also won $250 for a piano sonata, and I won $250 for an art song.

During the cold winter nights in Chicago, we used to sit around a large table in our kitchen—manuscript paper strewn around, Florence and I extracting parts for some contest deadline. We were a God-loving people, and, when we were pushed for time, every brown-skinned musician in Chicago who could write a note, would "jump-to" and help Florence meet her deadline. She insisted I would never write good orchestration—something that I feel I have disproved.

Our collective security stretched out a hand to visiting artists, and when composers like Will Marion Cook had an opportunity to present a Negro choir on NBC, I was sent to extract all of his choral parts, which, incidentally, he changed daily. Even now, when I write something for a choir and it's jazzy and bluesy and spiritual and Tchaikowsky all rolled up into one, I laugh to myself, "That is Will Marion Cook." No wonder Boulanger didn't quite understand what my music is all about.

The "so-called Negro" in America today is a marginal person. He is "neither white nor black." He is a Judeo-Christian by religion. Most times his blood is very mixed. His influences, if he is educated, are mostly European. He uses European techniques to express his talents. What other techniques could he possibly know?

In these few days since slavery is over, Negro America has given some fine composers. A few of them are Will Marion Cook; R. Nathaniel Dett; Nora Holt (founder of NANM); Florence B. Price; Camille Nickerson; John Work; William Grant Still; Hall Johnson; William L. Dawson; Jester Hairston; Clarence Cameron White; and Harry T. Burleigh. Their works range from settings of spirituals through art songs, ballets, cantatas, organ works, violin concerti, piano sonatas, symphonies and even operas.

—1967

Margaret Bonds

Marian Anderson sings "The Star-Spangled Banner" at the dedication,
on January 6, 1943, of a mural commemorating her free public concert
on the steps of the Lincoln Memorial, Easter Sunday, 1939.

# Elective Affinities: American Negro Singers and German Lieder

by Richard Plunt

OVER A hundred years ago, the great German writer Johann Wolfgang von Goethe published a novel that caused a scandal. His *Elective Affinities* exposed the secret thoughts of two married couples, each of whom was irresistibly attracted to a member of the other marriage. Using a term from chemistry, Goethe described two people whose minds and souls take to each other in a manner similar to certain substances which naturally and easily merge into new compounds. Nature, Goethe hinted, seems to have created some elements destined to be united with other elements and to bring forth a new substance. The hero and heroine of Goethe's tragic novel have no choice: their chemical affinities were predestined, and each would destroy his best qualities if he resisted the union with the other ego.

For a long time, observers of the musical scene have noticed how certain interpreters possess affinities to certain compositions, composers or types of music. In contrast to Goethe's blueprint, the consequences of this relationship are rather auspicious for all involved. They benefit the work of art, the interpreter, and, in the end, the public, participating in that nearly indefinable union which happens during a meaningful concert.

At this point, I hope I will be permitted to insert a few personal remarks in order to throw some light on the observations I have to make. For over 20 years, I have reviewed the American musical scene for German and Swiss papers and radio stations. The German radio outfits, in contrast to most American networks, faithfully report most American artistic events: if a new soprano makes her debut in San Francisco, if a far-out play has its première in a small Off-Broadway theatre, these outfits have a man on the spot. European listeners seem to manifest a stronger interest in everything concerning the arts than do American listeners. My own experience with colored singers, however, goes back to my youth in Germany when, as a freshman in college, I went to hear an unknown American artist, a woman presenting a program of German Lieder and American spirituals. When she walked on stage, the audience froze: here stood a stately Negro woman, tall and still. We had never heard a Negro singer—and, besides, she ventured to perform our beloved classics: Schubert, Schumann, Brahms. After the second or third song, however, the mood changed radically, as though clouds had been swept away by a gentle wind. The warm, powerful contralto filled the huge hall without effort; the musical phrases were timed to perfection. Nothing was rushed, nothing was done for effect alone; Schubert, Schumann and Brahms were speaking through her.

But there was more to stun the audience. The German words came through in flawless clarity. Most Americans get into trouble with a few devilish German vowels and consonants.

Here, there occurred no slurring of R's, no misshapen A's and O's. At the end of the first section, the performer sang Schubert's famous *Death and the Maiden*. It demands a flow of very low notes, sustained over a long stretch without a single interruption for breathing. Many singers cheat a little and take it a half note higher than the original. But here it was done as the composer had intended it: not only did this young colored singer from America command an inexhaustible supply of breath; those low, gentle notes floated through our old Victorian *Konzert Halle* like something produced by a true church organ. The audience, the rather stiff, reticent German audience, went wild. And there, bowing slightly to the roar of approval, stood Marian Anderson.

"As Schubert had intended it": this will furnish a further guidepost. A long time after this memorable recital, I bought Miss Anderson's recordings and listened to her Schubert, Mahler, Brahms, etc. At that time, I did not appreciate spirituals. My English was still too poor. Besides, the texture and mood of the spirituals, and above all their religious fervor, were alien to me. But Miss Anderson interpreted Schubert in such a manner that the concept of many native German singers appeared superficial in comparison. What Miss Anderson had caught and projected was a deeply ingrained sadness, a knowledge that life is a short procession of vanities, in which our most passionate longings can never be fulfilled. There exists, even in some of the light-hearted romantic Lieder, a profound melancholy, a biting feeling of isolation, of being shut off from the happier concerns of everyday life, of being different from those around us.

Number 20 in Schubert's cycle *The Winter Journey* is titled "The Guidepost." For the composer, the guidepost signals only in the direction of isolation, sadness and death: "Why forsake the beaten highways/Where the other travelers go?/Where to seek my hidden byways,/Through untrodden mountain snow?" The traveler goes on to explain why he has to shun people, why life appears like a vast desert. While the other guideposts for the everyday travelers point towards the bustling cities, his guidepost points its finger in the direction of darkness and solitude. One might say that this song, written by a young German composer in the early nineteenth century, is a sort of blues. It lays bare emotions like those embodied in numerous spirituals, blues and other songs created and performed by American Negroes. Perhaps this striking affinity came into existence because the German lyricists and composers of certain periods felt as unfulfilled in their society as did the Negroes in America. And so, both groups turned inward, so to speak. Of course a spiritual owes more to church music than to the German Lied, but the underlying moods are so similar that we can speak of elective affinities.

People shut out from the mainstream of their nation often find consolation in nature, and escape into the realms of fantasy and poetry. Here again, the poetry of America's Negro songwriters and the poetic style of German romantic vocal music display so many similarities that they can't be accidental. Their basic mood of sadness, alienation, helplessness before hostile ministries of power, lasts from the early products of Schubert to those of Gustav Mahler, who died in 1911. Mahler's two cycles, *Songs of a Wayfarer* and *Songs on the Death of Children,* might be called German spirituals. Both share a feeling of loss, of a despair so beyond words that only music can express it. And both, the often articulate German lyricists and the less trained colored workers, preachers, farmhands who produced the words, possessed the gift of conveying everyday life in poetic terms, of being close to nature—to the fields, the winds, the rivers; these bestowed their bless-

Dorothy Maynor

Roland Hayes

Adele Addison

Shirley Verrett

ings on everyone regardless of station or color, and they never betrayed you, because they were more constant than humans.

I also believe that some American Negro artists who don't feel at home in our Anglo-Saxon business civilization have unconsciously developed a capacity for appreciating, and entering into, alien cultures, alien languages. I have watched this as a reviewer for many years. I still have no facts to prove it scientifically—but just as Leontyne Price succeeded in making the pulsing vitality of Verdi her own, in flawless Italian, so did Marian Anderson capture the poetic melancholy of the German Lied. The rhythmically obsessive music of Spain, with its undercurrent of threat and splendor, can be felt as much in the rendering of De Falla's *El Amor Brujo* by the American Negro mezzo-soprano Shirley Verrett as in the version presented by Victoria de Los Angeles, a native of Spain. To me, however, the most striking affinity remains that between the German romantic Lied and the American colored singer—from the earlier days of Roland Hayes, Dorothy Maynor, Paul Robeson and Marian Anderson, to the prominent performers of today, such as Adele Addison, Shirley Verrett, William Warfield and the young tenor George Shirley.

It goes without saying that our contemporary singers are also at home in music of another character, that of Mozart and Handel and the French art songs of Duparc and Fauré. Though my theory does not apply here, I believe there exist other, equally complex, chains of reasoning which would furnish explanations. However, I leave this to future researchers, musicologists and psychologists. To me, the German Lied demands more than the dazzling technique, the sense of style asked for by Mozart, Handel and the French: it has to be felt from the heart; its deepest layer must be understood, caught and projected from a basement of the unconscious— and here the American Negro singers and the German romantic composers reveal that rare and stunning elective affinity which makes one the fated partner of the other.

—1967

# The African Heritage

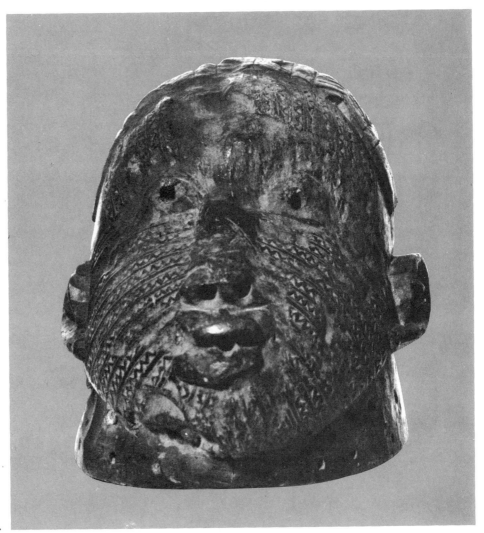

Yoruba mask. Ife, Nigeria.

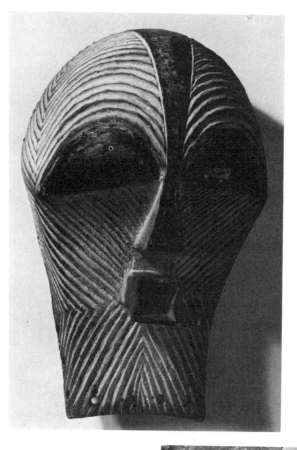

Basonge mask. Belgian Congo.

Pablo Picasso. "Les Demoiselles d'Avignon."
Oil. 1907. Museum of Modern Art, New York.
In the early 1900's, several French painters
became interested in African art. Though not
among the first to "discover" this art, Picasso was
the first to absorb into his work its subjective
approach—its portrayal of objects as the mind
conceives of them, not as the eye sees them.
The two figures on the right in this painting
postdate the rest of the work and were, in part,
almost certainly the fruits of Picasso's own
"discovery" of African sculpture. "Les
Demoiselles d'Avignon" was followed by
further experiments of Picasso's along similar
lines—experiments which led to the Cubist
movement, and which radically influenced the
course of twentieth-century art.

# Primitive Negro Sculpture and Its Influence on Modern Civilization

by Albert C. Barnes

PRIMITIVE Negro sculpture consists of idols made to be worshipped and of masks designed for use in heathen rites. The date of its origin is not known, although there are good reasons to believe that it goes back to the times of the ancient Greeks and Egyptians.

Twenty years ago, primitive African sculpture was a mere curiosity, of interest only to the anthropologist and ethnologist. Today its best examples are recognized by connoisseurs to be equal in artistic value to the great Greek, Egyptian and Chinese sculpture, and quite as difficult to obtain. People who saw the birth of the vital era in art, which began about two decades ago, were profoundly astonished to realize that its source of inspiration was the work of a race that was for centuries condemned to a servile status. Nothing could have seemed more unbelievable than that these idols and masks of the ancient Africans should have been responsible for the creative work in painting, music, sculpture and literature which has moved the whole cultured world so deeply during the past 20 years. Just at the moment when the art values of Negro sculpture had been discovered, contemporary European art seemed suddenly to have lost its creative powers. Art threatened to decline into a period of academicism and eclecticism like that which occurred in Italy in the sixteenth and seventeenth centuries. At that critical moment, the treasures of Negro sculpture were recaptured from the anthropologist and the antiquarian, and served as a new impetus toward creative work in plastic art, in music and in poetry in European and American civilization.

Primitive Negro sculpture was not the work of savages, for only a small part of the population of Africa was in a savage state. The sculpture was the manifestation of a life which was a stable organization, thoroughly adjusted to its surroundings, and was therefore able to find natural, authentic expression. Before the coming of the Portuguese into central Africa, in the sixteenth century, the Negroes had established a mode of life in harmony with their environment and congenial to their temperament. Their material wants were slight, food was abundant and they required little clothing and shelter. As they had no commerce with the world at large, they were free from economic pressure. Hence they had ample leisure for the free exercise of their powers, and especially of their vivid and dramatic religious instinct, enriched by their luxuriant imaginaton. Although they lacked scientific conceptions and their religious rites were consequently full of superstition, the very naïveté of their religion made it more colorful and dramatic. It was a religion into which they could pour all their instincts—their fondness for music, for the dance, for histrionics, for ceremony, in general for participation in a natural, spontaneous, rhythmic group-activity.

Guro mask. Ivory Coast.

Mossi mask. French Sudan.

Statuette of a priest or monk. Congo. Seventeenth century.

Into this paradise came the Europeans in the early sixteenth century, and very soon the natural life of the Negro was at an end. The material powers and prestige of the white race deprived the Negroes of their freedom, their self-confidence and their initiative. Reduced to a status of inferiority, they sought to imitate the Europeans, and their native art died.

What is there in these strange African carvings in wood, ivory and stone to justify the enthusiastic praise of modern critics, and what contributions to contemporary education and culture were inspired by them?

In any work of art, we must first of all realize what *not* to look for as well as what positive values to expect. Negro statues and masks express no ideals of physical beauty, nor of moral or intellectual character, and tell no interesting story. What they do possess instead of these extraneous kinds of appeal is *sculptural design.* And this design is a quality which we are apt not to see unless we are specially trained and are willing to put aside our usual ways of looking at a statue and learn instead to appreciate design.

What is meant by design in sculpture? Design is the essential characteristic of all works of art. It is achieved by taking certain basic themes or motifs, then repeating, varying, contrasting and interrelating them to form a unified, harmonious whole. For example, in music the composer's theme is certain melodic phrases and chord progressions; the painter takes lines, colors, spaces and areas of light and dark. In similar manner the sculptor uses grooves, ridges and contours of objects, surfaces of different curvature, angularity, texture and degree of smoothness, all of which he works into masses of different shapes, such as cylinders, spheres and the variations of these and other shapes. He selects a few particular forms which he varies and combines in countless different ways.

The repetition of similar lines, planes and masses gives an effect of *rhythmic sequence,* as of beats in music, which satisfies the instinctive craving for rhythm which all human beings possess innately. When a characteristic rhythm pervades the various parts of an object, we feel a *harmonious unity,* and this satisfies another universal, natural desire, that of order and equilibrium. But if the similarity of parts is too close, the design tends to become monotonous; consequently, an imaginative artist introduces unexpected and surprising *variations* and *contrasts,* but without destroying the sense of harmony.

Selection of certain aspects and elimination of others is the essence of all art, and a worker who merely copies nature, though he may astonish us with his technical skill, is more a counterfeiter than a creative artist. The sculptors of all the great past traditions departed from natural anatomical proportions in order to create the sculptural design which makes their statues works of art. In other words, the *distortion* which perplexes many observers in African art exists also in the statues of the ancient Greeks, Egyptians and Chinese. In Negro sculpture, however, the body is altered more freely and extensively, with the resulting achievement of a greater wealth of striking and different *rhythms* — just as the music of the Negro spirituals is infinitely richer in rhythms than European music. This rich and varied rhythmic harmony is what makes both authentic, natural forms of art that rank with the greatest achievements of the other civilizations of the past. Since these rhythms of Negro sculpture are composed of fully shaped masses as well as lines and surfaces, the typical Negro statue has a degree of vigorous *three-dimensional solidity* greater than that of any other sculpture.

The modern Negro's justifiable pride in his race, due largely to universal recognition of his musical accomplishment, has been powerfully fortified by the rediscovery of ancient

Negro sculpture and by the acknowledgment of the most important contemporary artists of the magnitude of their debt to it. It released them from the shackles of outworn traditions and gave a new stimulus to freedom of expression. It also revealed an unsuspected wealth of artistic endowments in the Negro race, a sense for the visible essentials of natural objects and an ability to arrange forms in varied, rhythmic, harmonious, moving designs which do not suffer by comparison with the most distinguished classic achievements of any of the other races.

It is no exaggeration to claim that the best of what has been developed in contemporary art during the past 20 years owes its origin to the inspiration of primitive Negro sculpture. In the painting and sculpture of the recognized leaders of our age—Picasso, Matisse, Modigliani, Lipchitz, Soutine and others—any trained observer can recognize the Negro motif. The music of the famous French group of composers known as The Six—Satie, Auric, Honegger, Milhaud, Poulenc and Tailleferre—is the ancient Negro spirit embodied in musical forms representative of the highest degree of musical culture and knowledge. Much of Stravinsky's best work belongs to the same category. Diaghilev, the director of the Russian ballet, fused the spirit of Negro sculpture with the essence of Russian music and dance and created some of the best pieces of the famous Russian ballet. The poetry and prose of Guillaume Apollinaire, Jean Cocteau, Max Jacob, Blaise Cendrars and Reverdy are likewise fundamentally Negro in emotional content and formal expression. The creations of the most artistic dressmaker of our age, Paul Poiret, of Paris, were inspired by his contact with Negro sculpture. Every informed visitor to the great Paris Exposition of 1925, Art Décoratif, was impressed with the predominance of the Negro motif in the really creative work of the decorators of all the nations represented at that exhibition. In Europe and America today, the posters that arrest the attention were unmistakably inspired by primitive Negro sculpture. All these great and widespread influences—in painting, sculpture, music, poetry, literature, decoration—are freely acknowledged by the creators of the worthwhile art of the past 20 years. They acknowledge also their great debt to Paul Guillaume, of Paris, who was the first to collect Negro sculpture and allow contemporary artists to study it.

Appreciation of this sculpture has been rare, and indeed the Negro spirituals were not properly valued until recently; but as this knowledge of the great art achievements of the Negro becomes more generally diffused, there is every reason to look for an abatement of both the superciliousness on the part of the white race and of the unhappy sense of inferiority in the Negro himself, which have been detrimental to the true welfare of both races.

—1928

Old wrought iron balconies of New Orleans.

# Negro's Art Lives in His Wrought Iron

WHILE scanning the horizon for debatable achievements of "the talented Negro" appropriate to his race, W. E. Burghardt Du Bois quite overlooked the first Afro-American art —the famous old wrought iron of New Orleans. It is solid and tangible proof that the Negro brought with him into his slavery the ancient art heritage of Africa.

The gracious iron balconies, the craftsmanlike grilles and charmingly designed lunettes, wrought by slave labor, have won their expensive place in the world of collectors, antique dealers and connoisseurs. The identities of the dark-skinned craftsmen who wrought the heavy bars of iron into beautiful and sensitive line have been sunk in obscurity by years of forgetfulness as impenetrable as the mists of antiquity that hang low over Africa. Only in the realm of our imagination may we come upon them—experiencing the artist's pure joy of creation.

Did they sing songs as they wrought? There must have been songs, because the Negro found songs for the rhythm of every labor. Did the rhythm of the hammer on the anvil strike new syncopations to his sensitive ear, unlike the anvil songs of Europe? The rhythms and the songs, too, have faded into the silence of forgetfulness. So forgotten are these craftsmen that Northern connoisseurs dismiss the idea with a smile.

"Well, maybe some of the cruder pieces," they admit, "under white supervision. But it's preposterous to think that ignorant Negroes could take a hybrid collection of French and Spanish motifs and fuse them into an art expression of their own, simpler than anything that was being done in Europe. No, no, there were European craftsmen on that job."

## WITHOUT WHITE DIRECTION

Thus is the cause of the first Afro-American artists dismissed without a hearing. The only flaw in the argument is that there were no white craftsmen in New Orleans at the time when the best of the iron was wrought. It was only after the War of 1812 restored the sea to America that the immigration of German artisans would begin—an immigration that would culminate around 1830 with riots of white artisans, because all skilled trades and crafts were monopolized by Negroes. To quote Booker T. Washington:

> The Southern white man did business with the Negro in a way that no one else has done business with him. In most cases, if a Southern white man wanted a house built he consulted a Negro mechanic about the plan and about the actual building of the structure. If he wanted a suit of clothes made he went to a Negro tailor, and for shoes to a shoemaker of the same race.

In such economic soil grew this first flowering of Afro-American art.

The Negroes were the smiths. Every plantation had to have its smiths, for the planta-

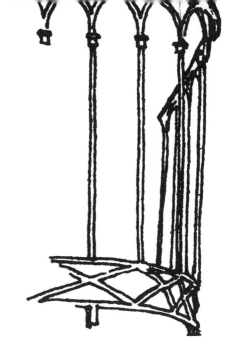

A graceful lunette

The sophistication of the classical revival translated into terms of smithing.

A strangely haunting Gothic quality

A medley of periods happily blended

tion existed in an age of iron. From wagon wheels to bolts, from plowshares to horseshoes, from locks to iron grave crosses in a stoneless country, the Louisiana plantation could not run a day without the blacksmith. Each master blacksmith had his learners—a relationship not so different nor more oppressive than was the apprenticeship system of Europe in the golden age of handicraft.

Craftsmanship is not usually considered a by-product of democracy and of the rights of the younger generation. And if you do not think that those Negro master smiths knew how to get the work out of black boys without the help of a white overseer, you need only wind up some ancient ante-bellum Negro, trained to work in the old regime, on the evil ways of a trifling younger generation.

There is another ante-bellum condition that must also be realized before we can recreate our black craftsman from the filings and shavings of history and set him against the red, glowing fires of his background. Not all the apprentices trained in the "industrial school" of the plantation were needed on that plantation. A particularly likely young blacksmith could be sent into New Orleans. Indeed, one of the sources of revenue of the Southern planter used to come from the wages paid to him for the work of his artisans.

The plantation did not waste its talent in the cotton field, but trained it into carpenters, wheelwrights, brickmasons, engineers, seamstresses or housekeepers. Never were talent and flair more scientifically turned into specialization. And if the whole system sounds rather like Rossum's Universal Robots to twentieth-century ears, there were mitigating legal circumstances never admitted by the abolitionists and probably never heard of by the poets and novelists who wrote so freely of tearing families apart and sending dusky brides "down the ribber."

There was a Black Code that protected the slave in his legal rights, and these were many. The legal right that bears directly on our art of wrought iron was that the slave had the right to buy his freedom for the set price of $500.

## THE CHANCE OF FREEDOM

The Black Code gave him the right, and the social and ethical code gave him the opportunity. The master's work took only so many hours out of his day. The hours left were his own time. On the plantation he could keep a garden or eggs for pin money, as farmers' wives do today. In the big house he could amass tips from visitors. As an artisan in the city he could work overtime in the same way. And rueful enough were the feelings of the master when an artisan for whom he had refused $3,000 bought himself for $500. Of course it was the exceptionally valuable and talented slave who had the ability and the continuity of purpose to save up $500 over the years. Yet public opinion damned the man who did not give his slave that sporting chance at liberty—just as shotgun public opinion saw to it that a master should not work his slaves on Sunday.

Of history's filings and shavings, then, we recreate no chain-bound bondsman quivering under a white overseer's lash, but a man of color who owned and operated his own blacksmith shop, or else a trusted slave who conducted a business for his master. Both men of dignity in their own eyes! Both artisans trained meticulously and uncompromisingly from childhood in the virile trade that requires skill, dexterity, speed and brute strength.

And there was work in plenty, for the city, too, yet moved in the iron age of handicrafts. There was work for every minute of the working day—a condition without which true craftsmanship cannot flourish, even if artistic temperaments may thrive on leisure. Here were the perfect historical conditions that in medieval countries used always to precede a flowering of wrought iron—diversified and necessary all-around blacksmith work, ready to be illuminated into art by the flame of talent and the torch of opportunity.

That torch of opportunity was pretty accurately a torch—the one that burned down the city in 1788 and started New Orleans building the stately Spanish city that has been preserved to the world in the Vieux Carré. Periods of building are always the opportunity of the artist. The particularly fortuitous opportunity for our incipient Negro artists was that the fine gentlemen with mansions to build were of French and Spanish lineage and desired to build in the French and Spanish tradition—which at the time meant going in for iron balconies and railings, and walled-in courtyards protected from the street by iron grilles and gateways.

As for the flame of talent, it was to come out of Africa—Africa of that primitive art whose discovery, a century later, was to stimulate the genius of Picasso and Matisse and create a cult of Negro sculpture.

## OF UNKNOWN ORIGIN

Tantalizing it is to wonder whence came the black craftsmen who wrought so well and so permanently in New Orleans. Did their fathers come from the Ivory Coast, where the art of Africa was most primitive, most hugely creative? Came they from Bushongo, where the portrait sculpture of long-dead savage kings seized upon characterization in character's intensest moments? Came they from the Sudan, where the influences of civilization had been percolating throughout the millenniums —where old Egyptian idols of 2000 B.C., conventionalized, traditionalized, have, as it were, gone back to nature? Secrets of vital importance, these, to the believers in the Negro's indigenous talent.

All we know is that, when opportunity came, training and talent were ready for the occasion.

Probably the blacksmith was given an engraving to follow—or more likely, since books were precious and blacksmiths' hands grimy, he was shown the engraving. Possibly the amateur gentleman-architect had done some sketching in Provence or in Palma; in both locales the general style of our Vieux Carré architecture prevailed. Sketching was a pleasing accomplishment of the period when a gentleman went on his travels. The practical builders of the eighteenth century, whose eye and hand were purified by handicraft, managed to achieve the abstract beauty of proportion without any more official architectural drawings.

What the Negro blacksmith did was to take the designs—the gorgeous curves and high modeling of the Rococo and the ultra-sophistication of the classical revival—and translate them into terms of pure smithing. There is a strangely haunting quality, too, of twelfth-century Gothic that pervades the workmanship. For there are certain curves and spirals, perpendiculars and junctions, that iron, given the same smithing technique, whatever the century, falls into naturally. So it is that we find many of the old medieval motifs reappearing after a break of centuries.

In Europe, since the closing decades of the thirteenth century, decorative wrought iron had passed out of the domains of pure smithing—for the very practical reason that Europe had passed out of the age of iron and into the age of steel. The armorer and the locksmith had got hold of the essential industries that used to be monopolized by the blacksmith. Smithing, once deemed worthy of Thor's high companionship when swords were wrought upon the anvil, deteriorated into a matter of shoeing horses. The iron to be wrought went to the armorer or locksmith, who brought to the business all the finesse of their crafts.

Heat they applied only in the preliminary stages. The greater part of the work was done on cold iron by file and saw. The Oriental metal-workers of Venice and Spain got into the game, adding to wrought iron the wiles of damascening and brass work and gold-smithing. Ornaments were cut out from sheet iron. Statuettes were carved out of the solid. Iron crackled and glowed with exquisite leaf-age washed in gold.

The achievement of this first Afro-American art is that it took an overcivilized craft, that had run its course because it had reached the ultimate of conquest over material, and over a span of 40 years did to iron only what blacksmiths could. Do not misunderstand. If the fine iron-workers of France, following the whims of architectural fashion, could achieve a finesse that our Afro-American art never even dreamed of, our dark-skinned New Orleans smiths had technical achievements of their own—just because they were smiths.

## THE DESIGN IS BOLD

It is only the blacksmith in constant practice who can work quickly enough in wrought iron to achieve final results before the white heat has faded to red. Hence the tendency of purely wrought iron to boldness of design.

Nor were there any modern mechanical aids to lessen the technical problems and to rob the designs of the delights of irregularities. Every curve was beaten out freehand by eye, instead of beaten out around the curve of a model, as is the standardizing way with the commercial "ornamental iron work" of our current elevator period. Every junction was riveted or strapped or fused and beaten at white heat, instead of fused cold with electricity.

Yet our muscular black artists were as innocent of periods as if they still hurled their spears in the jungles of the Congo. Spanish Renaissance, French Gothic and Rococo motifs were thrown together at random—but charm and naïveté are the result, instead of hodgepodge. The periods are blended happily, because only the lines and the curves were exacted of the iron that are legitimately of the smithy. "Iron is sweet stuff, if you don't torture her, and hammered stuff is all pure, truthful line with a reason and a support for every curve of her," says Kipling.

It would have been a satisfactory ethnological experiment had the wrought iron of the Negro blacksmith continued uninterruptedly for a century. To other art periods of iron, Fate has allotted at least a century for development. It was not to be. Fast on the blacksmith period was to press the mechanical period of cast iron, flooding the cities and plantations with manufactured articles. Skilled German artisans were to pour into New Orleans, fighting grimly for a foothold against competing slave labor. In iron, they brought with them the latest German methods of mechanical labor-saving devices. The foundries inevitably took the economic place of the smithies. Jolly fat Teutonic angels of cast iron began to decorate knockers and gardens. New Orleans fashions shifted to the lacey cast-iron galleries that are a charming period in themselves and quite another story.

The first Afro-American art can fairly be said to have ended in 1830—as all "decorative" art seems to end when it becomes exotic, unrelated to life and industry. Is it nature's provision, lest decoration disappear from the earth and its honorable place be cluttered up with "trimmings"?

—1926

Edward Mitchell Bannister. "Driving Home the Cows." Oil. 1881.

Robert S. Duncanson. "The Surprise." Oil. 1868.

# The American Negro as Craftsman and Artist

**by James V. Herring**

THE AMERICAN Negro's achievements in the concert hall, in the theatre and in the world of sports are generally well known; but probably few people know of his achievements in the crafts, and still fewer, no doubt, are aware of what he has done in the field of painting.

It is my aim to present the achievements of the American Negro in the United States in this realm of art. If the term "Art" strikes terror to the heart of the academic individual, it is as nothing compared with the sense of panic which its sound produces in the average layman of the radio audience; yet it should not, for since prehistoric times man has carved or painted his gods in his own image, and in the image of his ancestors.

To the average person, art almost invariably means painting. Architecture is generally considered to be the science of construction rather than an art. Sculpture, though considered an art in the Western world, plays a relatively small part in our lives today. But painting in one or another of its various forms is an everyday experience. In advertisements note our own "Buy Liberty Bonds" posters, magazine illustrations like those of E. Simms Campbell in *Esquire,* and wall decorations in our own public buildings, to mention only a few.

Thomas J. Watson reminds us that three great patrons have fostered painting through the long history of civilization. Priests have adorned temples, rulers their palaces and public buildings, private persons their homes and museums.

The Negro artist, even in these days of strife and narrow interests, has never been in doubt as to the relative importance of these patrons. His outstanding characteristics—tremendous emotional endowment, free imagination and a powerful individual expression—have kept him nearer to the ideal of man's harmony with nature than are many so-called practical-minded Americans. Although at times, like his brother artist, the Negro has served the church, the state and the individual patron, he has always thought of his art as an achievement, not as an indulgence.

## TOM DAY, CABINETMAKER

In the *Atlantic Monthly* for August, Mr. Kouwenhoven discusses the topic "Arts in America," but like so many of our writers he fails to mention the Negro in his sovereign group, either as craftsman or artist. Surely this was an oversight, for he must at some time have heard of Tom Day, a Negro craftsman, who was born in the late eighteenth century and was educated in Washington and Boston, later returning to North Carolina. He had become proficient in cabinetmaking and had a workshop as early as 1818. He moved to Milton, North Carolina, in 1823, in order to increase his business. It was then he bought the old Yellow Brick Tavern, where he manufactured mahogany furniture on a large scale, teaching his own slaves and a number of white apprentices. When he first began to practice his craft, he hired the slaves of white men; but he found that as soon as they became proficient as cabinetmakers their owners called them home and put them to work in their own interest. Day was thus compelled to become a slave-owner.

The output of his factory was considerable, and many homes of the wealthy in Virginia, the Carolinas and Georgia were furnished throughout with his work. The earliest existing example of Day's furniture, a large dining table with convertible ends, bears the date 1820. This, with other pieces, was made for a famous judge. One home of the descendant of a former governor of North Carolina is a veritable museum of the now scarce Day mahogany. Furniture was also made by this Negro craftsman for the governor's home at Raleigh, North Carolina.

> When stage coach and private equipage were the usual means of travel, this furniture was not nationally known, and there are many connoisseurs of antiques who have never heard the name. Those who own any [of this furniture] have usually inherited it and held it as a precious possession. Only direct need would cause them to part with it. In this way it has been carried from Maine to Texas, and from the Atlantic to the Pacific.

Caroline Pell Gunter, in the *Antiquarian* for September, 1929, tells the following story:

> An old gentleman of Milton has told of interesting days spent in the finishing room, where he could sit and listen to Tom Day giving orders and to the singing of the workers. While carving or polishing an eagle, which he sometimes used on large, heavy furniture, he would exclaim thus: "Bird of Liberty! Hover over the home of the owners of this wardrobe and bring them joy in its possession."

He enjoyed much success for many years, but owing to the unsettled conditions of the country just prior to the Civil War, when collections fell off, the price of mahogany rose and shipping facilities grew complicated, he, like so many white businessmen, failed. He died in 1861. It is of historic interest to note, to quote Caroline Gunter, "that Tom Day . . . free Negro and owner of Negro slaves, lived at a time and in a country where Anglo-Saxon supremacy precluded recognition of the Negro race save as laborers—yet he mastered the difficulties of life and used the wonderful talent that was given him to design and build."

There were many such Negro craftsmen during the nineteenth century in Philadelphia, Pennsylvania, Charleston, South Carolina, New Orleans, Louisiana, and other Colonial centers. By no stretch of the imagination could the works of these men be termed folk art, and when Mr. Kouwenhoven speaks of the "unique factor of a modern people's art" that we must include in our concept of arts in America, he must include these Negro craftsmen, whose achievements so greatly aided in the triumphs of our national genius.

## EDWARD MITCHELL BANNISTER, PAINTER

You may say that these were only craftsmen. But what of the work of Edward Mitchell Bannister, an early American Negro artist, born in St. Andrews, New Brunswick, in 1828? We are told in the *Atlantic Monthly* article of the excellence in technological design of—and of the attention Europeans paid to—American tools and machines at the Philadelphia Centennial Exhibition of 1876, but not a word is said concerning a first prize gold medal won by Mr. Bannister at this same centennial exhibition. The prize-winning picture, "Under the Oaks," was sold to Mr. Duff of Boston for $1,500, a large sum to be paid for any American work at that time. Mr. Bannister died in Rhode Island in 1901. The preface to the catalogue of the memorial exhibition of his work at the Providence Art Club reads thus:

> He early came to this city, and for 30 years was prominent in the Providence group of artists. His gentle disposition, his urbanity of manner and his generous appreciation of the work of others, made him a welcome guest in all artistic circles. Although he painted cattle, sheep and figures with life and force, yet he introduced them only as incident to the effective portrayal of his scene. He was par excellence as landscape painter, and the best one our state has yet produced. He painted with profound feeling, not for pecuniary results, but to leave upon canvas his impression of natural scenery, and to express his delight in the wondrous beauty of land and sea and sky. Had his nature been more self-reliant and adventurous, and had early opportunity been more kind, he might easily have been one of America's greatest landscape painters.

Another writer says, "Providence is today one of the chief centers for the cultivation of art in America, and this is due in no little degree to Edward Bannister." He was among the seven persons who incorporated the Providence Art Club in 1880.

In an exhibition of the art of the American Negro, assembled by the American Negro Exposition, July 4—September 2, 1940, in Chicago, Illinois, there were shown the works of at least six artists of national and international fame who were born in this early period, between 1821 and 1859. They were Bannister, Harper, Harleston, Patterson and Tanner.

## HENRY O. TANNER

Henry O. Tanner was born in Pittsburgh, Pennsylvania, in 1859. He is probably the best known of all of our Negro artists, although he spent most of his life in France and in the Near East. During his long career he painted racial subjects, seascapes, animal compositions, a few portraits such as those of the late Bishop Hartzell and Rabbi Wise; but his renown rests principally upon his romantic landscapes and his religious works.

He is represented in the Howard University gallery of art by one of his latest paintings, "The Return from Calvary." "The Two Disciples at the Tomb," in the Chicago Art Institute, is one of his best-known works, as it has been most often reproduced. His paintings are owned by all the great museums of the United States, as well as the Luxembourg Palace in Paris. His prizes, medals, and awards are too numerous to mention; he is one of our few American artists to receive the coveted Legion of Honor of France. He died in France in 1937. His whole career, says Dr. Brawley, is an inspiration and a challenge to aspiring painters, and his work a monument to sturdy endeavor and exalted achievement.

## THE SECOND GENERATION

Long before the close of this first period, the bold forerunners who spent their efforts directing the future towards a new mode in art had seen a younger generation, their pupils and followers, born between 1890 and 1900, become more and more distinguished in composition, figure painting and portraiture. These painters, William Edward Scott, a pupil of Tanner's in France, Malvin Gray Johnson, a student of the National Academy of Design, and Archibald J. Motley, Jr., who studied at the Art Institute of Chicago and abroad—to name only a few—are among those who form the second generation of Negro artists.

Perhaps the finest talent of all this second generation is Archibald J. Motley. Motley says he felt himself attracted to art almost from the first. Also, he was absorbed in contemplation of the contrast—often so suggestive and so luminous—between ancient expressions of his race and expressions such as manifest themselves today. The river of emotional and intellectual reaction to life he sees as a "deep river," flowing out of the mists of the past, through the present, and off into the veiled potentialities of the future.

Born in New Orleans in 1891, with a background of slavery still fresh enough to leave its impression upon his mind, Motley was taken, two years later, to St. Louis. Thus his childhood was not spent in the "Deep" South, where racial ties may be said to be felt most powerfully. To have lived there long enough to absorb into his being the vivid atmosphere of post-slavery plantation life might have proved of inestimable value; on the other hand, because Motley possessed a genius for picking up scattered threads, for visioning and reporting upon the varied existence of black people plunged into the great American crucible of change, it was perhaps as well for the subsequent versatility of his canvas that stakes were pulled up when he was still very young.

The family did not remain long in St. Louis. It eventually moved to Buffalo, and the final stopping-place was Chicago, where Motley has lived for about 37 years. On leaving high school, Motley took up art work seriously. The president of the Armour Institute in Chicago urged him to become an architect and offered a course gratis. But Motley knew that he wanted to be instead a painter, and he stuck to his ambition. He was then about 21 years old. Looking back over the early stages of his progress, he says the man from whom he learned the most about painting was Earl Buehr, while John Norton instilled in him a knowledge of the technique of drawing. Mr. Norton's method Motley found particularly to his liking. Instead of working directly from nature, meticulously copying the model, he would draw a few simple lines, as a child does, to designate a human figure. Posture would dictate the position of these lines. Afterward the figure would be modelled in and built up after nature upon this primitive scaffolding. To this day Motley works in that manner.

## MOTLEY ONE-MAN SHOW

The years of study at the Art Institute produced a great increase in technical proficiency; also, they developed the young man's sense of self-sufficiency. But he left the institute at 25, full of doubts regarding the future. It was not until 1921 that he sent pictures to the Art Institute exhibitions. In 1925, an article published in Paris about his work aided in turning the tide in Motley's favor. Life became more interesting. More of Motley's work appeared in exhibitions in this country. His remarkable portrait, "A Mulattress," won the Frank G. Logan medal and prize at an exhibition held in the Chicago Art Institute. In 1928, he held his first one-man show in New York City.

The exhibition alluded to was significant both because of the quality of the paintings themselves and because it represented, so one understands, the first one-man show by a Negro artist to be held in New York. This painter, fighting against perhaps more than the usual odds in his determination to liberate the creative urge within him, has already contributed eloquently to the artistic accomplishments of his race.

In his paintings of the Voodoo mysteries, in the interpretations of modern American Negroes at play, in the weird allegorical canvases and in the portraits, Motley directly or by subtle indirection lays bare a generous cross-section of what psychologists call the subconscious—his own and that of his race. The ancient traits and impulses of his ancestors in Africa, Haiti, or wherever they found their habitation, are a milestone on the unending march; but the phantasmagoria bears the imprint of the modern molds into which so much of the old race-life has been poured. The same fundamental rhythms are found, whether the setting be a jungle presided over by witchcraft or a cabaret rocking to the syncopation of jazz. Motley was given the Harmon Foundation Award, gold medal and

Archibald J. Motley, Jr. "Chicken Shack." Oil. Harmon Foundation.

Elton C. Fax. "A Nigerian Patriarch."
Lithograph crayon and ink.

Archibald J. Motley, Jr. "The Octoroon Girl."
Oil. Harmon Foundation.

prize, and, in 1929, he received a Guggenheim Fellowship. The group of which Motley is the leader paved the way for a phase of painting which has prevailed among the younger Negro artists since 1900, the phase which is unrepresentational, subjective, or abstract.

## THE THIRD GENERATION

In March, 1939, the *Survey Graphic* magazine carried this brief note:

> In accordance with its policy of having the museum serve the people of the whole community, the Baltimore Museum of Art has held the first exhibition of work by Negro artists to be shown in that city, whose population is more than one-fifth colored. Paintings, prints, drawings and sculpture by some 30 Negro artists were assembled from all over the United States with the aid of the Harmon Foundation, New York. They represent, the art critic of the Baltimore *Sun* points out, a so-to-speak first generation of Negro artists. Yet they work in varied styles, and without self-conscious, strained efforts to produce a racial art.

It is disconcerting to me that an art critic on the Baltimore *Sun* should speak of these artists as belonging to the first generation of Negro artists. In that exhibition in 1939, the younger artists of the third and present generation were represented. Among this group were Elton Fax, James L. Wells, James A. Porter, Charles Sebree, Charles Sallee, Lois M. Jones, Hale Woodruff, Hilda Wilkinson and many others. In fact, Miss Mary Beattie Brady, director of the Harmon Foundation, says in an article in *Opportunity* for May, 1931:

> From its vantage point in the pilot house, the foundation has observed the widening channel of the broader horizon ahead. Mr. Harmon's firm belief in the conquering power of straightforward public information as a weapon against prejudice has been justified as far as his awards are concerned. The next problem to be faced is how wisely and effectively to cultivate more

ground. With a total acreage, one might say, of more than 11,000,000 people, it seems impossible to believe that the scant list of approximately 700 names which the foundation has on its records can in any way represent the total outstanding achievement of Negroes which is worthy to take its place in the first ranks, without regard to race.

## A SUMMING-UP

Albert C. Barnes, in the *Survey Graphic,* March, 1925, says, "That there should have developed a distinctively Negro art in America was natural and inevitable." A new people of African origin, transported into an Anglo-Saxon environment and held in subjection to that fundamentally alien influence, was bound to undergo the soul-stirring experiences which always find expression in great art. "The contributions of the American Negro to art are representative because they come from the hearts of the masses of a people held together by like yearnings and stirred by the same cause." It is a sound art because it flows from the spirit of the Negro, which an alien culture has been unable to harness. "It is a great art because it embodies the individual traits of the race and reflects its suffering, aspirations and joys during a long period of acute oppression and distress."

In the United States it is difficult to say how much we owe culturally to each of the racial groups which make up America. All of these racial elements, like ourselves, are immigrants from the Old World, with widely differing backgrounds, but always aware that they are in a new land, a land that their ancestors came to as strangers, and a land which they have occupied only a few centuries and in which they are making their own contribution through a slow evolution. Negroes, like other groups, are making their contribution to the art life of America.

—1942

# The Second Heritage
# and Its Dilemma

Palmer Hayden. "Midsummer Night in Harlem." Oil. Harmon Foundation.

Romare Bearden. "The Street." Collage. 1964.

# The Negro Artist and Modern Art

by Romare Bearden

FOR THE moment, let us look back into the beginnings of modern art. It is really nothing new, merely an expression projected through new forms more akin to the spirit of the times. Fundamentally, the artist is influenced by the age in which he lives. Then for the artist to express an age that is characterized by machinery, skyscrapers, radios and the generally quickened cadences of modern life, it follows naturally that he will break with many of the outmoded academic practices of the past. In fact, every great movement that has changed the ideals and customs of life has occasioned a change in the accepted expression of that age.

Modern art has passed through many different stages. There have been the periods of the Impressionists, the Post-Impressionists, the Cubists, the Futurists and hosts of other movements of lesser importance. Even though the use of these forms is on the decline, the impression they made in art circles is still evident. They are commendable in the fact that they substituted for mere photographic realism a search for inner truths.

Modern art has borrowed heavily from Negro sculpture. This form of African art had been done hundreds of years ago by primitive people. It was unearthed by archaeologists and brought to the continent. During the past 25 years it has enjoyed a deserved recognition among art lovers. Artists have been amazed at the fine surface qualities of the sculpture, the vitality of the work, and the unsurpassed ability of the artists to create such significant forms. Of great importance has been the fact that the African would distort his figures if by so doing he could achieve a more expressive form. This is one of the cardinal principles of the modern artist.

It is interesting to contrast the bold way in which the African sculptor approached his work with the timidity of the Negro artists of today. Their work is at best hackneyed and uninspired and is only a rehashing of the work of any artist who may have influenced them. They have looked at nothing with their own eyes—seemingly content to use borrowed forms. They have evolved nothing original or native, like the spiritual, or jazz music.

Many of the Negro artists argue that it is almost impossible for them to evolve such a sculpture. They say that since the Negro is becoming so amalgamated with the white race, and has accepted the white man's civilization, he must progress along his lines. Even if this is true, they are certainly not taking advantage of the Negro scene. The Negro, in his various environments in America, holds a great variety of rich experiences for the genuine artists. One can imagine what men like Daumier, Grosz and Cruickshank might have done with a locale like Harlem, with all its vitality and tempo. Instead, the Negro artist will proudly exhibit his "Scandinavian

Landscape," a locale that is entirely alien to him. This will of course impress the uninitiated, who, through some feeling of inferiority toward their own subject matter, only require that a work of art have some sort of foreign stamp to make it acceptable.

I admit that at the present time it is almost impossible for the Negro artist not to be influenced by the work of other men. Practically all the great artists have accepted the influence of others. But the difference lies in the fact that the artist with vision sees his material, chooses, changes and, by integrating what he has learned with his own experiences, finally molds something distinctly personal. Two of the foremost artists of today are the Mexicans Rivera and Orozco. If we study the work of these two men, it is evident that they were influenced by the continental masters. Nevertheless, their art is highly original, and steeped in the tradition and environment of Mexico. It might be noted here that the best work of these men was done in Mexico, of Mexican subject matter. It is not necessary for the artist to go to foreign surroundings in order to secure material for his artistic expression. Rembrandt painted the ordinary Dutch people about him, but he presented human emotions in such a way that their appeal was universal.

Several other factors hinder the development of the Negro artist. First, we have no valid standard of criticism; secondly, foundations and societies which supposedly encourage Negro artists really hinder them; thirdly, the Negro artist has no definite ideology or social philosophy.

Art should be understood and loved by the people. It should arouse and stimulate their creative impulses. Such is the role of art, and this in itself constitutes one of the Negro artist's chief problems. The best art has been produced in those countries where the public most loved and cherished it. In the days of the Renaissance the townsfolk would often hold huge parades to celebrate an artist's successful completion of a painting. We need some standard of criticism, then, not only to stimulate the artist, but also to raise the cultural level of the people. It is well known that the critical writings of men like Herder, Schlegel, Taine, and the system of Marxian dialectics, were as important to the development of literature as any writer.

I am not sure just what form this system of criticism will take, but I am sure that the Negro artist will have to revise his conception of art. No one can doubt that the Negro is possessed of remarkable gifts of imagination and intuition. When he has learned to harness his great gift of rhythm and pour it into his art, his chance of creating something individual will be heightened. At present it seems that by a slow study of rules and formulas the Negro artist is attempting to do something with his intellect which he has not felt emotionally. In consequence, he has given us poor echoes of the work of white artists— and nothing of himself.

It is gratifying to note that many of the white critics have realized the deficiencies of Negro artists. I quote from a review of the last Harmon Exhibition, by Malcolm Vaughan in the *New York American:* ". . . but in the fields of painting and sculpture, they appear peculiarly backward, indeed so inept as to suggest that painting and sculpture are to them alien channels of expression." I quote from another review of the same exhibition, that appeared in the *New York Times:*

> Such racial aspects as may once have figured have virtually disappeared, so far as some of the work is concerned. Some of the artists, accomplished technicians, are seen to have slipped into grooves of one sort or another. There is the painter of the Cézannesque still life, there is the painter of the Gauguinesque nudes and there are those who have learned various "dated" modernist tricks.

There are quite a few foundations that sponsor exhibitions of the work of Negro artists. However praiseworthy may have been the spirit of the founders, the effect upon the Negro artist has been disastrous. Take, for instance, the Harmon Foundation. Its attitude from the beginning has been of a coddling and patronizing nature. It has encouraged the artist to exhibit long before he has mastered the technical equipment of his medium. By its choice of the type of work it favors, it has allowed the Negro artist to accept standards that are both artificial and corrupt.

It is time for the Negro artist to stop making excuses for his work. If he must exhibit, let it be in exhibitions of the caliber of the Carnegie Exposition. Here, among the best artists of the world, his work will stand or fall according to its merits. A concrete example of the accepted attitude towards the Negro artist recently occurred in California, where an exhibition coupled the work of Negro artists with that of the blind. It is obvious that in this case there is definitely created a dual standard of appraisal.

The other day I ran into a fellow with whom I had studied under George Grosz, at the Art Students League. I asked him how his work was coming. He told me that he had done no real work for about six months.

"You know," he said, "I sort of ran into a blind alley with my work; I felt that it definitely lacked something. This was because I didn't have anything worthwhile to say. So I stopped drawing. Now I go down to the meetings of the Marine and Industrial Workers' Union. I have entered wholeheartedly into their movement."

We talked about Orozco, who had lost his arm in the revolutionary struggle in Mexico. No wonder he depicted the persecution of the peasant class Mexicans so vividly—it had all been a harrowing reality for him.

So it must be with the Negro artist—he must not be content with merely recording a scene as a machine. He must enter wholeheartedly into the situation which he wishes to convey. The artist must be the medium through which humanity expresses itself. In this sense the greatest artists have faced the realities of life, and have been profoundly social.

I don't mean by this that the Negro artist should confine himself only to such scenes as lynchings, or policemen clubbing workers. From an ordinary still-life painting by such a master as Chardin we can get as penetrating an insight into eighteenth-century life as from a drawing by Hogarth of a streetwalker. If it is the race question, the social struggle, or whatever else that needs expression, it is to it that the artist must surrender himself. An intense, eager devotion to present-day life, to study it, to help relieve it—this is the calling of the Negro artist.

—1934

Charles Sebree. "Still Life." Oil.

# *The Gestation*

Haywood L. Oubre, Jr. "Mother
and Child." Plaster.

Edward L. Loper. "Twelfth Street Gardens." Oil. Harmon Foundation.

Edward Harleston. "The Old Servant." Oil.
Harmon Foundation.

William E. Scott. "The Lord Will Provide." Oil.
Harmon Foundation.

# Negro Art and the Depression

by Vernon Winslow

HAVE YOU heard how the Depression rescued the Negro artist from almost complete social impotence?

Since common opinion evaluates the artist as a pathetic accident, and since popular conversation refers to the Depression in those terms, perhaps the story of how the one helped the other might contain more than ordinary significance. At any rate, our story is one of truth . . . and we hope one of interest.

However, before we relate our narrative there is one point that calls for common understanding. By drawing your attention to this point I wish to emphasize what I consider a fundamental concept, the precise scope of which cannot be too clearly apprehended. In fact, the destiny of most art touching our daily lives seems to shape itself around this principle. In citing this concept, I am fully aware of the danger of excessive presumption; nevertheless, having been duly impressed by its worth in my own judgment, I feel safe in this belief: that the forces of art and the forces of industry must freely interpenetrate before there can grow any complete expression of, or any sincere regard for, true art. And by true art I refer to that which grows from the dominant interests surrounding the masses of people. That is, from ordinary laymen such as you or me.

And now for our story.

Time: around 1914. Place: a restless world torn between the ideologies of imperialism and humanitarianism—a world tossed and writhing in the throes of an undigested industrial revolution. Germany had just served her ultimatum upon the Allies; the Balkans counted their days with pistol shot and cannon, while the United States, nervously wealthy, construed all booming sounds as ominous. Against this background, interpreting, as it were, the spirit of evolution, the tempo of incessant speed and the impact of machine-made strength, a convincing artistic expression began to take root—an expression which touched all the fields of fine arts, including literature, sculpture, painting and architecture. In literature there emerged the poetry of Sandburg and the plays of Eugene O'Neill.

A special instance of this expression can be found in Carl Sandburg's "Smoke and Steel":

In the subway plugs and drums,
In the slow hydraulic drills, in gumbo or gravel,
Under dynamo shafts in the webs of armature
    spiders,
They shadow-dance.

The adapted classicism of William Zorach and Heinz Warneke was next. Graphic arts were prolific, for under this heading were noted the first works of Reginald Marsh, Georgia O'Keefe and Rockwell Kent; and who is there that does not remember the daring architecture of Frank Lloyd Wright? All these represent but a scant description of our first great force, artistic expression—an expression supported by common enthusiasm for the new and powerful industrial discoveries making their appearance in every phase of American life. This brings us to our second important force, industrial expression.

Now, by some peculiar method, our artistic utterances on the one hand seem to anticipate our industrial realizations on the other. Then both in turn thrive and grow. If you will, think of two plants, art and industry, whose roots interlock beneath the earth, and whose leaves and stems respond to the same rainfall and sunlight, the growth of one depending upon and yet determining the other. This stem of industry, apparently accepting the challenge of artistic expression, bursts forth with products containing, to a great degree, excellent design and craftsmanship, such as the motion picture with sound and color, the skyscraper, the radio with bakelite and plastic cabinets, the mechanical refrigerator, synthetic fabrics and a thousand successful experiments in cello-glass, plexiglass, cellophane, pliofilm, linoleum and metal alloys—each in itself an example of American art which seems to voice the same messages found in the earlier verse of Sandburg, the plastic design of Zorach or the illustrative work of Rockwell Kent.

To return to our original premise, the correlation between the spirit of art and the spirit of industry is a powerful reality, echoing and re-echoing itself until finally there is created what is called national art. Already, aspects of this can be seen in the presence of streamlined kitchenware, the adoption of tubular furniture or the popularity of Walt Disney's animated pictures. Furthermore, these same aspects were no doubt contained in the mummies of Egypt, the pottery of early Greece and the oil paintings of the Italian Renaissance, all of which evince the same artistic–industrial relationship. And now for the other side of the picture.

Presumably, all of us are Americans, main-taining an effusive interest in American art; but some are also Negroes, and, as such, we would like to hear, perhaps, what happened to us in this cycle of contemporary industry and art. So again, let us turn the pages of our histories back to the days of 1915.

Here we find taking place an epochal migration from the fields and streets of the South to the opportunities provided by the industrial centers of the North. Beckoned by blazing headlines in the Negro weeklies and prompted by the Jim Crow of the South, our folk, blind to the new cruelties of climate and labor, pushed themselves into every Northern occupation that would accept them. But despondency and suffering followed their trek for security and civil rights. Chaos and the confusion of adjustment extended a dismal reception. However, these provided a spawning place for our first "Negro Renaissance." Though our bodies seemed to stagger, new voices were born—the voices of Langston Hughes and Countee Cullen, of Richmond Barthé and Augusta Savage, of Hale Woodruff and Malvin Johnson, of William Du Bois and James Weldon Johnson. These comprised the artistic force of the American Negro.

For instance, listen to the chant of Langston Hughes in his "Our Land":

> We should have a land of sun,
> Of gorgeous sun,
> And a land of fragrant water,
> Where the twilight,
> As a soft bandanna handkerchief. . .

These were the voices which glorified— only in darker tones—the same panorama extolled by the bards of white America; but where the messages of the white artist were recaptured by white industry, ours fell upon an impoverished, helpless group without industrial ownership or participation.

True enough, the Negro possessed an abundance of abstract scholarship and artistic sensitivity, but he pathetically lacked any means of industrial translation. He could not build a skyscraper or a massive bridge, despite a possible inspiration for steel and concrete; even if trained to do so, he could not produce a motion picture of any proportions; neither would his presence be tolerated, except as a janitor, in any of the experimental laboratories working on tubular furniture, plexiglass or synthetic fabrics. On the contrary, he had to consider himself fortunate to be classed as a poor farmer, a day laborer or a menial, in which event unemployment and insecurity were but a step away. And hands that are denied the healthy choice of craftsmanship grow weary of contributing to its inspiration.

As a result, the normal plant of art and industry, with its roots pushing two stems above the ground, did not exist for us. Instead we found ours with only one stem, sadly overworked and with very weak roots which nourished no twin. Talent and creativity were here rendered impotent for want of industrial participation. And yet, it is a known fact that before the man in the street can benefit by any abstract beauty, literary or graphic, it must be translated to him in some material form, preferably a form that is shaped by the crucible of his own industry.

But as it stood, the Negro in the street could not feel with full manly response the living message implied in the scholarship of Du Bois, the poetry of Hughes or the paintings of Woodruff. And any race with an active mind and shackled hands risks the eventual prostration of its own talent.

So here was our dilemma:

While, in the white world, painters, in addition to the traditional work on canvas, were contributing to the knowledge of commercial photography, of advertising design and of architectural chromatography, our artists were largely restricted to easel painting alone. Likewise, while the white sculptors assisted in the designing of the modern automobile, the shaping of ornamental fixtures and the fashioning of hundreds of articles such as the electric iron, modern glassware, radios and telephone apparatus, our sculptors were limited to the making of allegorical figures. Meanwhile, the economic importance of oil painting and allegorical sculpture was becoming more and more limited. At the same time, more and more importance was being attached to advertising art and industrial design.

And then the worst happened: yes, it was the Depression.

The Depression. A catastrophe which snatched gold from the wealthy, swept security from beneath the moderately comfortable, and left the poor to suffer more intensely and in larger numbers. To be sure, the Negro had known poverty before 1929, but his fate was made easier by the generous profusion of crumbs falling from the tables and the cupboards of his white friends. But now, even those crumbs were greedily sought by an increasing number of poverty-stricken whites. Naturally enough, the Negro artist suffered the same deprivation. Public support was scarce enough before the Depression, but now the scarcity was terrifying; oil paintings and sculpture were sold for whatever they could command, while many artists scanned the ranks of unskilled labor for possible employment. Something had to be done.

Fortunately, however, within this catastrophe were sown the seeds of a sweeping reaction which finally burst forth with a towering brilliance. The United States government had suddenly decided to lend a hand. The tenant farmer, the sharecropper and, above all, the artist were to receive a chance to begin again. With a hearty response, the Negro painter welcomed the NYA and the WPA; and in turn there sprouted almost overnight such services as public parks, schools, libraries and hospitals, all of which were designed, decorated and in many cases furnished, under the supervision of the government. With equal rapidity, community art classes were established to answer adequately this enthusiastic correlation between industry and art. And then, recapturing the vision of American tradition, our poverty-stricken hordes flocked to learn the basic trades of contemporary industry. Silk-screen work, furniture design, show card work, weaving, architecture and photography seemed to flourish with a new pride; and for the first time since the plantation days artists began to touch new materials, to understand new tools and to accept eagerly the challenge of black poetry, black song and black scholarship.

Following this, a new art agency was born —an agency with a timely response to the collapse of the community and with a valuable answer to the thousands searching for a chance to be of some use to a culture which apparently had forsaken them. As a practical instrument born in times of extreme need, the community art center, in order to survive, was forced to make its program all inclusive. The artist, the craftsman, as well as the man in the street—all found themselves in dire need. Hence it was a simple step to conclude that the contribution of all three was a natural and most effective method of reorganizing the community. For example, the creation of an electric iron needs first an artist to place the design upon paper, then a craftsman to shape the materials and, finally, a sympathetic consumer whose taste and demands will spur the artist and craftsman to their highest efforts. Simple, is it not? And yet, despite the simplicity, this new approach was the first step which allowed the Negro to see his significant function, as a man, in the whole process of community creativeness.

This simple observation has finally placed under the same roof creative imagination and mechanical ingenuity, where both feed on the new vigor of the community. In this new setting the painter has multiplied the range of his vision, for he not only reaches a greater market, but he sees his painting in relationship to the production and use of other contemporary expressions. Wholesome experience for anyone who considers himself an artist! As a result, modern painting is now executed in relation to its environment of skyscrapers, of diesel engines and of cellophane packaging. While on the other hand, the craftsman who views the painting can more readily understand it. Why? Simply because its message contains the language that he himself inspired—the language of skyscrapers, of diesel engines and of cellophane packaging.

Consequently, that which had been destroyed by the Depression was rebuilt to a much more democratic perfection. Democratic, of course, because the new art center excluded the limitations based on the color of one's skin. More perfect because it promises to assimilate completely our social environment. Representing the most recent achievement in this direction, the South Side Community Art Center in Chicago has been added to the list of those dedicating their program to the strengthening of art through industry. Both in turn will enlarge the meaning of democracy. Thus, in its true function—to articulate and aid in the problems of life and of living—art now presents a new meaning to the American Negro.

—1941

# Negro Art in Chicago

*by Willard F. Motley*

IN CHICAGO there is a small group of young colored artists who paint where they can—in garages, in tiny studios, in bare back rooms. They paint for the love of it. There is much talent in the group. They are following the trail blazed years ago by William E. Scott, Archibald J. Motley, Charles C. Dawson and William Farrow. Today these older, established artists are working more slowly, less spectacularly, while the young group, allowed to express itself through the assistance of the Federal Art Project, is painting feverishly.

This present generation hasn't found itself yet and realizes it. Some of the artists are still students. But one day they undoubtedly will have something powerful to say. At present they are making a beginning by staging what amounts to a debut—a small, informal exhibition at Hull House which is an interesting show in many ways.

There are 72 paintings in the gallery. For the most part they depict the homes of the artists and the people of nearby neighborhoods. Most of the canvases have a decisive, finished appearance—disproving the opinion of many white critics who feel that the Negro artist should have something primitive in his soul that should find its way to the canvas, that his work should be crude and unfinished, regardless of the fact that his environment in a large city is much the same as that of the white artist of like economic status.

There are some powerful paintings by Charles White—"Lust for Bread," "Gussie" and "Evangelist." Eldzier Cortor, perhaps the most original of the group, displays his remarkable versatility in such paintings as "Brother and Sister," "And So to Bed" and "Where Once a Dwelling Stood." Bernard Goss's "Always the Dirty Work" is much commented upon. Charles Davis has a number of outstanding canvases, chief among them "Low Cost of Living," which is handled in almost a Utrillo tone. William Carter, Henry Avery, Ramon Gabriel, Charles Sebree and Earl Walker are among those showing finished technique. Fred Hollingsworth is the lone primitive.

Having looked at the artists' work at the gallery, let us take a trip to their studios to learn where they work and to understand their privations and struggles.

## CHARLES DAVIS

World-famed Michigan Boulevard speeds past, a smooth, sophisticated avenue, sleek with motor cars. One steps off the sidewalk just south of 31st Street on Michigan, crosses a vacant lot and knocks loudly on a garage door. One climbs a narrow, rickety flight of dingy steps and enters Charles Davis' studio where it stands on the alley, a dirty vacant lot in front of it, one stretching toward Wabash Avenue behind it. Telephone pole wires drape across the windows; the alley is heaped with garbage and ashes. But the studio is a beautiful old place. One forgets the alley, the vacant lots, the vegetable peddler who keeps his wagon and his potato sacks on the floor below. The studio has an atmosphere that reminds one of Paris—of artists struggling in garrets. A whitewashed brick wall is one boundary of the studio. Doors, fastened together, partition the other end. There is a small, wood-burning stove, a home-made bookcase piled with rich old books, mostly about art. There are three other rooms. There are many canvases. Davis is a prolific worker.

Charles Davis grasped my hand, drew me into a chair, brewed tea in a coffeepot. He showed me his antiques, his books. He was reluctant to talk about himself. It was from his wife, Hazel, who also paints, from his artist friends, all of whom have a great admiration for him, that I got most of my information. His sincerity is absolute. He is an artist first, last, always. He often works on two or three canvases at a time. He paints almost every waking hour. Once he worked from eight to eight washing dishes and came home to paint until two or three in the morning every night without fail. At another time he was employed as a pick and shovel man on the WPA at the airport. He became ill and had to go to bed. Even that didn't stop him. He sat up in bed and painted. At the Hull House exhibition, only one of his seven canvases is the property of the art project. The others were done on his own time. When he needs shoes and has the money, he goes around in slippers and buys paint.

Davis is handsome, slim, has a small mustache and a pleasant smile. He is 28, married, has three children and yet seems a boy. He has the modesty, directness and enthusiasm of a boy and gives the illusion of being in his teens. He was married when he was 18. His oldest child is almost 10. He has always wanted to paint but has had to learn by himself. He had little academic training. Two

months at the Art Institute and art classes at Hull House comprise his formal study. He has passed through all the stages, from copying the pictures of movie stars from magazine covers, to portraits in oil. He has had a family to support while he learned and painted.

Davis says: "I live here because I have a deep sympathy for the people who live here. These people and the whole neighborhood have something to say. I want to paint real people and real places. I am not interested in making a lot of money out of painting. I paint because it is the only thing I want to do, because I love it."

## ELDZIER CORTOR

Eldzier Cortor lives in a little house behind a big house on Chicago's southeast side. The little house is painted white, and on the second floor I found Cortor in his beautiful little three-room studio apartment. It is artistically, almost lavishly, furnished. There are two bookcases crowded with the works of the old masters, contemporary best-sellers, and volume on volume concerning art. There is a new desk, a typewriter, an easel, an oil-burning stove, harmoniously upholstered chairs, a soft couch against a window. Next to the wall is a large stand with many tubes of paint and other containers of colors Cortor has made himself. His brushes are in a large vase on a table. The doors are arched; the walls are white, and on them hang Cortor's works. Each is both original and individual. Here is a lithograph, here a pallet-knife portrait, here a painting done in paint-tube technique, here something influenced by African sculpture, here a woodcut, here a mural worked out on a small scale, here a sketch impressive in its simplicity of line and its living mood. And each has the stamp of Cortor's originality.

Cortor is 24. His deep brown eyes shine when he talks about art; his small mustache wrinkles with his smile. He has a pleasing personality and a generous friendship. He sat cross-legged on a modern chromium tube chair while we talked.

When Cortor graduated from Englewood High School, he enrolled in the Art Institute night classes and worked during the day. He met discouragement everywhere. Many thought he was a crackpot because he wanted to be an artist. Nevertheless, by washing dishes, being a bus boy, and doing a hundred odd jobs, he managed to be true to himself and get in a year of nights at the institute. A year of day school followed. There a woman, Miss Kathleen Blackshear, a teacher of the history of art and composition at the institute, and, incidentally, a Texan, took a keen interest in him. She bought several paintings from him, enabling him to work on. Peter Pollack, of the Illinois Art Project, who then had a private art gallery on Michigan Boulevard, purchased some of his paintings. At the end of the second semester he was employed on the art project with full assurance that he could do the one thing he wanted to do—paint. Meanwhile, he had met Felicia Brown, who is studying to be a school teacher, and they are now engaged.

Cortor says: "I would like to travel through the South and depict Negroes as they are there. I want to paint, never reach any set goal, always work toward an ideal."

## CHARLES WHITE

Charles White's easel is the back of a chair in a crowded dining-room at 210 East 53rd Street, where he lives with his mother. His mother has been a great influence and inspiration. She has been tolerant and sympathetic. His eyes smile as he remembers that she gave him his first oils when he was seven years old. His father died when he was eight. His mother has always worked. Because of her interest in him and his own intense study, he is today one of the most promising young artists of the group.

Only 21 years old, he has gone fast and far. He is the best draughtsman of the group and credits this to the influence of Rubens and El Greco. At Englewood High School, in 1936, he won a nation-wide high school pencil-sketching contest. This was followed by a $240 scholarship to the Art Institute, which carried him a year. Always a giant for work, he finished two years in one. In competitions he won scholarships conducted by the Chicago Academy of Fine Arts and the Frederick Mizen Academy of Art. He is now studying fresco painting at the Hull House Art Center. Employed by the Illinois Art Project, he is working on a large and strikingly powerful mural entitled "Five Great Negroes."

White has had to work hard to educate himself and to buy materials. He has been a newsboy, delivered groceries for the A & P stores, washed dishes for Thompson's restaurants, scrubbed floors at Jack and Jill ice cream parlors. He has been a cook and valet. He was employed at one time as a houseboy for an artist while studying at the institute. Both his education and experiences have made him an intelligent, interesting and well-rounded young man.

White says: "It is a little hard to say what I want to do finally. I do know that I want to paint murals of Negro history. That subject has been sadly neglected. I feel a definite tie-up between all that has happened to the Negro in the past and the whole thinking and acting of the Negro now. Because the white man does not know the history of the Negro, he misunderstands him.

"I am interested in the social, even the propaganda, angle of painting; but I feel that the job of everyone in a creative field is to picture the whole social scene. The Old Masters pioneered in the technical field. They have done that work. I am interested in creating a style of painting that is much more powerful, that will take in the technical end

Eldzier Cortor. "Night Letter."
Oil. Harmon Foundation.

William Carter (below). "Still Life." Oil.
1941. Harmon Foundation.

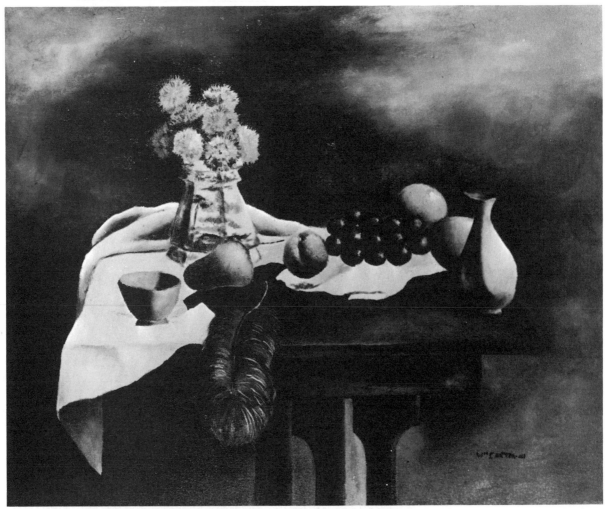

Charles Davis. "Tycoon Toys." Oil. Harmon Foundation.

Charles White. "Paper Shelter." Collage and Chinese ink and stick.
1965. Heritage Gallery, Los Angeles.

and at the same time say what I have to say. Paint is the only weapon I have with which to fight what I resent. If I could write, I would write about it. If I could talk, I would talk about it. Since I paint, I must paint about it."

## WILLIAM CARTER

The old mansion on the northwest corner of 30th and Ellis is falling into decay. An iron fence on a stone embankment surrounds the estate. Inside the fence the grass is rusted. The paint scales away from the building, the mortar crumbles from between the bricks, the wooden columns under the portico-porch are rotting. There has been no paint on them for years. The door opens. The aged housekeeper stands in the shadows. A musty smell permeates the great, high-vaulted hallway. A candle burns in a red cup on a rickety table. A winding staircase climbs the far wall and lifts itself to a beautiful stained glass window that lets in the gentle bars of light. Dust lies over the bare floor, the balustrade rail. The wallpaper hangs in little withered leaves from the ceiling and wall. This, once the estate of a wealthy citizen of Chicago, is almost like a haunted house.

The old woman leads the way to a door on the second landing, knocks. The door opens and William Carter stands there in a soft green jacket, a neckerchief knotted about his throat. The room is dingy, the windows small, the ceiling high. In a dark corner an old coal stove feebly tries to warm the place. The furnace has been taken out of the building. The rooms have stoves, and coal is stored in the closets.

Carter's room is the size of two. In a bucket on the table is a bunch of celery. On the table is a loaf of bread, butter, cans of vegetables. On the floor are a number of empty milk bottles. All about the room are vases of oak leaves and pussywillows—the touch of an artist.

Pictures hang against the nude walls, stand on the floor. There is a cot against the wall. The floor is bare, dirty. Carter apologizes for this, says he has time only for his work. But a clean-scrubbed floor would spoil the effect. On the easel is Carter's latest painting for the art project. Carter handles his canvases as if they were children. He takes pleasure in showing them.

Carter is 30 years old. He has had little formal training and has gained no revenue from his paintings. With two dollars in his pocket he went to the University of Illinois and managed to stay a year. His were the usual jobs—scrubbing floors, washing dishes. In 1930, he went to the Art Institute and was able to get in two years there. Since then it has been a struggle for handholds—working at odd jobs, painting in bare rooms with poor light. He has been represented by occasional exhibitions here and there. Then the art project and security, a chance to work.

Carter says: "Here in Chicago the trend is toward propaganda in art. There is no social significance in my work. I want to be a good, representative painter—not necessarily limited to racial representation. I have always exhibited with others. I am planning a one-man show so that I can get opinion on and criticism of my work."

\*    \*    \*    \*    \*    \*

There are many more artists, but space prohibits telling of each of their lives in detail. One and all, they are working, studying, dreaming, painting. And it would surprise no one familiar with their work if out of this group some day there developed a great American artist whose name would be acclaimed around the world.

—1940

# *At Long Last, Recognition*

Horace Pippin. "The Lilies." Oil. 1941. Harmon Foundation.

Jacob Lawrence. "Going Home." Gouache. 1946. International Business Machines Corporation.

Jacob Lawrence. "Street Orator." Gouache. 1936.
Collection of Mrs. Jacob Lawrence.

Jacob Lawrence. "Interior." Gouache. 1939.
Collection of Mrs. Jacob Lawrence.

# Advance on the Art Front

by Alain Locke

THE RECENT advances in contemporary Negro art remind me of nothing so much as a courageous cavalry move over difficult ground in the face of obstacles worse than powder and shell—silence and uncertainty. I have only read one book on military strategy, and remember only one or two sentences. But these happen to be appropriate. One said: "It's not the ground you gain but the ground you can hold that counts"; the other: "Even retreat, organized, is safer than disorganized advance." So, sobering though it may be, before we lose our heads and handkerchiefs in hysterical hurrahs for the brave lads who press forward, let us look at the cold strategy of our art situation and ask a few pertinent questions.

After all, we cannot win on the art front with just a thin advance line of pioneering talent or even the occasional sharp salient of genius; we must have behind this talent and this genius the backing of solid infantry and artillery support and the essential lifelines of supply and communication. In short, we must have for the most effective use of our art proper public appreciation, adequate financial support, competent and impersonal criticism and social and cultural representativeness. We must first of all support our artists, or our art will fail—fail outright or, what is quite as bad, fail to represent us. We must consolidate our art gains, or their cumulative effect will be lost as mere individual and "exceptional" achievement. Finally, we must capitalize our art, for it is, after all, as the most persuasive and incontrovertible type of group propaganda, our best cultural line of defense.

Surely, after the recent Marian Anderson case, this is self-evident. But why should we wait upon a mis-maneuver of the enemy or hang precariously on a fumble of the opposition? The essence of strategy is planned action and the tactics of internally organized resources. As illustration, imagine the educative public effect of a permanently organized traveling exhibit of the work of contemporary Negro artists. Or visualize the social dividends on such a representative collection as part of the Golden Gate Exposition or of the New York World's Fair. I heard the subject debated for months pro and con, and in the end, I believe, positive action was impaled on the horns of the usual dilemma. That old dilemma of the persecuted, which the successful always dare to ignore! Imagine confronting a Polish artist with the alternative of a national *or* an international showing; if he had as few as two pictures the answer would be "one in each." At the World's Fair practically every nation is reinforcing its share in the international showing with national collections under its own auspices; and the Union of South Africa, including as a prominent part of its art exhibit the rock drawings of the prehistoric Hottentots and Bushmen, makes it seem as though consistency was the enforced virtue of the disinherited.

So while we rejoice over a few well-earned inclusions of the works of some of our younger artists in the exhibit of contemporary American art at the Fair, let us frankly lament and take the blame for the lack of a representative unit collection of the best work of contemporary Negro artists. And while we glow over the increasing number of one-man shows by Negro painters and sculptors, let us regret that thus far no comprehensive and representative permanent collection of the work of Negro artists exists.

Too, I have heard Negro artists and critics in some strange befuddlement question the relevance of African art to our cultural tradition. Try to buy, beg, borrow or steal that prehistoric African art from the state collections of the Union of South Africa! Question, if you must quibble on something, the relevance of the African art in the imperial museums and colonial expositions the world over or the often concealed transfusion of African style in contemporary modernist art. Art belongs where it is claimed most or where it functions best. Bohemian art was in strange and sad succession Bohemian, German, Polish, Austrian, Czechoslovakian and now, I dare say, will become "German" all over again. Art doesn't die of labels, but only of neglect—for nobody's art is nobody's business.

Negro art is and should be primarily our business, and deserves to be our glory to the extent that it has been our concern. Happily enough, as in the art of Miss Anderson, the more deeply representative it is racially, the broader and more universal it is in appeal and scope, there being for truly great art no essential conflict between racial or national traits and universal human values.

Within the field we are reviewing, two illustrations will clinch this point. The intuitive genius of a New York lad, using the Haitian historical materials of the Schomburg Collection in the 135th Street Branch Library, reinterprets in 41 modernistic tempera panels the life of Toussaint L'Ouverture and the whole course of the Haitian revolution. It would be hard to decide which cause owed the greatest debt to Jacob Lawrence's talents, Haitian national history, Negro historical pride, Expressionism as an appropriate idiom for interpreting tropical atmosphere and peasant action and emotion, or contemporary Negro art. As a matter of fact, all scored simultaneously when this brilliant series of sketches was exhibited in a special gallery at the Baltimore Museum of Art's recent showing of Negro artists.

Or again, let us take the "Mother and Son" group exhibited for the first time in the recent one-man show of Richmond Barthé's sculpture at the Arden Gallery in New York. Here is a subject racial to the core—a Negro peasant woman kneeling and mournfully cradling in her arms the limp, broken-necked body of her lynched son. Though striking enough to be more potent anti-lynching propaganda than an armful of pamphlets, this statue group is, as a work of art, universalized, and would move a spectator who had never heard of lynching or an art critic merely interested in the problems of sculptural form and tradition that have come down to us from the days of classical sculpture.

What should concern us primarily, then, is how to encourage and support our artists, assuring them that artistic freedom which is their right, but buttressing their creative effort with serious social and cultural appreciation and use.

As for the present, if it had not been for the Federal Art Project and its direct and indirect support, almost all of our art gains would have been snuffed out in the last few

Richmond Barthé. "Boy with Flute."
Bronze. 1940. Harmon Foundation.

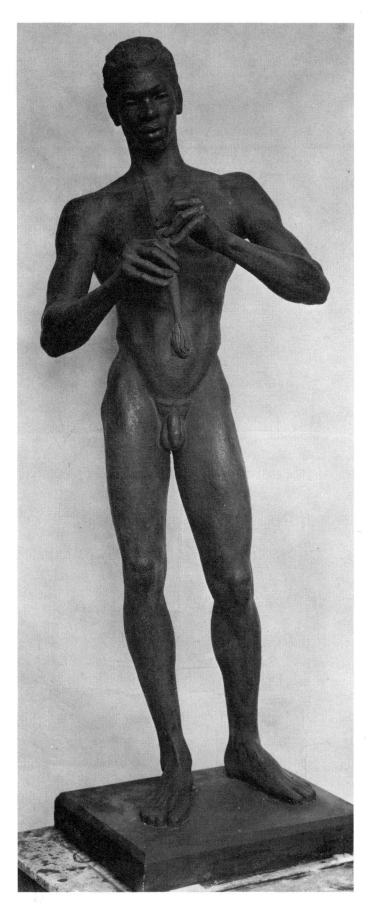

Richmond Barthé. "Judith Anderson."
Bronze. Harmon Foundation.

Malvin Gray Johnson. "Southern Landscape, No. 1." Oil. Harmon Foundation.

William H. Johnson. "Flowers to Teacher."
Oil. Harmon Foundation.

Lois Mailou Jones. "Letitia et Patrick." Oil.
1964. Howard University Gallery of Art.

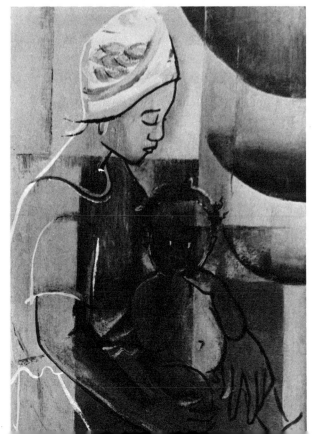

Allan R. Crite. "Last Game at Dusk." Oil. 1939.
Harmon Foundation.

years. More power to this project, but, in addition, we need the reinforcements of voluntary and sacrificial outside support, such as that of the Harlem Citizens' Sponsors Committee that guarantees rental and materials for the Harlem Community Art Center; or that admirable initiative of the Baltimore Negro Citizens' Art Committee that was back of the Baltimore Museum of Art's exhibit of Contemporary Negro Art; or that pioneer offer of Le Moyne College of quarters for the Federal Art Gallery in Memphis. These things, let us hope, are the beginnings of a movement for the popular support of the Negro artist.

On the artists' part, there have been signs of remarkable activity. In Boston, one-man shows of the work of Allan Crite and of Lois Jones have been held recently; in Philadelphia, at the A.C.A. Gallery, Sam Brown exhibited a striking series of water colors, most of them from Nassau, the Bahamas, in a joint show with Hen Jones, who exhibited a new series of oil landscapes and figure studies in a successful modernistic change of style. The same gallery later had an exhibit of the black and whites and lithographs of one of our most skillful technicans in these media, Dox Thrash. In New York, the Labor Club recently held a stimulating exhibit of the work of younger Negro artists, and at the Harlem Art Center, under the enterprising direction of Gwendolyn Bennett, a whole series of exhibitions has been held, culminating in interest, from our point of view, in the third annual group exhibit of the Harlem Artists Guild. Here, in this group, we have probably the nucleus of the younger Negro art movement, for in rapid sequence it has brought forward the talents of promising young artists like Georgette Seabrook, Norman Lewis, Sara Murrell, Ernest Crichlow, Vertis Hayes, William Blackburn, Ronald Joseph and Jacob Lawrence.

The New York season has also seen one-man showings of the work of William H. Johnson at Artists' Gallery and of Aaron Douglas at the A.C.A. Gallery. Each of these somewhat older artists has modified his earlier style, Mr. Johnson by moving somewhat extremely to the artistic left of disorganized Expressionism and Mr. Douglas by a retreat from his bold earlier style to mild local-color Impressionism which, though technically competent, gives little distinctively new or forceful either in his Negro-type studies or his series of Haitian landscapes.

\* \* \* \* \* \*

But certainly the outstanding artistic events of the season thus far have been the Baltimore Museum of Art's well-chosen and brilliantly arranged show and the equally well arranged and unusually comprehensive one-man sculpture show of the work of Richmond Barthé. Barthé, by his industrious application, has developed a seasoned technical proficiency: 37 subjects in five media, ranging from portrait commission busts to heroic figure compositions like "Mother and Son" and the 40-foot bas-reliefs of "Exodus" and "Dance" for the Harlem River Housing Project, attest to original talent and steadily maturing artistic stature. Critics, both conservative and modernistic, agreed in their praise of undeniable proficiency and versatility. The adaptation of style to subject is Barthé's forte. Always seeking for a basic and characteristic rhythm and for a pose with a sense of suspended motion, he shows an almost uncanny emphasis, even in his heads, of a symbolic type of line, like the sinuous patterned curves of the Kreutzberg figure, the sensuous ecstatic posture of the "African Dancer," the sagging bulbous bulk of the "Stevedore," the medieval-medallion-like faces and figures of the *Green Pastures* Exodus scene, or the lilting lift of "Benga," the sophisticated African dancer. Carl Van Vechten is right in his statement that Barthé is actually seeking "the spiritual values inherent in moving figures." This sensitiveness to moods and temperaments makes Barthé an excellent character portraitist, as his portrait busts of John Gielgud, Maurice Evans, Kreutzberg, Jimmie Daniels and Rose McClendon show unmistakably. However, it is in figure sculpture of racial types that his talent expresses itself most capably and with greatest promise of making a unique contribution to Negro art.

The Baltimore Museum show was in many respects the Negro art event of the year. In the first place, it represented the first regular showing of Negro art in a Southern municipal museum. In this, several factors played a role of progressive collaboration: the timely initiative of the Baltimore Negro Citizens' Art Committee, under the chairmanship of Mrs. Sarah C. Fernandis; the new liberal policy of the museum management under the leadership of Mr. Henry Triede; the cooperation of the Harmon Foundation, the pioneer organization in the exhibition of the work of Negro artists; and the selective taste of the museum's acting director, Mr. R. C. Rogers. As a combined result, there ensued a selective showing of the advance front of Negro art with a decided emphasis on modernism in style, and technical maturity. Black and white, oils and sculpture, were well represented, with the emphasis on the graphic media. Among the sculptors, Sargent Johnson, Barthé and Henry Bannarn were well represented. There was the first American showing of a strong newcomer, the Jamaican-born modernist sculptor Ronald Moody. Moody's work, even though influenced by cosmopolitan Expressionism, has a healthy primitivism about it, especially in works like "Une Tête" and "Midonz," which makes him a welcome adjunct to the growing group of representative Negro sculptors. His talent would undoubted-ly benefit from closer contact with racial types, either West Indian or American.

In painting we have already mentioned the sensational series of Jacob Lawrence's Haitian tempera sketches, which attracted favorably both lay and professional attention. Archibald Motley was well represented by a competent series in his later style; Elton Clay Fax had a strong self-portrait and three competent oils, "Coal Hoppers," "Steel Worker" and "Lunchtime"; Palmer Hayden had two vigorously naive racial interpretations, "Midsummer Night in Harlem" and the "Janitor Who Paints"; Sam Brown had several water colors of clever conception.

The chief attraction in the oils section was a most carefully selected group of the works of the late Malvin Gray Johnson that was an object lesson in direct and sincere approach and convincing evidence of what contemporary Negro art lost in the premature death of this young genius. Whether Virginia landscapes or rural Negro types or rural labor themes, all of Gray Johnson's pictures in oil and water color were done with sincerity and power, hinting at that decline among our artists of both imitativeness and derivative exhibitionism, which is the main hope for the future of the younger generation of Negro artists. Miss Florence Purviance, a Baltimore artist, made a creditable debut, and in the black and white section James Lesesne Wells, Hale Woodruff, Dox Thrash, Robert Blackburn and, most especially, Wilmer Jennings, gave evidence of maturing powers of technical execution and conceptual grasp. With a request invitation for this show from the Dallas, Texas, Museum, we may justifiably say that Negro art has inaugurated a new phase of public influence and service.

—1939

Merton Simpson

Charles Alston

John Biggers

Ellis Wilson

# The Harmon Awards

by Evelyn S. Brown

SEVERAL years ago, a Negro artist was seen at work in his studio by the late William E. Harmon, founder of the Harmon Foundation. His work showed a finish and perfection that interested Mr. Harmon to the point of inquiring of him what his charge was for a portrait. The reply given seemed out of all proportion to the ability shown in the production, yet the artist said, "Because I am a Negro I cannot command a price which is commensurate with the amount of training I have had, the time consumed or perhaps the actual ability which I have shown in my production."

This meeting had much to do with the starting of the William E. Harmon Awards for Distinguished Achievement among Negroes, for Mr. Harmon, who had long been interested in the economic progress of these people, was probably more impressed than ever by the necessity of putting performance on the basis of its merits rather than considering it as good work for a Negro. The field of fine arts was but one of the eight fields of creative work which were considered in the series of awards during the five-year experimental period; yet, in this particular division, the achievement has been of a more tangible nature.

It has not been possible to cover at one time the total achievement of Negroes in this country in farming and rural life, in education, in literature, in music, in science, in business or in religious service. One or more endeavors could be singled out in any of these fields and looked upon as outstanding and worthy of recognition. Yet, in fine arts, it has been possible for the Harmon Foundation to keep closely in touch with a large number of creative workers and to bring to the attention of the public, during a period of several years, the high quality of their productions.

This has been accomplished through five exhibitions in New York City, one of which is now current, and through three traveling art shows which have visited the principal cities of the country and been shown in the leading galleries. It is estimated that more than 350,000 people have seen the productions of Negro artists through traveling exhibitions, and several thousand each year view the work as it is shown in New York. Thus the art of the Negro, which had so much to do with bringing the Harmon Awards into being, has very largely outgrown these recognitions at the present time and now stands quite apart from them in the program of the foundation's work.

When the entries were received in the first year of the fine arts award (1926), they were housed in an empty room at the foundation's offices on Nassau Street. It became clear, as soon as they were hung for the consideration of the judges, that they were vivid and alive beyond the usual range of pictures submitted for judgment. As soon as the judges had passed on them, it was the intention to send them immediately back to the artists. Word of the collection spread, however, through various channels, and many people, entirely unsolicited in any way, came to see them.

The foundation realized that this interest was genuine and that in another year the pictures should have a public showing. International House, on upper Riverside Drive, offered a space which was open equally to white and colored groups and fairly central to both in New York. While the gallery itself was small, the charming cordiality of International House itself furnished a fine background for the early exhibition work.

Neither the foundation nor the Commission on Race Relations of the Federal Council of Churches, which was administering the awards and cooperating in the exhibition, had had any experience in putting on an art showing; and yet, in those early years, workers from the two organizations did everything, from unpacking the material, through the hanging, the publicity, the making-up of catalogues, to the final packing for reshipment to the artists. Approximately 3,000 people attended that first exhibition, and the snowball of interest rolled larger in size. It was readily apparent that this was a work which would have to continue.

After the second showing, letters from many sections of the country began to arrive requesting the use of the exhibit in interracial projects and Negro Week programs, so that in 1929 a portion of the work that had been shown in New York was assembled and sent out "on the road" by the Commission on Race Relations. The following year, still more cities desired the exhibition, and this time there was a wider range of interest, carrying through to museums and fine arts galleries along the Atlantic Seaboard, into the Middle West, and out to the Pacific Coast. This has been continued to such an extent that two traveling shows were conducted during the past year, and, in addition, a portfolio of photographic reproductions of more than 100 selections from four New York exhibitions was prepared for clubs and small gatherings.

In 1931, it was apparent that the small gallery of International House could not again be used to accommodate the large numbers who had indicated that they were closely following the development of the Negro artist. The Art Center, through Mr. Alon Bement, the director, arranged with the foundation for the use of its entire first floor, and 123 productions, including paintings by Edward M. Bannister, lent by Dr. John Hope of Atlanta University, and some by Henry Tanner, lent by Mr. John E. Nail and the Grand Central Galleries, were displayed.

This is the largest exhibition which the foundation has thus far sponsored, but it was assembled at a great deal of effort—so much so, that the foundation realized that an exhibition each year was not giving the artists sufficient time to study and produce, and that there would have to be a pause before another showing could be made. The present exhibition, which is now being held at the Art Center through the cooperation of the National Alliance of Art and Industry, has borne out this theory, for it has come about entirely through the requests of the artists themselves and what has practically amounted to the demand of the public. The foundation had felt that, with the present business conditions, it would not be possible to sponsor an exhibition this year, but with these earnest urgings the opportunity was one which could not be set aside.

In watching the work as it has come in from the artists over the six-year period, the foundation has been able to note a very definite advance this year over the work of other years. It is not only apparent in the actual productions that have come to its attention, but also in the efforts that are being put forth by the artists toward a means of expression that may be individual and bring out the richness of the environment, custom and experience that lies in their background. It is true that those who are painting today have not experienced scenes of tribal or jungle life, have not known conditions of repression in slavery which brought forth so much in Negro music, and that they have had—where training has been possible— their study in art with the white artist; yet it is believed that these strong influences of the past, together with the African note (which is among the basic arts of the world), will emerge as the American Negro gains in his confidence and expression. This unique background, combined with the Negro's growth in the Western world, will gradually blend into something new, distinctive and fine, which will take an important place in American culture and the art history of the world.

—1933

Lois Mailou Jones

Warren L. Harris

Richmond Barthé

Jacob Lawrence

Henry O. Tanner. "Jews by the Wailing Wall." Oil. 1908. Harmon Foundation.

# Negro Artists Gain Recognition after Long Battle

by James A. Porter

THE AMERICAN Negro should take pride in his achievements in art over the past 50 years. Whereas, at the turn of century, the Negro artist was generally seen even by his own people as a cultural sport or misfit, foolishly swimming against the tide, today he stands on the threshold of world recognition as a contributor to Western art. By 1905, Henry O. Tanner, Meta Warrick Fuller, William A. Harper and others had already demonstrated a sense of their profession as a calling and a responsible field of endeavor. Embarrassed by vicious racist propaganda, snubbed by white publishers who preferred the scurrilous "darky" representations created by Frost and Kemble and other white illustrators to honest versions, and irked by discriminatory restrictions on their attempts to show their work, they nevertheless persisted until the respect and admiration of many whites and a few appreciative Negroes were won. In fact, they were the heralds of better days for the Negro artist.

Tanner alone among these early Negro artists of this century enjoyed a truly international fame. He was made a member of the French Legion of Honor. In the United States, the National Academy of Design honored him with an associate membership. His works were purchased for or presented to several important American museums of art. Private collectors vied for acquisition of his best paintings. His deserved artistic triumphs abroad enforced recognition of him at home.

From 1900 to 1925, Negroes generally had to make their own opportunities in the fine arts. They had to wangle opportunities for study and travel and literally wheedle their way into the studios of white master artists under whom they wished to study. Later, to exhibit their work, they were forced to use the churches, the vestibules and reading rooms of public libraries and YMCA buildings, or the classrooms of public school buildings. Occasionally, they received help through well-intentioned race leaders, broad-minded educators or white patrons of means. They were also handicapped by the absence of that critical interest in their work which is usually exercised for good or ill by the art critic or connoisseur.

## "REALIST" PAINTERS

Through such vicissitudes arose the first group of "realist" painters and sculptors around 1910. Concerned principally with earning a livelihood, a number of these early twentieth-century artists were at the same time keen observers of reality. John Henry Adams, Jr., Clinton DeVillis, W. O. Thompson, Richard Lonsdale Brown, Samuel Collins and W. E. Scott won praise for their portrayals of character, life and landscape.

Though none was a great artist, they did achieve results comparable in some respects to the work of their white contemporaries, the realists Glackens, Luks, Henri and Shinn, who were once derisively called the "Ashcan School" painters.

## THE DOMINANT URGE

In art, as in literature, science, education and other walks of life, the alert Negro felt the dominant urge to defeat the theoretical, the fanciful and the real misconceptions and prejudices entertained of the Negro by the white world. The struggle to do just that was most intense throughout the first 25 years of this century. Knowing this, we can understand why the realists were dominated by their interest in factual renderings of the Negro. Later they were to build on the materials thus discovered. Sculptures symbolizing the Negro's cultural and historical contributions, his aspirations, his sufferings, were done by Meta Warrick Fuller with enchanting power. May Howard Jackson and Edward A. Harleston, in direct portraiture of Negro leaders and fine character studies, proudly enriched Negro art with dignified types. Yet, adverse circumstances kept these pioneer artists from utilizing their creative energies to the full.

The isolation of the American Negro artist of the middle period from the mainstream of culture is well illustrated by the fact that the great New York Armory Show of 1913 made little impression on him until the late 1920's. That show had shocked even sophisticated white Americans into attentiveness to the advanced modernism of European art. For fully 15 years after its closing, young Negro artists were still preoccupied with academic realism or with a belated Impressionism of manner, while all around them the old complacency of American art was losing ground.

## "NEW NEGRO MOVEMENT"

In fact, the Negro artist was not disturbed by the aftermath of World War I until the middle of the third decade. When unemployment and bad housing in our larger cities, and the first ominous signs of the great Depression, began to inspire serious racial conflict, out of the effort to understand and interpret these mass disturbances and shifting conditions was born the so-called "New Negro Movement." Then, for the first time in our American history, was world attention focused on the cultural heritage and the living arts of the American Negro.

With the establishment of the Amy Spingarn Awards for achievement in literature and art in 1924, and three years later the Harmon Awards for achievement in art, literature, science and other fields, the third decade became a landmark of the practical advancement of our effort in the creative arts.

## SHOWS BY NEGRO ARTISTS

One very immediate result of the deliberate encouragement and publicity given Negro artists was the multiplication of individual and group shows by Negro artists. As opportunities would in the course of time lead to recognition, it was understandable that more and more youthful talent was recruited to the standard of art. Most of the younger artists, like their predecessors, were easel painters or modelers of small sculpture. Their work ranged from portraiture to still life and genre. The influence of the "New Negro" propaganda was evident in their preference for race themes. But very little that they produced evinced any bitterness or critical social feeling.

Possibly but little agreement can be had on the matter of which were the most representative artists of the Twenties. The paintings of Harleston, of the late Laura Wheeler Waring, W. E. Scott and Palmer Hayden testified to the maturity of their authors. But the new work by Archibald Motley, Malvin Gray Johnson and a number of others compelled attention.

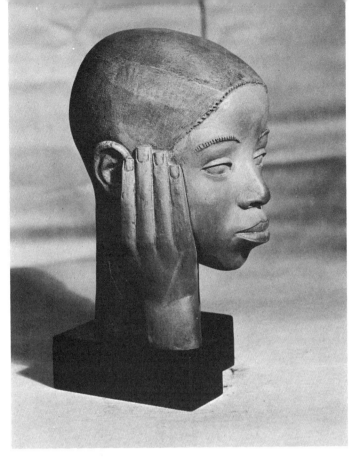

Sargent C. Johnson. "Chester." Plaster.
Harmon Foundation.
Meta Warrick Fuller. "Water Boy." Bronze.
Harmon Foundation.

James L. Wells. "St. Francis and the Birds." Oil. 1957.

Albert Alexander Smith. "Generations." Oil.
1929. Harmon Foundation.

Aaron Douglas. "Were You There?" Book cover design.

## AFRICAN SCULPTURES

The Armory Show had revealed to America certain currents of influence in modern European art. Among those currents, that of African Negro art had impressed Picasso, Braque, Derain, Matisse, Van Dongen and other European moderns. These artists had summoned the world to behold the beauties of a formerly disprized art.

Stimulated in their turn not only by the African art itself, but also by the enthusiastic writings of great critics like Dr. Albert C. Barnes of Merion, Pennsylvania, some of our own artists began at this time to study the contours and rhythmic patterns of African sculptures.

But the Negro artist was not yet to have entirely clear sailing. The very strangeness of African art, and the widespread public misconception of the background of the Negro, joined with the American plantation tradition to raise one more stumbling block in the way of free creativity. It was difficult for Negro writers and artists of the 1920's to find well-established white publishers for their work. Traditional preconceptions of the Negro character held by certain whites prevented a fair point of view toward either the content of Negro writing or the forms of Negro art. The much-abused words *naive* and *primitive* were reserved as prejudgments of Negro culture, art and character. Yet these chains, too, were finally loosed from the wrists of the Negro artist.

## BROADER EDUCATION

Broader educational opportunity was rapidly made available to the Negro artist. More Negro art students were sent abroad to study in the third decade of this century than were sent during the entire nineteenth century. In addition to this, certain educational institutions serving Negroes began to strengthen their long-standing offerings in art, and to call upon Negro artists for help with the planning and teaching of art programs.

At Howard, the first art gallery completely under supervision of a trained Negro staff was established in 1930. Under the direction of Professor James V. Herring, this gallery now ranks both as a fine university art gallery and as a force in Negro education. Since 1942, Atlanta has held its annual competition in painting, sculpture and the graphic arts exclusively for Negro artists.

## ART APPRECIATION

Many Negro colleges in the South now have courses in art appreciation or, indeed, in studio practice.

One of the most influential factors in the change of regard for the Negro artist in recent years has been the historical and critical research done in the history of Negro art. The writings of Murray, Brawley, Locke and Porter have considerably broadened our perspectives of Negro art history. Not only the so-called "ancestral African arts" but also the Negro's artistic achievements in the Western Hemisphere have been thus illuminated. It is now possible to look on our twentieth-century accomplishments as in part the fruitage of more than a century of creative effort.

For the present-day artist, however, the most stimulating factor has been the definite, if sparse, recognition accorded him by a respectable number of American museums and art galleries, and important private collectors. Also significant is the fact that Negro artists have been regularly winning regional and national art awards for the past 20 years.

## CREATIVE WORK

Mass recognition and acceptance of the Negro artist came in with the creation of the Works Progress Administration and affiliated agencies during the Roosevelt regime.

Federal subsidy opened art workshops and other training opportunities, and teaching and creative projects which theretofore had been denied Negro and white alike.

To the Federal opportunity were added at the same time opportunities supported by state or municipal or private organizational means. These were the adult education workshops, the municipal art centers such as the St. Louis Art Center and the Harlem Art Center, and various welfare agencies giving employment to artists.

## MURALS AT FISK UNIVERSITY

Probably no Negro artist since Robert S. Duncanson had tried his hand at serious mural painting until, in the 1930's, Aaron Douglas of New York painted subjects drawn from Negro history on the walls of the Fisk library. Soon thereafter, mural paintings appeared at Talladega, at Hampton, at Howard, and in Negro-staffed libraries and YMCA's.

During World War II, several Negro artists carried out murals on the walls of USO canteens, officers' clubs and PX units in this country and abroad.

## TOP WOMEN ARTISTS

In sculpture and painting, colored women have been among the foremost contributors. Selma Burke, winner of a Rosenwald Fellowship, has conducted several successful one-man shows of sculpture. Among women painters, the most outstanding is Miss Lois M. Jones of Howard University.

## COMMERCIAL ART

Gains in the less creative field of commercial art are not nearly so spectacular. The names Elmer Stoner and E. Simms Campbell of New York loom large in illustrating and cartooning. Campbell has for some time drawn special features for *Esquire* magazine and various newspapers.

## COLLECTOR'S ITEMS

Since the mid-1920's when the first etchings of Albert Smith became collector's items, Negro artists have worked increasingly well in the various techniques of the graphic arts. For truly fine accomplishments in lithography, wood carving and etching, Alan Freelon, James L. Wells, Dox Thrash, Wilmer Jennings, William E. Smith, Charles Sallee and Robert Blackburn may be cited.

The Negro artist should look toward complete integration in American art. Though he belongs to a minority group, there is no reason for him to accept cultural segregation as the inevitable state of things. Two or three years ago he was upset over the decision to boycott exhibitions of all-Negro art. But such a question or practice is only superficially related to the main problem—that of serious and continual production, against which neither time nor prejudice will prevail. Of course, the strategic and political aspects of free art practice must never be neglected. Therefore, let the Negro artist join with his white fellow-artists in fighting cultural segregation and all the provincial, regional and class brands of philistinism that now hamper cultural growth in America.

—1950

# The Young, the Hopeful and the Rebellious

Richard Dempsey. "Fear." Oil.

# Four Rebels in Art

by Elton C. Fax

IF YOU are looking for an appraisal of artists and their art all done up in fancy esoteric jargon, you will not find it in the paragraphs I have written here. This is a statement about four distinguished Americans whose works speak to the world in forceful reproach at what they see and feel as gross injustice. They are Negroes—three men and a woman. Their mood is rebellious. Because they are true artists, they speak in voices strong, articulate and shattering to the national conscience. By voices that shatter the national conscience I mean voices proclaiming that the mantle of dignity and greatness fits our nation badly because Uncle Sam has become grossly overweight from excess of fear, bigotry and hatred.

To understand the how and the why of the rebellion in these artists, one has to look long and honestly at the times and places that bred them. One has to also remember that there have always been many Negroes who have not met adversity with a smile and with negative placidity. Thus, viewed in the order of their arrival on the scene, the quartet is led by Elizabeth Catlett.

## ELIZABETH CATLETT

She is a sculptor, painter and print-maker. She is tall, strong, handsome and not given to easy smiling, small talk or idle chatter. For the last decade she has lived in Mexico.

There, amid the shades of Hidalgo, Morelos, Obregón and other great Mexican freedom fighters, Elizabeth Catlett draws, carves, and rears her family. Disdainful of tourist attitudes, this university-trained woman lives with Mexicans in the manner of Mexicans. In return, she finds an acceptance she never found in Washington, D.C., where she was born—or in Iowa, Louisiana, Texas, Virginia and New York, where she pursued the study and practice of her craft. Deep and eternal is her compassion for oppressed human beings, and her portrayal of them glows with a warmth that is as real as it is unsentimental.

The year was 1915. Eighty Negroes and 13 white men were lynched by U.S. mobs. The nation's colleges and universities awarded Bachelor's degrees to 281 Negroes, and a daughter, Alice Elizabeth, was born to the Catletts. Before she was five, Elizabeth had come to know the small child's terror of mob violence. She also learned that her people were not hesitant to strike back in defense of their lives and property.

A group of white soldiers, sailors and marines on leave in Washington launched an unprovoked attack upon Negro citizens of the city's Southwest section. The attackers, infuriated over the social acceptance overseas of Negro servicemen by Europeans, had taken that means of "putting the Negroes in their proper place." That was on Saturday, July 19, 1919. The next day the assailants,

Jacob Lawrence. "Meat Market." Gouache. 1964. Collection of Mrs. Monroe Golden.

reinforced by white civilians, raided streetcars and other vehicles, dragging Negroes from them and beating them into unconsciousness. One Negro was beaten in front of the White House. Three hundred others were wounded by gunfire and assorted weapons.

Another siege, planned for the next day, found Washington's Negroes "ready"; and the raid on a large Negro section resulted in the death of four whites and two Negroes, the wounding of scores of whites, *and the end of the Washington riot!*

Six years later, a Ku Klux Klan parade two hours long marched down Washington's Pennsylvania Avenue. The Klansmen were in full regalia, and their demonstration had the permission of the U.S. government. Elizabeth Catlett was 11, quite old enough to understand—and to remember. Today she remembers Negroes less "privileged" than she was—workworn men and women of the slums and the rural cabins. And she remembers their children with whom she went to school, and played, and fought.

When Elizabeth Catlett draws humble working people and their children, whether they be Mexican or American Negro, they spring alive under her skillful hand. When she carves them she is superb. Her sculptures of Negro mothers are awesomely strong, and, like her terse conversation, they are bereft of all non-essentials. Their heads tilt upward at defiant angles, and their feet are planted squarely under them. And why not? Elizabeth Catlett learned early that to survive as an individual she would have to lift her own head and plant her own feet firmly on the good earth.

## JACOB LAWRENCE

Following the outbreak of World War I, Negroes migrated from the South to Northern cities in two massive waves. The first occurred between 1916 and 1919, the second between 1921 and 1923. By the thousands they streamed into New York, Chicago, Philadelphia, Pittsburgh, Cleveland, Detroit and St. Louis looking for work. They were also seeking better treatment from white folks than they had been getting in Dixie. Jacob Lawrence's family came with that first migration. They tried Atlantic City, where Jake was born. Later they moved on to Philadelphia, but by the time Jake was 12 his folks had arrived in Harlem.

The Harlem of 1927 was indeed the legendary Harlem of the Roaring Twenties—the Negro capital of jazz, of sultry night spots owned by white mobsters, of policy kings, bootleggers, assorted hustlers and fabulous stage personalities. It was the Harlem of writers, painters, hard-working domestics and day laborers, Bojangles, the Barefoot Prophet, Kid Chocolate and Ethel Waters. And it was also the Harlem of A'Leilia Walker, whose mother, a one-time laundress, made an enormous fortune ironing the "naps" out of Negro hair.

Ten years earlier Negroes had occupied only a section of that legendary Harlem. As they poured in from the South, whites began to flee the area. But there were always more migrant Negroes than there was room in Harlem, and soon a ghetto was formed. The housing shortage and the fact that most of New York's Negroes were being forced into that one area created profits for rapacious landlords and grave problems for Negroes. The situation grew tense—terribly tense. And then came Marcus Garvey.

The squat, flamboyant and electrifying black printer from the island of Jamaica proclaimed himself the Messiah of the Negro. By 1920, through oratorical skill, a weekly newspaper, the *Negro World*, and an uncanny knack for collecting money from the Negro masses, he had captivated throngs of Negroes all over the nation. Garvey's thunderous promises to Negroes of a merchant

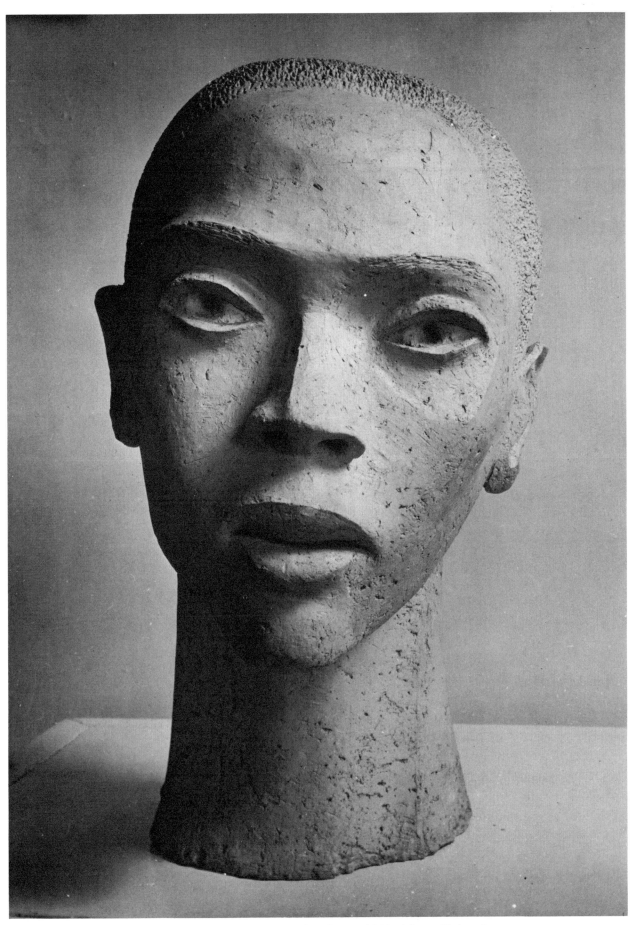

Elizabeth Catlett. "Young Girl." Plaster. 1946. Atlanta University.

marine of their own (the Black Star Line), and his plans to establish them as a black colonial power in Africa, were hard for a suppressed people to resist. He did purchase three boats, one of which (the *Frederick Douglass*) foundered in Virginia waters on its intended maiden voyage to Cuba. Established Negro leadership, who had fared badly under Garvey's lashing oratory, waited for the Jamaican's schemes to collapse. They did; and Garvey was jailed, pardoned and deported, but not before he had made at least one lasting contribution. *Marcus Garvey made white America aware, for the first time, of the Negro masses' great disaffection for Jim Crow. And he gave the lowliest Negro a reason to be proud of his badge of blackness.* Such was the background against which 12-year-old Jacob Lawrence would later begin a unique career.

The Depression hit Harlem like a thunderbolt. Half of its congested population depended upon unemployment relief in 1933. Its infamous "Lung Block" housed more than 4,000 Negroes, whose death rate from pulmonary tuberculosis doubled that of all white Manhattan. Rats and roaches swarmed through its fetid tenements. Rags and old newspapers were stuffed into broken windows and chinks to keep out the winter blasts, and Negroes paid from 40 to 50 per cent of their slim incomes to live in such hovels. The Harlem of the gay and reckless Twenties was no more. "Depression Harlem" was the Harlem Jake Lawrence lived in and came to know so dreadfully well. It was the Harlem of his early paintings.

A blind man is led along a squalid street. A child pauses hungrily before a dingy shopwindow where hang a few scrawny chickens. Children play their games in the dense concrete forest littered with refuse and filth. The colors are flat and sombre, with contrasting areas of black and white balanced within the composition. Figures, buildings, pavements

and sky bite into the consciousness of the viewer. This is HARLEM, man! It is the dozens of Harlems all across America, seen through the sensitive eye and mind of an aroused inhabitant. In those early days the career of Toussaint L'Ouverture fascinated Jake Lawrence, and he made a series of 41 paintings of the great Haitian general. Later he did series commentaries on John Brown, the struggles of the American Revolutionists, and the powerful group called *The Migration*.

As he continues to paint, one notes Lawrence's technical advancement. Even more striking is the constancy of the artist's awareness of the changing scene. The current demonstrations of Negro youth against fearful white tyranny and the cruel ineptness of that tyranny in meeting youth's challenge is a theme Lawrence handles with strikingly personal symbolism. To those of us who know him closely, Jake Lawrence matures in a way that is beautiful to see. The fires of outrage burn bright within him, and deep inside the flames he forges the tools of retaliation. When he replies, either orally or in paint, he does so with a deadly clarity. Jake Lawrence shakes you up. With his experiences and his power to transmit them he has every right to.

## CHARLES WHITE

Like Jacob Lawrence, Charles White was born in poverty during the first wave of the Negro migration. Chicago is his hometown. His mother worked in domestic service and his father toiled in the steel industry before entering the U.S. postal service.

The year before Charley White was born a gruesome massacre took place in the southwestern Illinois city of East St. Louis. Between one and two hundred Negroes were shot, burned to death and hanged by white mobs of men, women and children. Six thousand Negroes were driven from their homes. Negro laborers, newly arrived from the South, had been used as strikebreakers

Charles White. "Two Brothers Have I Had on Earth—One of Spirits, One of Sod."
Charcoal and Chinese ink. 1965. Collection of the Government of Guinea.

John Biggers. "Web of Life." Mural (detail). University of Texas.

at three major meat-packing houses. Fear, suspicion and hatred spread throughout the white community, and mobs quickly formed to drive all Negroes from the city. They nearly succeeded.

Anti-Negro feeling in Chicago was on the upsurge. Between 1910 and 1920, the city's Negro population tripled. One-fourth of the laborers in the Armour stockyards were Negroes, and the spectre of even more employable Negroes migrating to Chicago panicked white workers, who had been led to believe that Negroes were too shiftless to be considered serious labor competition. Whites therefore demanded a subservience of Negroes in employment opportunities. The latter, many of them battle-conditioned veterans of World War I, were having no part of it. In the three-day riot that ensued, 13 Negroes and 11 whites were reported killed. Such was the climate in which Charley White spent the first year of his life.

The youngster had scarcely reached his third birthday before 25 bombs had been thrown at the homes of Chicago's Negroes who could afford to buy homes. Eight bombings occurred on the residences of whites who had dared to sell to Negroes; but nobody bothered to waste bombs on the houses occupied by the White family and the other Negroes who lived on their block.

Chicago, 1925: *Boom!* Another hate bomb smashed the north side of the newly acquired Negro Bethesda Baptist Church. No one was injured. Damage estimated at $50,000. Charley White was seven years old. When he tells us that he began to draw at the age of seven, we conclude that right then and there he at least sensed *why* he had to draw and what he had to draw about. He speaks about having rebelled against most formal schooling. Yet he made it through high school with honors! With professional study at Chicago's Art Institute, the Art Students League of New York, and the Taller de la Gráfica in

Mexico, White was on his way to a powerful mode of self-expression and communication.

Charley White paints murals and makes lithographs and woodcuts. What he does not remember about the science and art of draughtsmanship alone would do a lesser professional a lot of good. His theme: the struggle of the American Negro for the dignity of full manhood. In both murals and prints he reflects a serious study of the Mexican masters of those crafts. The Orozco influence is particularly strong in White's panel installed at Hampton Institute. Titled "The Contribution of the Negro to American Democracy," it depicts Negro abolitionists, educators, soldiers and working people welded in a strikingly rhythmic and solid design. This is Charley White's answer to those who would deny the Negro's strength. He gives us a portrait of a people who have withstood lynching and privation, who have come through the great Depression of the Thirties and who have given America its current young Negro leadership. This panel embodies the forces that organized the sit-ins, kneel-ins, wade-ins and the March on Washington. And there are those also who, tomorrow, will free the nation from her own bondage. All of this is said and implied in one painting because of what Charley White has been forced to feel and see from childhood.

Today his statements of conviction roll across our land with the resonance of sustained thunder. Only a man fully and proudly aware of what he is and what he will yet be can speak in tones so commanding. Charley White is that kind of man.

## JOHN T. BIGGERS

The drawings, paintings and sculpture of John T. Biggers that brought him initial acclaim speak for the anonymous Negroes of the rural South. His are the interpretations of the hopes and aims of those who, spurning migration, remain behind to carry on the freedom fight on the hottest lines of battle. The Negroes whom Biggers draws are the rustics whose manners and customs are ridiculed and rejected by many whites and middle-class Negroes. More recently, John Biggers has been to Ghana and to Nigeria. Out of that experience he has given us a magnificent book, *Ananse: The Web of Life in Africa;* and in typical Biggers fashion he has reported mainly on the common folk of the towns and villages he visited in those two West African countries.

The youngest of these four artists, John Biggers is a native of Gastonia, North Carolina. While his home state is not considered one of the "hard core" areas of segregation, neither can it be considered a Southern oasis of pro-Negro attitudes. In the 35 years preceding Biggers' birth (1924), North Carolina had lynched over 40 Negroes. It had lynched seven more before young Biggers had reached his eighteenth birthday.

Gastonia is a thriving mill town whose 1955 population was 23,000. A serious mill strike in 1929 brought national attention to the workers' conditions and to the low wages of the workers there. Negroes in surrounding rural communities work the land yielding cotton for the mills. They are the people from whom John Biggers draws inspiration for his murals and prints.

Early schooling in North Carolina was enlarged upon when Biggers attended Hampton Institute in Virginia. There he met Victor Lowenfeld, who later headed the Department of Art Education at Pennsylvania State University. "It was Victor Lowenfeld who helped me firm up my convictions of who I really was," Biggers says. This artist is that rare combination of high academic and high esthetic achievement who knows that it is certainly not his doctorate that makes him an important artist.

As a muralist, he looks for inspiration to Orozco and Charles White. "The Contribution of American Negro Women to American Life and Education" is the subject of the Biggers mural panel for the Negro YWCA of Houston, Texas. This panel is an expertly organized interpretation of the moral matriarchy embodied in the subject. The artist is no less skillful when handling smaller works. His drawings and lithographic prints have a monumental grandeur that lends a unique dignity to the simple people represented in them. John Biggers occupies a place of distinction with the three other artists already viewed here.

Collectively they voice their dissatisfaction with their country's default to its own declared principles, and that collective voice is clear, resolute and eloquent. Just think of it. We are the only people on earth who could produce this particular quartet of artists, together with Odetta, Miles Davis, Sidney Poitier, Mahalia Jackson and Ray Charles— all swinging on the same beat.

—1961

# Magic Stones and Totem Poles

by John Torres

WHO AM I, and how did I come to be here on this farm, shoveling dirt onto a pasture lined with magic stones and totem poles? From what I can understand now, I feel that I am just a stonecutter who is breaking his back to become a sculptor. The word "sculptor" implies distance and wisdom combined with excellent hand control, which I do not have at this time. It also implies accuracy of inner strength, so that individual projects are allowed to go their full gestation period. Many of my pieces appear to me as though they were hurried because a show had to go up, or a bill had to be paid. Sculpture doesn't want to know from hang-ups. It wants what it needs: to be fantastically beautiful or strong, or both. Make no mistake—I participate in my own growth, and recognize that, as stonecutters go, I can damn sure swing a hammer with anyone my age. But greatness *is,* period. And the sooner I get me a piece that can stand next to one of those from the Middle Kingdom Egyptians, the better I'll like it.

In some ways, my education, like many others', was a miracle. A 20-year-old young man, home from two years of western wandering, arrived in New York with $9.00. I started school at the Art Students League in September of '59. My first classes were with Frank Reilly. That turned out to be largely a disaster, mostly because I didn't connect to Mr. Reilly's philosophy, but at least it was a start, and it gave me something to react to and against. I then changed my class to Sidney Dickenson's painting class, mostly because I had met two young men in the class who seemed to be really serious about what they were doing. One was Hal Moore, and the other was Mike MacDonnell. These two guys were really unusual in their dedication. Both of them had had previous art training, and when I met them they certainly could be considered advanced students. They took me into their studio and showed me concretely, by painting right beside me, what the new words I was learning—composition, value, chroma, color, drawing—could mean.

I then changed to what I had originally wanted to do, which was sculpture, and I began studying with John Hovannes. Perhaps the most fortunate thing that ever happened to me was to find Hovannes teaching the morning sculpture class at the Art Students League.

At that time, my work day went something like this: I'd appear at school between seven-thirty and eight-fifteen, sneak in the entrance where the garbage cans were collected and begin work as soon as I could get into my old clothes. I'd work by myself until the school opened at nine, and then be part of the formal class until twelve-thirty. I'd eat lunch, then, if I had the money, and go to work at a mail-order house where I was a stock-boy. At the end of the three-and-a-half years I worked for this particular mail-order firm, I was general manager. The owner of the business was absolutely sure that I was not an artist, but I made a lot of progress in my art during those three years, and I made sure that when I had a show, he had an invitation to it, so there would be no misunderstanding between us. My hours at the mail-order company ran from one in the afternoon until about eight or nine at night. During the Christmas rush, I would work later. So my day started at seven in the morning and ended around ten at night. I did this for three years. Sometimes, when I was particularly excited about a piece I was working on, I would go back to the school at nine-thirty or ten and hide in the cloakroom until everybody went home and the janitor turned out the lights. Then I would turn on one single light and work on my own piece until, sometimes, two in the morning.

I think this kind of single-mindedness is absolutely essential to becoming a sculptor. I remember very vividly that the administration of the school didn't particularly like the sculpture department, because there was a group of us in there who were absolutely serious about what we were doing, and we got there too early, and we stayed too late, and we were messy. From these points of view, I can't blame the school, for, in a sense, having a little bit of a dislike for the way we were conducting our affairs.

In 1961, I decided to marry a girl that I had met one day in the smoking room on the third floor. I had been hurting inside that day, I remember, and, in order to ease that hurt, I had been sitting alone in this small concrete cubicle, reading Edna St. Vincent Millay aloud, and she came in. I asked her if she would mind if I kept reading. She said, "No." Later, I found that this particular wonderful young woman was able to complete parts of me that had seemed to be missing for years, and that armed with what she taught me about love, I was able to begin to use the idea, the

power and song of love in my work. Her name was Margaret Alexandra Clarke. I married her because I loved her, and more than that, I saw something: that she would one day be able to make something of great beauty, and when I say she taught me about love, I mean it, and as an illustration, I give to you one of her poems:

To John
I make a poem: your name
against the noises and disasters
of the city.
I make an incantation to find
hope amid the concrete same-
greyness of long corridors
of subway doors
closing.

I make a poem: your name
to magic-wand the apple
trees to bloom, to bring
the summer closer and cause
the lilacs to bloom in my
dooryard.

I make a poem: your name
to hold in darkness
against the fear and
tempest of the longing
night.

That was the springtime that she unleashed in me a torrent and shower of stone, and a run of words, like this thing from a concert we went to together. I sat scribbling in the margin of the program:

In the springtime I was caught
by the greenness of your eye
and the play of light in your
red-brown hair.
And when I was that young,
I saw that you had not been touched,
but, even then, that you were complicated
by the promise of a child.
There on the bridge, at the end of winter,
you were wrapped in a heavy woolen shawl.
The night caught you,
. . . . . . . . . . .
In the springtime, I was caught
by the greenness of your eye,
and the play of light in your
red-brown hair.

During the first couple of years of marriage, I guess we were like many other young married people with one of the partners trying to get through school. Margaret worked, and I went to school full time and worked full time. It was hard, but it was what we wanted, and that's what we did.

The problem was that we were being pushed toward a crisis. In order to become a truly significant creator, a person has to spend an awful lot of time doing his work. And that means that all of the time that he's working to earn money, tension is mounting as he begins to find out more and more about his art. The deeper I got into sculpture, the more demanding it got, and the more necessary it became to have complete focus, complete attention and complete silence available for the sculpture voice to develop and to be heard.

In May of 1963, I had a one-man show in New York. I didn't expect to be reviewed, and I didn't expect to sell anything, but I did know three or four people I considered to have very good eyes, and I wanted them to take a look at the work and tell me what they saw. I remember three of the people came, separately, and they all said the same thing: "I don't care what you're doing. Whatever you're doing now, stop it and carve, because you're very close to making a significant breakthrough, for yourself and for sculpture."

It was at this time that I had to choose between quitting my job and working full time on my sculpture, or staying with my job and becoming an executive of the corporation. I chose to carve. On May 30, I left my job, with nothing in the bank, no money to feed myself or my wife, and things got so bad that summer that I had to send Margaret off to friends in Maine, just so that she would be able to eat. I stayed in the city and carved every day, as long as I could raise the hammer. I was living on thirty cents a day for food. At the end of the summer, I had an appointment to show my work to the Whitney Museum, the Guggenheim Museum and the Steven Radich

Gallery. When I showed them my work, the museums were polite, but noncommittal, and Steven Radich was critical, but encouraging.

I began the fall by enrolling for school without knowing how I was going to pay for it. Then I got a job with the Henry Street Settlement, so my work day changed slightly. At school at seven-thirty in the morning till two-thirty in the afternoon, then down to the settlement house to teach, from three in the afternoon until ten at night. By this time, we had a small antique shop to try to raise money to support my studio, so that when I got home from the settlement, at ten-thirty, I had to stay up till two in the morning refinishing antiques. We did this all of '63 and '64.

By the spring of 1964, my spirits were on the verge of tears. Margaret was pregnant, I didn't have enough money for my studio, I didn't have enough money for school tuition, which was $40 a month, and I was still crying for a space to work and for someone outside my immediate circle to acknowledge that what I was doing had some value—a wider audience than just myself.

In the first week of April, Hovannes gave me an application to the MacDowell Colony and asked me to fill it out. He told me that the school would act as my sponsors. I submitted the application and forgot about it. Meanwhile, my finances went down hill, and around May 1, I received my first eviction notice. If you have never faced the prospect of having to move your books, your records and your laundry onto the street where your friends walk by on the way to do their shopping, you have been excused from a severe pain over the eyes. And the morning that the eviction came, I went to school, tried to work, but couldn't. So I went to the telephone and called the MacDowell Colony office in New York and said, "I assume that I have not been awarded the fellowship to the colony. May I pick up my photographs?"

The secretary said, "Please spell your

name. I think you are one of the winners."

Dazed, I picked myself up off the floor of the phone booth. From that moment my life changed. I took my eviction notice to Rosina Florio, the registrar of the Art Students League, and told her that I could no longer afford to continue my studies. She asked me to return the following day. As I was leaving, I told her about the colony fellowship. Then I went into the park, and I sat down on a bench for a long time, with tears in my eyes. The following day, Miss Florio told me that my tuition fees had been waived for the rest of the year.

That summer of 1964, I was given a studio at the MacDowell Colony, with a place to sleep and three meals a day.

It was a dream come true, almost impossible to imagine. My studio was a barn, with marvelous soft light and the smell of hay—and silence. At first the silence frightened me, but then I began to use that silence that had never been available to me before. I began to listen to what my carvings wanted, and during that summer I discovered that, for me, sculpture was the sense of touch. I began to close my eyes and see through my finger tips, and my work changed. I think it became more personal, more beautiful and more professional.

By not having any interruptions from nine in the morning until six at night, I was able to focus in a new way, which gave me a hint that my life could be very productive. I was using hand tools for carving stone, and a light trimming axe for cutting wood. That summer I think I did about 10 sculptures in three months.

For the first time in my life, I had enough space in the studio to hang up the majority of drawings that I had been doing for the last two years. Some of the drawings were six feet tall, and it gave me a marvelous feeling to be able to cover the inside of a barn, from floor to ceiling, with the nudes of my life.

At the end of the summer, on October 4, a new miracle occurred. Alexandra Valeria Torres was born. I was in New York, working for the Henry Street Settlement, and Margaret was in Peterboro, at Monadnock Community Hospital, because it was cheaper and because it was such a beautiful area to do anything in, including having a baby. When mother and baby could travel, we went down to New York in an old, battered 1953 Dodge pickup truck, in the middle of October, with no heater.

When we got to New York, I had the feeling that I had to try to earn more money, so besides the teaching job at the settlement, and running an antique shop, I started using the weekends to obtain fireplace logs in New Hampshire, which I brought down and sold in New York. I've already described my schedule on weekdays. The wood business required that I get up on Saturday morning around three and load logging equipment into the old truck and drive for about six hours. I would arrive in New Hampshire around nine and go up into the woods, where I had permission to cut down trees on the MacDowell Colony land. I'd knock down as many trees as I could, and saw them into 18-inch logs, and load the truck.

This would usually take me all day, so I couldn't start back to New York until after eight P.M. I'd get to New York with the load about two or three in the morning. Then I would have to unload the truck into the back of my studio, which would take me another two or three hours, so that I usually ended up working 24 hours in a row, at least. Then I would sleep four or five hours, get back up, go to the studio, split the wood, and carry it back out to the truck and deliver it to the people who had ordered it. Sometimes I would have to carry 80 logs up five flights of stairs. The logs were so heavy that I couldn't lift more than four or five at a time. That's the way I spent all day Sunday, usually until

John Torres

John Torres. "The Monument." Plaster. 1963.

John Torres. "Horse Sketch." Bronze.
1963. Collection of Mr. and Mrs. J. Weinberg.

about nine at night. Then I'd go home, pull all the furniture off the sidewalk in front of the antique shop, eat dinner and fall into bed and try to get up at seven the next morning.

I had one big break, though, about school: the Ford Foundation was paying my tuition, so at least I didn't have that to worry about. They also paid a small monthly allotment for materials.

My work at the settlement seemed to be getting more and more complicated, because as my experience with handling children grew, the responsibilities the settlement wanted me to handle grew also. I started out just teaching a couple of woodworking classes, and the next thing I knew, I was working almost full time, dealing with boys and girls in woodworking, from the ages of six to 18, plus working with "difficult" groups—a program for pre-delinquent gangs. Then the sets for the teen-age stage productions had to be made, and sometimes the scenery for the plays alone would keep me at the settlement until two or three in the morning. It was a hard way to live. I felt like I went months without ever seeing my wife and baby.

In the winter of 1964–65, the settlement got involved in a strike, so I was without a salary for 11 weeks. This put us way behind on our bills, so our financial situation didn't seem to be improving. In the summer of 1965, a man I had met through the settlement asked me to lead a summer work-camp project in southwestern Massachusetts. The problem was to move a 90-foot barn six miles, which involved taking the barn apart, moving it across town, and putting it back up again. But before we could do the moving job, we had to prepare the site for the barn when we got it there. All this labor, which is quite a long story in itself, was to be done by 13- and 14-year-old boys and girls. To make a long story short, we did it, but by the time the summer was over, there was evidence that I was bleeding internally.

September 1, I went back to the Mac-Dowell Colony to work on three pieces of sculpture which I wanted to submit to the Tiffany Foundation competition, as I had been chosen as a finalist in that competition. I finished my pieces just in time to start teaching again, and by now my sense of fatigue was extreme. I felt as though I hadn't had a rest or a day off for about three or four hundred days. But I had a family to support and a career to support, so I just tried to get back in the harness—going to school in the morning and teaching afternoons and evenings, refinishing furniture at night and logging on the weekends. Once more, the scholarship was offered, so I didn't have to pay for my school, but my little girl was getting older, and her needs were increasing, as were my sculpture needs. I began to yearn to just carve, without going through so many gyrations just to stay alive. In the middle of November, I had an automobile accident. I was so tired I fell asleep while driving the big truck. I came within about six feet of killing myself. Two weeks later, I had an accident in the woods with the chain saw. I got within about an eighth of an inch of chipping the bone in my knee. After that, I just decided to throw in the towel. I figured that whatever I was doing, I was doing it wrong, and that all I really wanted to do was just carve. So I began to apply for assistance. I needed about $2,000 for tools and materials and living expenses for my family, so I could carve for four months without working for a living, and I tried every single door I heard about.

Finally, one of the doors opened, and the Studio Club of New York offered $800 if I could find someone else to put up the other $1,400. Julia Green Sturgis offered the other $1,400, and all of a sudden I was free.

The MacDowell Colony gave me a fellowship for four months, starting in January of '66, and with the money I had enough to get power equipment for carving and finishing. I got into the MacDowell Colony in the winter, and I started to carve like I had lost my sanity. I worked night and day, 14 hours a day some days, and I got into a rhythm and a momentum that was so beautiful and so perfect that I was able to work on five or six pieces at the same time. There were so many different sculptures at so many stages of becoming that I could spend 14 hours in the studio without making one false gesture. As the momentum built up, I was able to do a year's work every eight days. I finished 38 stone carvings in five months. I did 300 yards of drawings and about 20 poems.

I completely and thoroughly exhausted myself, so that at the end of the fifth month I found myself one day at the dining hall table with tears streaming down my face. I could not explain in words the reason for the tears, but I knew that I had come through something very important, and what I had gone through had been so meaningful in terms of sculpture that other people could feel it.

There seemed to be a great press around me. My immediate neighbors visited my studio, and I sold a lot of work to other artists, many of whom couldn't really afford to buy a sculpture but who were impressed by the tremendous sense of power in what they saw.

I did 38 carvings and sold about 35 of them, which meant that I had enough money to stay out in the country and continue working; so after the colony residence was over, we looked for a house with a barn that we might be able to rent, where I could be with my family and continue my work. We were lucky enough to find a house through a friend, a writer named Richard Frede, who told me that Margaret Mead's daughter and her husband had a farm in Hancock, New Hampshire, that we might be able to rent for two years, as they were going to the Philippines to teach and do research.

And I suppose that is part of the story of how I happened to be shoveling dirt on this meadow lined with magic stones and totem poles.

—1967

Robert Reid. "Track." Oil. 1965.

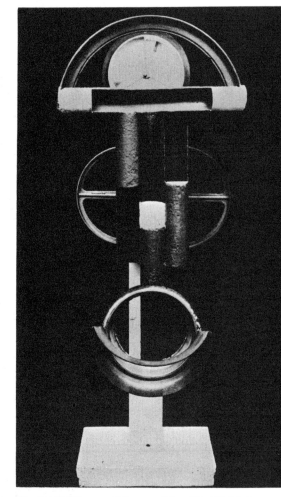

Todd Williams. "Coney Island." Welded
steel and iron, painted mobile. 1965.

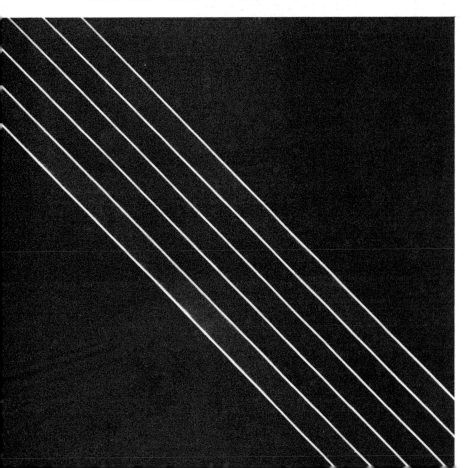

Sam Gilliam. "Tempo."
Acrylic on canvas. 1965.
Collection of Gerald Nordland.

# Artists of the Sixties

**by Hale Woodruff**

WHAT CRITERIA are appropriate to the valid assessment of the art of a people? For the answer, one must look first to the interacting forces which shape the artist as well as his art and, in the process, guard against oversimplification, for these forces are far more complex than they seem. There is, of course, the obvious factor of those broad cultural conditions which form the artist's immediate environmental experience. But there is also the factor of the artist's own interpretation of, and reaction to, his cultural experience. Thus, while culture and environment may provide ideas and themes, they are always, as art, filtered through the artist's own mode of formulation—his personal language. This combination of forces effects a primary particularization of the art in question. In concert, interacting among a group of artists, these forces become virtually a dialect.

But we must strive even beyond subject content and esthetic language to get at our roots, for perhaps the most valid measure of any art lies in the impact of qualities outside the obvious. Certainly, in the domain of the spirit and the senses, intangible but real, are forces which grip the very nature of art.

For the Negro American artist these forces may be especially significant. While he is naturally responsive to the general environmental culture of which he is a part—a culture which, incidentally, has fostered many of the broad and varied concepts of contemporary art, he seems sometimes to have pursued a tangential and independent search for an appropriate esthetic dialect. There is speculation, if not certainty, that this search stems from present-day social motivations. On the other hand, his quest may simply come from overriding concern with the broader problems of art itself. Whatever the reasons, it seems clear that the Negro artist has approached his art with a peculiar dedication, singularly avoiding the traps of mere journalistic narrative and literal banality to which so many other groups have fallen prey.

Thus, there are notable instances in which true and impressive achievements of artistic dialect have been realized by Negro artists. Some of them have undoubtedly been characterized by a kind of "racial quality"—at least they show indications of reaction and interpretation involving the experience of being part of a culture in which Negroes are a minority. For the greater part, however, the foundations upon which the Negro American has constructed his artistic language have been those which are rooted in the larger body of art itself, perhaps because they see in this larger body the opportunity for a totally free "universality" of artistic expression. The situation has given rise to claims that the Negro artist in America is an eclectic and that his eclecticism has obscured, if not obliterated, his more valid racial qualities.

Granted that the claim contains a certain

measure of truth, the allegations are superficial since they are generally based upon a superficial viewing of the outer crust of stylistic mannerisms rather than upon a closer, and more revealing, examination of the qualities which lie beneath. There, if one takes the trouble to look, will be found an intensity of spirit, a profundity of the senses, and a vitality of statement.

Moreover, while no attempt to justify eclecticism is intended here, it ought to be pointed out that eclecticism has characterized the development of art throughout history. The formal qualities of art have constantly been drawn upon by artists of varying cultures; the test is whether these qualities have been given new meanings and fresh significance.

It is equally risky to weigh the relative efficacy of art derived from broad environmental culture against that which emanates from more narrowly oriented racial sources. Not that these relative considerations must necessarily be overlooked, but the work of art must, finally, be judged upon its own merit.

Let us examine Lawrence. Here is a painter who, with a forcefully compelling sense of design rising from experience, brings us into immediate contact with a world which we know only too well. He has, in a sense, triumphed in the quest for an esthetic language which formulates reaction to environmental experience. Achieving a compatibility of subject, form and content, he has established an artistically harmonious fusion of three qualities which are often regarded as irreconcilable.

Robert Reid tends toward poetic imagery, projecting forms and symbols that have little to do with nature in the everyday sense of the term. Reid also resorts to playful brushwork, vitalizing abstract concepts and static space with a lively animation they might not otherwise possess.

Sam Gilliam, on the other hand, has declared allegiance to the current trend called "Hard Edge" painting—a style that is gaining popularity not only in America but in other parts of the world. The precision and purity of Gilliam's geometric forms are commensurate with the clean propriety of his bold colors, used in a way suggesting that he intends them chiefly for the purpose of evoking a response of pure sensation.

As Gilliam is dedicated to the "New Painting," so does Todd Williams subscribe to the "New Sculpture." The mechanical-like forms of his works combine functioning organic unity of movement with spatial dynamics. Despite this, however, Williams rescues his compositions from the cold rigidity of a machine through his amazingly imaginative creativity. In effect, his work challenges the claim that this form of art rests solely on a soulless world of technology and its mechanistic instruments.

Another of the younger group, Richard Hunt, showed promise of becoming one of the leading sculptors of the day at the very outset of his career. He now seems to be reaching fulfillment. Although Hunt's work may be categorically referred to as abstract, it seems to be based on a figurative motif. At least this is suggested by the nature of his forms. The true impact of Hunt's sculpture derives, however, from the warm humanness with which he tempers and qualifies it.

Barbara Chase, likewise, has her own distinct form and style. "Big little sculptures" is perhaps the most consummate and direct way to define her work. In this context it is obvious that "bigness" is not synonymous with size or scale; it refers instead to the magnitude of ideas and interpretations embodied in sculpture that speaks strongly, eloquently, and with conviction.

Both Hunt and Chase are keenly aware of the role played by the material used in their works. For them, the medium of metal contributes a vital factor to the visual totality of their ideas. There seems little doubt that had these works been executed in stone or wood the forms, as well as sensory response to them, would have been quite different.

Indeed, the restrictions imposed on the artist by his medium are often exploited by him to significant esthetic advantage. The graphic works of William Majors and Norma Morgan are cases in point. Etched in metal plates, Majors' delicate lines become enchantingly visual poetry. Morgan, too, engages a wide range of linear and textured variations, and the works of both artists, through the light-to-heavy weights of line and surface treatment, rise crescendo-like, then descend, to lead us over an elegant deployment of surface patterns and shapes.

The works of Charles White, now active primarily as a draughtsman, can be broadly characterized as "graphics." Apparently quite remote from the purposes of Majors or Morgan, his aim seems to be to bring us immediately face to face with his subject and the characters involved in it. Although his characters are often obliquely symbolic in their treatment, the unequivocal reality of each of them, not as *a* person but *all* persons, is a reminder to us of the travails, perhaps agonies, that mankind has always known.

Emilio Cruz surrounds his figures with voluminous shapes of color. Indeed, in Cruz's hands, color dominates imagery. His figures appear to come under the pervasive spell of harmonious and contrasting colors, moving chameleon-like as they take their places within the total spectrum.

It seems obvious, then, from the diversity of even so compact a collection as this, that the works of contemporary Negro American artists run the full gamut of expression. Is there a single thread which serves either as a racial or esthetic bond to link these works in a unified purpose? The answer must come—as answers almost always do—from examination of the works themselves. They are faits accomplis. They speak for themselves. And they augur well for the future.

—1966

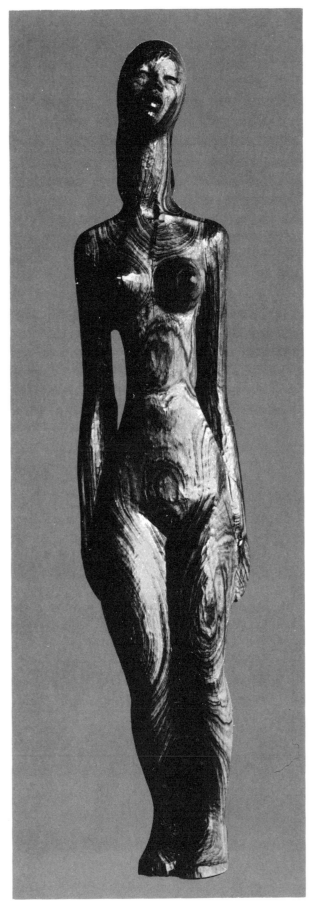

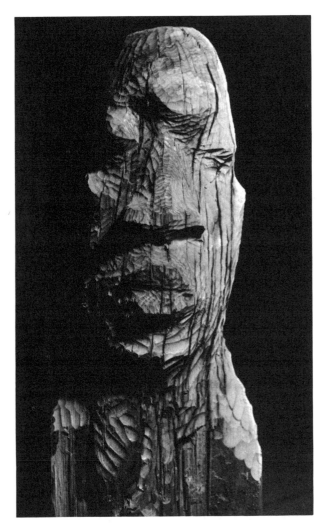

Arnold Prince. "Zulu." White oak.

Warren L. Harris. "Mattie." Plaster.

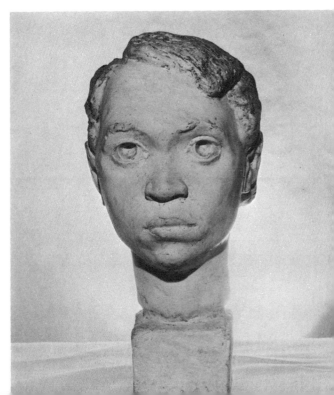

John W. Rhoden. "Female Figure." Wood.
Atlanta University.

## More Artists of the Sixties

SOME OF the most exciting art in America today is being done by black artists—but the black artist is still not being represented in the major exhibitions. There is a new awareness, a new fighting spirit. Black artists are organizing and protesting their exclusion, and at the same time their art is discovering all over again that black is beautiful. One cannot, of course, label their work black art, for it reflects the individual artist's experiences. Some artists do look upon all art executed by blacks as black art, but others feel that black art has to be visibly recognizable as "black." Today the black artist is working in a variety of mediums and in styles ranging from the abstract to the representational.

In addition to the "Artists of the Sixties" cited by Hale Woodruff, more artists working today can be found on the following pages.

—1969

Sue Jane Smock. "Priestess of Orosun." Woodcut. 1966.

Ellis Wilson. "Island Cemetery, Haiti." Oil.

Hughie Lee-Smith. "Cliff Grass." Oil.

Betty Blayton. "Childhood's End." Oil.

Rosalind Jeffries. "Composition No. 3." Charcoal.

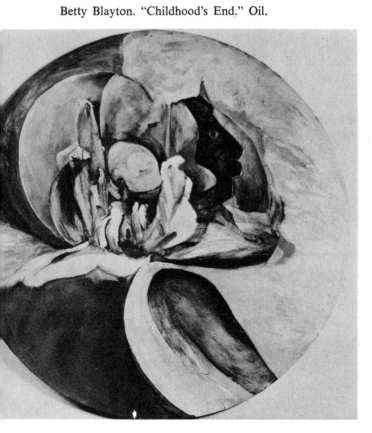

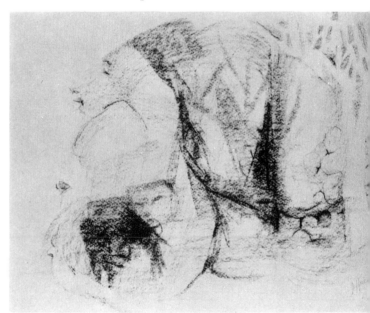

Faith Ringgold. "Mr. Charlie." Oil. 1964.

Reginald Gammon. "Freedom Now."
Acrylic on cardboard. 1965.

Joseph Delaney. "V-J Day, Times Square." Oil. 1945.

George Wilson, Jr. "Mother and Child." Oil. 1962.

James D. Parks. "Artist's Model." Oil.

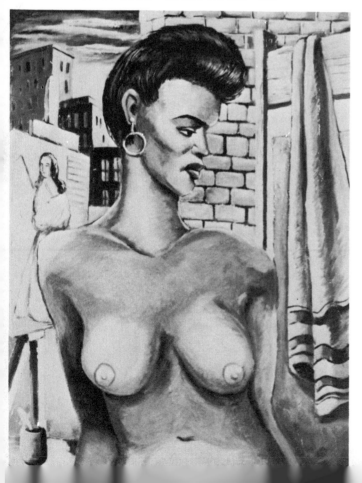

Clarence Edward Young.
"A Loud Sound of Silence." Oil.

Tom Feelings. "Big Band Blues Singer." Collage. 1961.

Shirley Woodson. "Beach Scene." Gouache.

A. C. Hollingsworth. "Reflection No. 2." Mixed media.

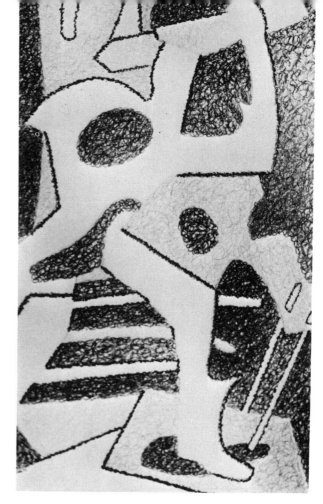

John Howard. "The Violin." Oil. 1961.

Haywood L. Oubre, Jr. "Conflict." Pencil.

Carroll Simms. Scene from *The Miracles of Christ*.
Stained glass window.

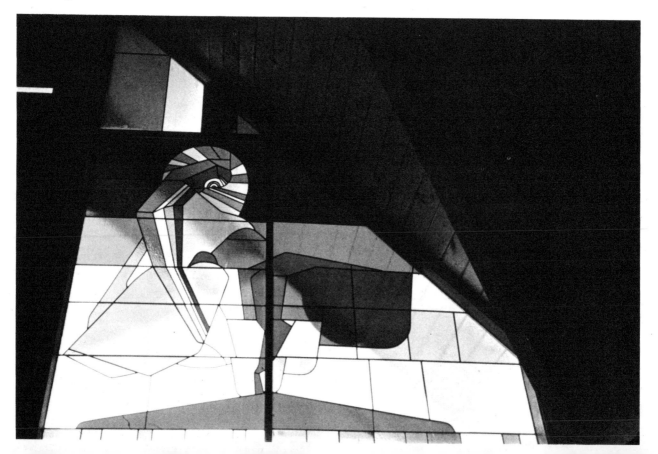

Thomas Sills. "Sea." 1960.

David C. Driskell. "The Pines." Encaustics on canvas. 1962. Collection of Mr. Louis K. Rimrodt.

Claude Clark. "Ignition." Oil.

Merton Simpson. "Confrontation III." Oil. 1967.

Archie Jefferson (left). "Mantantalus." Solart 3-DD.

Simon Outlaw. "Planes in Black and White." Oil. 1960.
Collection of Mr. Richard V. Clarke.

Walter Davis. "Monk's Now." Oil.

Floyd Coleman. "Remembrance of Things Past."
Mixed acrylics on canvas.

Hugh Harrell. "The Junkie." Oil.

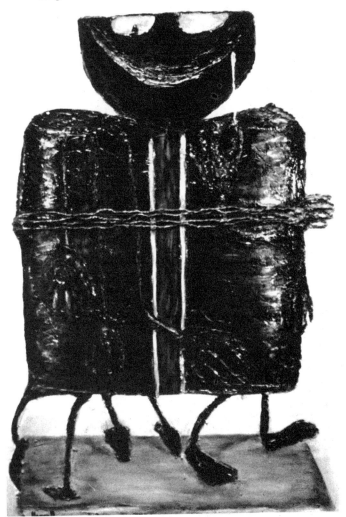

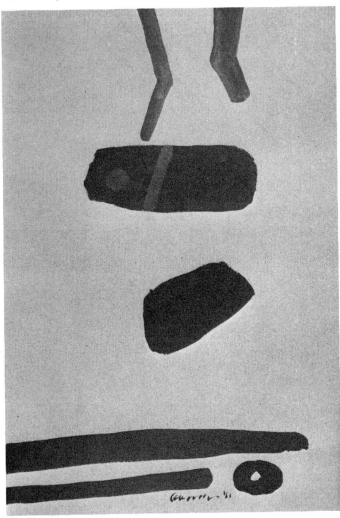

Yvonne C. Meo. "Mother and Child."
Steel engraving. 1967.

Scotland J. B. Harris. "Nude No. 3."
Woodcut. 1967.

# Biographies

ABDUL, RAOUL ("The Current Scene"), is a graduate of the Vienna (Austria) Academy of Music and Dramatic Arts, and has served as drama and music critic for the *Cleveland Call Post,* the *New York Age* and the Associated Negro Press.

BARNES, ALBERT C. ("Primitive Negro Sculpture and Its Influence on Modern Civilization"), educated at the University of Pennsylvania and in Heidelberg, Germany, was well known as an art collector and as creator of the Barnes Foundation.

BEARDEN, ROMARE ("The Negro Artist and Modern Art"), one of America's leading painters, has long encouraged young and talented artists. He lives in New York City.

BONDS, MARGARET ("A Reminiscence"), one of the nation's most outstanding woman composers, has won numerous honors and awards for her compositions and for her contributions in giving a "helping hand" to artists of all races. She is the composer of "The Ballad of the Brown King."

BONTEMPS, ARNA ("Rock, Church, Rock!"), a former librarian at Fisk University, is a prolific author. He is now public relations director at Fisk, from which he took a leave of absence to be a guest professor at the University of Chicago for the 1966-67 academic year.

BROWN, EVELYN S. ("The Harmon Awards"), is assistant director of the Harmon Foundation.

BROWN, STERLING A. ("Negro Producers of Ragtime"), was professor of English at Howard University. He is the author of many books and articles on the Negro in literature and music, and is co-editor of *Negro Caravan.*

CAMPBELL, E. SIMMS ("The Blues"), is known primarily for his cartoons, which have appeared in *Esquire* and *Playboy* magazines for many years.

DAVIS, FRANK M. ("Modern Jazz Is a Folk Music That Started with the Blues"), is one of the early writers on modern jazz.

DU BOIS, W. E. B. ("Of the Sorrow Songs"), educated at Fisk and Harvard Universities, was a professor at Atlanta University and editor of the *Crisis* magazine. He was also the author of numerous books, including the classic *The Souls of Black Folk.*

EWEN, DAVID ("Marian Anderson"), is a longtime observer of America's musical scene, both classical and popular. He is the author of many books on music and musicians.

FAX, ELTON C. ("Four Rebels in Art"), is an artist, writer and lecturer. He has toured both Africa and South America for the State Department, under its cultural program.

GLEASON, RALPH J. ("Rhythm and Blues [Rock and Roll] Makes the Grade"), is one of the nation's outstanding jazz critics, and has written and edited many books on the subject. He is editor of *Jam Session: An Anthology of Jazz.*

HANDY, W. C. ("Memphis Blues: A Bungled Bargain"), was called the Father of the Blues. His most famous tune was "St. Louis Blues."

HARE, MAUD CUNEY ("The Source" and "Musical Pioneers"), was a pianist, lecturer and writer. She graduated from the New England Conservatory of Music and was one of the first persons to write extensively on the history of the Negro in music. Her chief work is *Negro Musicians and Their Music.*

HERRING, JAMES V. ("The American Negro as Craftsman and Artist"), has been one of the first persons to write extensively on the Negro artist and his problems.

HOBSON, WILDER ("New York Turns On the Heat"), is well known as a writer on jazz and jazz musicians.

HOEFER, GEORGE ("Bessie Smith"), is a noted writer on jazz, who contributes regularly to major magazines such as *Down Beat* and *Esquire.*

HURSTON, ZORA NEALE ("Spirituals and Neo-Spirituals"), was highly regarded for her folk tales and studies. During her lifetime she also won many awards and fellowships for her novels and short stories.

JOHNSON, JAMES WELDON ("Negro Songmakers"), was the well-known poet and writer. With his brother J. Rosamond Johnson he wrote librettos and lyrics for the musical comedy stage. He was the author of *Black Manhattan.*

LOCKE, ALAIN ("The Age of Minstrelsy"), was a graduate of Harvard and a Rhodes Scholar. A professor of philosophy at Howard University, he was also the author of many articles on the theatre and on the Negro in literature and art.

MOTLEY, WILLARD F. ("Negro Art in Chicago"), was the brother of the painter Archibald Motley. Though he evinced an interest in art at an early age, he turned in later years to writing. He was the author of the best-seller *Knock on Any Door.*

PATTERSON, LINDSAY (editor of this anthology), is a native of Louisiana and was educated in North Carolina and Virginia. He has traveled to most of the major capitals of the world, living for periods in Europe and Mexico. He is a writer of fiction as well as non-fiction.

PETRIE, PHIL ("The Negro in Opera"), a native of Tennessee, was educated at Tennessee State College. He has done criticism and reviews for *Freedomways,* and has worked for the New York Welfare Department. He is an editor at Holt, Rinehart and Winston.

PLAUT, RICHARD ("Elective Affinities: American Negro Singers and German Lieder"), is a professor of German at the College of the City of New York. Dr. Plaut lectures widely on the Negro in classical music, and regularly contributes reviews on the Negro in the arts to European newspapers and to Swiss radio. He also writes frequently for leading American publications such as the *Saturday Review* and the *New York Times.* He is co-author of the American opera *Lizzie.*

PORTER, JAMES A. ("Negro Artists Gain Recognition after Long Battle"), was chairman of the Department of Art at Howard University for many years. A well-known artist in his own right, Dr. Porter was the author of *Modern Negro Art.*

RUSSELL, WILLIAM ("New Orleans Music"), writes frequently on jazz.

SMITH, CHARLES EDWARD ("Billie Holiday"), wrote the first serious study of jazz to appear in this country (*The Symposium, 1930*), and was author of the script for the first network jazz program. He is co-editor of the book *Jazzmen.*

SMITH, STEPHEN W. ("New Orleans Music"), is a jazz critic and writer.

THURMAN, HOWARD ("The Meaning of Spirituals"), is one of the nation's leading theologians and for many years was dean of the Boston University chapel.

TORRES, JOHN ("Magic Stones and Totem Poles"), is a more than promising young sculptor.

WINSLOW, VERNON ("Negro Art and the Depression"), an artist as well as writer, has tried to bring a historical perspective to the evaluation of the work of the Negro visual artist.

WOODRUFF, HALE ("Artists of the Sixties"), is a professor of art at New York University, and is considered one of America's most accomplished painters. Perhaps his best-known work is the *Amistad* mural series.

YELLEN, JACK ("Popular Negro Composers"), a noted American songwriter, has given us such tunes as "Happy Days Are Here Again," "Down by the O-Hi-O," "Ain't She Sweet" and "Hard-Hearted Hannah."

# Bibliography

## MUSIC

ALLEN, WILLIAM FRANCIS, WARE, CHARLES P., and GARRISON, LUCY McKIM. *Slave Songs of the United States.* New York, 1867.

AMES, RUSSELL. *The Story of American Folk Song.* New York, 1955.

ARMSTRONG, LOUIS. *Satchmo: My Life in New Orleans.* New York, 1955.

ARNOLD, BYRON. *Folksongs of Alabama.* University, Ala., 1950.

AUSTIN, WILLIAM W. *Music in the 20th Century.* New York, 1966.

BALLANTA-TAYLOR, NICHOLAS G. J. *Saint Helena Island Spirituals.* New York, 1925.

BALLIETT, WHITNEY. *The Sound of Surprise.* New York, 1959.

BARTON, WILLIAM ELEAZAR. *Old Plantation Hymns.* Boston, 1899.

BERENDT, JOACHIM E. *The New Jazz Book.* New York, 1962.

BLESH, RUDI. *Shining Trumpets: A History of Jazz.* New York, 1958.

BORNEMANN, ERNEST. *A Critic Looks at Jazz.* London, 1946.

BRADFORD, PERRY. *Born with the Blues.* New York, 1965.

BROSSARD, CHANDLER (ed.). *The Scene before You.* New York, 1955.

BROWN, STERLING A. *The Negro in Music.* Research memorandum for the Myrdal-Carnegie Study. New York, 1940.

BURLIN, NATALIE CURTIS. "Negro Music at Birth," *Musical Quarterly,* V (January 1919).

BUTCHER, MARGARET JUST. *The Negro in American Culture.* New York, 1956.

CERULLI, DOM, *et al. The Jazz Word.* New York, 1962.

CHARTERS, SAMUEL BARCLAY. *The Country Blues.* New York, 1959.

————. *Jazz: New Orleans, 1885-1963.* New York, 1963.

————, and KUNSTADT, LEONARD. *Jazz: A History of the New York Scene.* Garden City, N.Y., 1962.

CHASE, GILBERT. *America's Music: From the Pilgrims to the Present.* New York, 1956.

CHOTZINOFF, SAMUEL. *A Little Nightmusic.* New York, 1964.

COURLANDER, HAROLD. *Negro Folk Music, U.S.A.* New York, 1963.

DANCE, STANLEY (ed.). *Jazz Era.* Vol. I. London, 1961.

DE TOLEDANO, RALPH (ed.). *Frontiers of Jazz.* New York, 1947.

DENNISON, TIM. *The American Negro and His Amazing Music.* New York, 1963.

DETT, R. NATHANIEL. *Religious Folk-Songs of the Negro.* Hampton, Va., 1927.

DEXTER, DAVE, JR. *Jazz Cavalcade.* New York, 1946.

————. *The Jazz Story.* Englewood Cliffs, N.J., 1964.

DU BOIS, W. E. B. *The Souls of Black Folk.* New York, 1961.

EWEN, DAVID. *Men and Women Who Make Music.* New York, 1949.

————. *Panorama of American Popular Music.* Englewood Cliffs, N.J., 1957.

————. *Popular American Composers.* New York, 1962.

FEATHER, LEONARD. *The Book of Jazz.* New York, 1957.

————. *The Encyclopedia of Jazz.* New York, 1960.

————. *Inside Be-bop.* New York, 1949.

FINKELSTEIN, SIDNEY. *Jazz: A People's Music.* New York, 1948.

FISHER, MILES MARK. *Negro Slave Songs in the United States.* Ithaca, N.Y., 1953.

FLENDER, HAROLD. *Paris Blues.* New York, 1957.

FLETCHER, TOM. *100 Years of the Negro in Show Business.* New York, 1954.

GLEASON, RALPH J. (ed.). *Jam Session.* New York, 1958.

GOFFIN, ROBERT. *Horn of Plenty: The Story of Louis Armstrong.* New York, 1947.

GROSSMAN, WILLIAM LEONARD, and FARRELL, J. W. *The Heart of Jazz.* New York, 1956.

HADLOCK, RICHARD. *Jazz Masters of the Twenties.* New York, 1965.

HANDY, W. C. *Father of the Blues.* New York, 1941.

HARE, MAUD CUNEY. *Negro Musicians and Their Music.* Washington, 1936.

HARRIS, REX. *The Story of Jazz.* New York, 1955.

HARRISON, MAX. *Charlie Parker.* New York, 1961.

HENTOFF, NAT. *The Jazz Life.* New York, 1961.

————, and MCCARTHY, A. J. *Jazz.* New York, 1961.

HOBSON, WILDER. *American Jazz Music.* New York, 1939.

HUGHES, LANGSTON. *Famous Negro Music Makers.* New York, 1955.

————. *The First Book of Jazz.* New York, 1955.

JACKSON, GEORGE PULLEN. *White and Negro Spirituals.* Locust Valley, N.Y., 1944.

JOHNSON, JAMES WELDON. *Black Manhattan.* New York, 1930.

————. *The Book of American Negro Spirituals.* New York, 1925.

————. *The Second Book of Negro Spirituals.* New York, 1926.

JONES, LEROI. *Blues People.* New York, 1963.

KEEPNEWS, ORRIN, and GRAUER, BILL, JR. *A Pictorial History of Jazz.* New York, 1955.

KEMBLE, FRANCES ANNE. *Journal of a Residence on a Georgian Plantation in 1838-1839.* New York, 1961.

KENNY, ANNE. *The Negro Spiritual and Other Essays.* Cairo, 1943.

KREHBIEL, HENRY E. *Afro-American Folksongs.* New York, 1914.

LANDECK, BEATRICE (comp.). *Echoes of Africa in Folk Songs of the Americas.* New York, 1961.

LANG, IAIN. *Background of the Blues.* London, 1943.

LOCKE, ALAIN. *The Negro and His Music.* Washington, 1936.

————. *The New Negro: An Interpretation.* New York, 1925.

MOON, BUCKLIN (ed.). *Primer for White Folks.* Garden City, N.Y., 1945.

NELSON, ROSE K., and COLE, D. J. L. *The Negro's Contribution to Music in America.* New York, 1941.

OLIVER, PAUL. *Conversation with the Blues.* New York, 1965.

PARRISH, LYDIA AUSTIN. *Slave Songs of the Georgia Sea Islands.* Hatboro, Pa., 1965.

PROCTOR, HENRY HUGH. *Between Black and White.* Boston, 1925.

RAMSEY, FREDERIC. *Been Here and Gone.* New Brunswick, N.J., 1960.

STEARNS, MARSHALL W. *The Story of Jazz.* New York, 1956.

THURMAN, HOWARD. *Deep River.* Oakland, Calif., 1945.

————. *The Negro Spiritual Speaks of Life and Death.* New York, 1947.

VARLEY, DOUGLAS HAROLD (comp.). *African Native Music.* London, 1936.

WHITE, NEWMAN I. *American Negro Folk-Songs.* Cambridge, Mass., 1928.

WILLIAMS, MARTIN. *Jazz Masters of New Orleans.* New York, 1967.

WORK, JOHN W. *Folk Song of the American Negro.* Nashville, Tenn., 1915.

## ART

BARDOLPH, RICHARD. *The Negro Vanguard.* New York, 1959.

BARNES, ALBERT C. "Primitive Negro Sculpture and Its Influence on Modern Civilization," *Opportunity,* VI (May 1928).

BEARDEN, ROMARE. "The Negro Artist and Modern Art," *Opportunity,* XII (December 1934).

BRAWLEY, BENJAMIN. *The Negro in Literature and Art in the United States.* New York, 1921.

BROWN, EVELYN S. "The Harmon Awards," *Opportunity,* XI (March 1933).

COLE, NATALIE ROBINSON. *Arts in the Classroom.* New York, 1942.

DOVER, CEDRIC. *American Negro Art.* Greenwich, Conn., 1960.

FORD, ALICE. *Pictorial Folk Art: New York to California.* New York, 1949.

H. B. L. "Negro's Art Lives in His Wrought Iron," *New York Times Magazine* (August 8, 1926).

HALE, ROBERT B. *100 American Painters of the Twentieth Century.* New York, 1950.

LOCKE, ALAIN. "Advance on the Art Front," *Opportunity,* XVII (May 1939).

————. *The Negro in Art.* Washington, 1940.

————. *Negro Art: Past and Present.* Washington, 1936.

MOTLEY, WILLARD F. "Negro Art in Chicago," *Opportunity, XVIII* (January 1940).

PORTER, JAMES A. *Modern Negro Art.* New York, 1943.

RODMAN, SELDEN. *Horace Pippin: A Negro Painter in America.* New York, 1947.

SUTTON, DENYS. *American Painting.* London, 1948.

WINSLOW, VERNON. "Negro Art and the Depression," *Opportunity, XIX* (February 1941).

WOODRUFF, HALE. *Ten Negro Artists from the United States.* Dakar, 1966.

Further information on American Negro artists can be found in the following exhibition catalogues:

"Annual Art Exhibitions by Negro Artists." Atlanta University, 1942-1966.

"Contemporary Negro Art." Baltimore Museum of Art, 1939.

"Eight New York Painters." University of Michigan, Ann Arbor, 1956.

"Exhibit of Fine Arts by American Negro Artists." Harmon Foundation, New York, 1929.

"Exhibit of Fine Arts by American Negro Artists." Harmon Foundation, New York, 1930.

"Exhibition of the Art of the American Negro." American Negro Exposition, Chicago, 1940.

"Exhibition of Productions by Negro Artists." Art Center, New York, 1933.

"Exhibition of Works by Negro Artists at the National Gallery of Art." Washington, 1933.

"The Negro Artist Comes of Age." Albany Institute of History and Art," 1945.

"Negro Artists: An Illustrated Review of Their Achievements." Harmon Foundation, New York, 1935.

"The Portrayal of the Negro in American Painting." Bowdoin College Museum of Art, Brunswick, Me., 1964.

"75 Years of Freedom." Library of Congress, Washington, 1940.

# Picture Credits

The author is grateful to the following for their aid in the search for unusual and interesting photographs with which to illustrate the text. Those pictures which have not been listed are in the private collection of United Publishing Corporation, Washington, D.C.

Key:   T: Top;   B: Bottom;   L: Left;   R: Right;   C: Center

Raoul Abdul, New York: 169TL, 189B
Bill Anderson, New York: 193
Atlanta University: 261
Margaret Bonds: 191
Richard V. Clarke: 286BR
Geoffrey Clements, New York: 274TL
Columbia Artists Management: 187
Dinsmore: 266, 271R
Terry Dintenfass, New York: iiBC, 238BL, BR, 258
*Down Beat* Magazine, Chicago: 51, 92BR, 130TL, TR
David C. Driskell, Nashville: 285BR
Elton C. Fax, New York: 217BL
J. Feierbaacher, New York: 237
Larney Goodkind, New York: 173
Gunter's Studio, Nashville: 254
Harmon Foundation, New York: 1, 5, 7, 212B, 217T, BR, 219, 226, 234B, 235T, 241R, 242T, BL, 243, 250, 253TL, BL, BR
Heritage Gallery, Los Angeles: 235B, 263T
Howard University, Washington: 242BR
Langston Hughes Collection, New York: 73, 74, 76TL, 122TR, 197TL, BL, BR
Hurok Attractions: 154, 159, 162, 168TL
International Business Machines, New York: 238T
William Kahn, New York: 246BR
Henry Kier: 63, 76BR
Library of Congress: 194
Louis Mélançon, New York: 168BR
Milton Meltzer: 31
Metropolitan Opera Association, New York; 168TR, BL, 169BL
Monclova Photographers, Brooklyn, New York: 189T
William Mullaney: 271TL
Museum of African Art, Washington: 212T
Museum of Modern Art, New York: 200B
National Broadcasting Company, New York: 160, 161
New York Public Library–Schomburg Collection: 48, 165TL, TR, 172, 174, 249BC, BR
*New York Times Magazine*: 206, 208
Haywood L. Oubre, Jr.: 2
San Francisco Opera Company: 188
Duncan P. Schiedt, Indianapolis: 23, 32T, 52, 57, 64, 82–84, 86, 87, 92T, BL, 93TR, BL, 104, 130B, 137, 140TL, B, 153TL
Merton D. Simpson, New York: iiBL, 199, 200T, 202, 203
Charles Stewart, New York: 122B
University of Texas, Austin: 263B
Maynard Frank Wolfe, New York: 111T
WPA Federal Art Project–Illinois, Chicago: 224, 234T
Jack Yellen: 121, 122TL, 127BL

# Index

Page numbers in *italic type* refer to illustrations.